U0514792

本书获得大连外国语大学学术专著出版资金资助，

为大连外国语大学 60 周年校庆系列成果之一。

DISCOURSE
IN
INTERPRETING

口译中的
话 语

—— 分析与重构

Analysis and Reconstruction

邹德艳 著

社会科学文献出版社
SOCIAL SCIENCES ACADEMIC PRESS (CHINA)

前　言

翻译实践及教学的研究，一直以来都是翻译研究的核心课题。20 世纪 90 年代开始，翻译教学随着翻译需求的增加而更加专业化，当时全世界 60 多个国家中有超过 250 所大学开设了翻译课程，世界各地的译员培训学校和课程数量也急速增多。进入 21 世纪，我国为了顺应社会对于高水平翻译人才的需求，自 2006 年教育部批准设立翻译本科专业（BTI），到 2007 年为培养高层次、应用型翻译人才设置翻译硕士专业（MTI）以及 2014 年对培养更高层次翻译人才的翻译博士专业（DTI）设置进行探讨，再到 2022 年 DTI 被列入教育部新版《研究生教育学科专业目录》，主管部门、行业协会、高等院校一直积极推动翻译专业学科发展和翻译专业人才培养。目前，我国有翻译本科专业院校 301 所，翻译硕士专业院校 316 所，后者的招生人数由 2008 年约 350 人，增长到现在每年招生超过 1 万人，累计招生约 9.7 万人，毕业生约 6.8 万人（《2022 中国翻译及语言服务行业发展报告》）。这种数量空前的翻译专门人才培养给翻译教学带来了挑战，也提出了更高要求，需要大力推进翻译教学研究。

除教材外，涉及口译教学的著作并不多见。国外研究者在针对国外的翻译实践及教学情况进行调研时发现，很多译员是全职工作，但也有一些译员仅以口译作为兼职，而他们的本职工作可能是家庭主妇、学生、医疗工作者、工程师或者记者，这凸显了科学正规的翻译教育的必要性和重要性。蒙特雷国际研究院口笔译学院前院长威廉·韦伯（Wilhelm

Weber，1984）曾指出：只有那些极少数特别有天赋的人可能在不受影响的情况下顺利发展自己的口译事业；在我的职业生涯中，只遇到过一两个这样的人；大多数没有受过相关训练的人，都会在工作过程中形成不好的习惯，犯下严重的错误，进而影响其职业生涯。科学正规的翻译教育可以帮助学员将其翻译天赋发挥到最大，快速成才，同时可以提升译员的职业地位；相比实践经验和自我训练，正规训练可以帮助学员更好发展翻译技能，避免或缩短探索期和试错期。

对于口译初学者来说，即便对于有了一定训练经历的口译学习者来说，他们经常感到头痛的问题往往是口译中记不住又翻不出的尴尬和无助。尚未学习笔记的时候还好些，学习了笔记就更加把握不住，不知是用脑记还是用笔记，试图多记些，结果反而记不到，最终只能产出零碎的、笔记上尚能看得懂的星星点点。这样的表现皆因初学者尚未形成积极分析口译话语的习惯，尚未习得话语理解和话语构建的能力，具体体现在：不能形成整体印象；不能分辨主要信息和次要信息；不能分辨问题和用来说明问题的例子等。总之，不能超越单词层面建构话语。想要跳出这个怪圈，与原文保持适当的距离，做到理解及时到位、产出准确流利，就需要凸显积极分析和主动记忆、话语理解和话语重构的重要性。

我们认为，口译中的话语与一般话语比较起来，既有共通性，又有特殊性。口译中的话语分析与重构，在教学中怎样强调都不为过。首先，口译话语与一般话语之间存在差异。有效的话语分析和重构有助于处理这些差异，更好地完成口译任务。其次，笔记无法替代话语分析。只有通过有效分析，笔记才有价值。否则，笔记也无法弥补分析的不足。

本书从话语的形式和话语的理解入手，从话语难度、信息权重、信息结构、信息推进的角度探讨口译中的话语分析，从话语生成、话语整合、口译脱壳、口译分脑的角度探讨口译中的话语重构。通过这些探讨，我们旨在提高口译从业者对话语分析重构的重视，进而提升口译表现和效果，改进口译教学内容和方法，形成完善的话语分析和重构框架。这些研究成果不仅对口译实践有重要意义，也为口译教育教学和翻译人才培养提供了新的思路和方法。总的来说，有效的话语分析和重构是提高口译水平的必要途径，也是口译教育和翻译人才培养的重要环节。我们希望本书能引起广泛关注，推动相关研究和实践，从而最终提高口译教学质量和翻译人才培养效果。我们也期待能与各位口译从业者和教育工作者交流合作，共同探讨，致力于不断完善和改进这一领域，为培养高素质的口译人才作出贡献。

目　录

第一章　话语的形式

我们首先从口语书面语、话语的模式、口笔译跨界、口译的话语四个方面来了解话语的基本形式。

1.1　口语书面语

口语先于书面语出现，书面语是在口语的基础上发展起来的，而且是在书写行为之后才出现的。另外，读写能力是在人类开始说话很久之后才逐渐发展起来的，以满足口头模式无法满足的需求。当需要对事实、信息或想法进行某种永久记录时，写作就变得非常重要。所以我们看到，在一个社会中识字之所以被接受，是因为它实现了口头手段不具备的功能和无法达成的目的。语音和写作已经演变为在不同的语境中服务于不同目的的两种语言形式，口头语言更适合某些社会功能，书面文字则更适合其他社会功能。人们在不同社交场合使用不同形式的语言，一种语言是否适合特定的交互，取决于正在与谁交谈、正在谈什么以及对话目的是什么。

那么，为什么要从面对面交流转变为书面交流呢？口语是人们在日常生活中使用的自然、随意的语言表达方式，与书面语相比有一些独特的语音和语用特点，绝大多数人都可以使用至少一种童年时期学习的母语以及一生中学习的其他语言进行交流。口语经常与书面语形成对比，事实上，两者存在许多显著差异。在所有人类文化中，口语早于书面语。

书面语是口语的一种表现形式，它通常遵循自己约定俗成的规则和惯例。人们可能会或者可能不会仅凭一种口语来推断这些约定。并非所有口语都有书面形式的对应，这取决于说话者的文化和语言背景。

有人认为，由于文化的变化，写作的演变是为了满足一群人生活方式中出现的需求。当某些很久以前的祖先群体将他们的整个生活方式从狩猎采集转变为农业时，一系列非常复杂的事件开始发生了。当时狩猎和采集社区的人们往往生活在小的、流动性很强的群体中，并且不断地从一个地方移动到另一个地方以寻找食物、住所和逃离敌人。他们的文化共享和有价值的知识是通过许多言语行为口口相传的，例如讲述祖先的传说、历史和史诗故事。写作没有任何收获，因为有价值的知识可以通过面对面的交流口口相传。然而，其中一些群体在有利的地点定居。他们种植粮食，放牧动物并建造更多永久性住所。群体变得越来越庞大，需要组织起来让人们和平共处，他们的文化模式发生了根本性的变化，有必要将语言简化为一种持久的形式，以便在必要时可以再次提及。于是有必要保留记录，使这些较大的群体能够规范他们的活动，尤其是涉及跨越距离和时间的商品和服务的销售和交换时。至此，"作为过程的语言"必须转变为"作为产品的文本"，也就是一种可以看到、可以触摸、可以处理和可以参考的东西。

书写的发展意味着语言现在可以满足各种功能需求。书写可以用来为商品交易开具发票，记录税款，制作财产清单。它可以用于记录以前以口头方式流传的法律、历史、宗教内容和各种叙事故事。在西方社会的历史上，识字能力的发展是一个跨越了几个世纪的过程。正如我们所见，书写发明这一非凡现象给人类体验带来了深刻的变化。人们能够以新的方式处理和利用知识和信息，有价值的手稿都是手工抄写的，只有少数人学会了阅读和书写来承担这些任务。15 世纪，英国印刷机的发明标志着一个新时代的开始，它可以相对快速地打印材料，使人们可以获得更多的阅读材料并且价格更低，并且书面文字接管了以前由口头方式承担的一些功能。从口头语言到印刷文本作为文化知识和思想的主要存储场所，这一过程发生了重大转变。

语言和文字在我们的生活中扮演着截然不同的角色，缺少任何一个，我们的生活都会变得不一样。写作和口语显然是相互关联的，因为它们都使用同一种语言来创造意义。然而，每个人都以不同但同样复杂的方式调用语言，演讲者和作家通常以不同的方式与他们的听众建立联系。

演讲者与其演讲的对象有面对面的接触。这意味着说话者和听者通常彼此认识，分享大量关于正在讨论主题的信息，或者可以相互地建立知识领域。也就是说，在听者不明白的地方，说话者可以提供必要的细节来帮助听者理解其说话的内容。说话者可以观察自己说话的效果，并根据听者的反应修改对话，听者可以要求在有误解的地方澄清。在演讲中，演讲者可以假设听众知道"我们""他们""当时""我们的"等指代是什么。当说话者和听者生活在一个信息共享的世界里时，说话者不必向听者解释很多事情。因此，口语交流时，我们可以假设很多知识已经被共享了。事实上，如果我们提供听众已经了解的大量细节，他们可能会说："我知道，我知道，继续吧！"

文本的读者可能处于时间或空间上的不同地方。也就是说，读者可能在第二天、下周甚至下个月才阅读报纸上的文字。他们甚至可能与作者不在同一个城镇、国家或地区，而作者可能对他们的读者一无所知。写作行为是经过深思熟虑的——作家会审读、编辑和改写他们的作品。书面文本与其书写的空间可能几乎没有或完全没有联系。所以我们可以说，演讲者与听众息息相关，而作家则与读者分离。作者与读者的这种分离是作者必须"编码"文本中所有含义的原因之一，因为读者无法要求作者解释或澄清所写内容。

口语是普遍的，每个人几乎都在生命的头几年学会使用他们的第一语言。口语有方言变体，说话者会使用停顿和语调，说话通常是自发的和无计划的；但不是每个人都可以学会书面语的读写，同一种语言的书面语应符合语法和拼写的标准形式，大多数写作都需要时间，作者可以返回并更改已写的内容。说话者使用声音（音高、压力、节奏）和身体（手势、面部表情）来帮助传达意思；作家必须依靠页面上的文字来表达意思。演讲者对在场的听众讲话，听众会点头或皱眉，打断或提问；对于作者来说，读者的反应要么延迟，要么根本不存在，作者只有一次机会传达信息，并且需要文字内容足够有趣和准确以吸引读者的注意力。演讲可以有很多重复，演讲者可以暂停，提议重新开始或改述，而不失去话语的意义；写作则更正式紧凑。

通常，书面文本比口头文本更密集。也就是说，书面文本包含更多具有意义的词，即词汇项。我们可以通过将词汇项显示为单词总数的百分比来测试这一点，这是口头文本和书面文本之间的一个主要区别，书面文本的词汇项占单词总数的比重比口头文本的词汇项要高得多。所以我们可以说，相对而言，口语和书面语之间的区别在于信息密度：书面语比口语更密集，因为文本中的信息以大"块"词汇项的形式呈现，这会影响其可读性。然而，某些时候的口语也可能比书面语更"复杂"。口语和书面语各有各的复杂之处，这两种交流媒介都使用从非常正式到非常不正式的不同风格。这些风格体现在我们所使用的语言中。口语和书面语之间的大部分差异来自两个主要方面。

第一个方面是情境。在使用书面语进行交流时，我们假设接收信息的人不在场。也就是说，书面交流本质是为了向不在场的听众传达信息，因此它不涉及面对面或直接的互动。由于听众不在场，有必要仔细准确地构造句子来尽可能明确要传达的信息。然而，口语交流假定说话人和听话人都在场，这使他们能够通过手势来辅助说出单词或短语，并通过言语或眼神确认听众已经理解了信息，听众的反馈几乎是即时的。因此，口语不一定必须包含完整或语法正确的句子。

第二个方面是传输语言的工具。在书面语中，我们使用的是页面上的文字符号，这些符号组合成单词和有意义的句子。然而，这些符号本身并不能代表发音，也就是说，页面上的符号并没有给出如何读出这些词语的指示。例如，不同语言的数字可能用相同的符号书写并具有相同的值，但通常它们在不同语言中的发音不同。也就是说，即使在页面上的数字 1、2、3 看起来相同，但这些数字在不同语言中的实际发音也可能存在差异。

信道是处理阅读和听解信息的一种重要感知特征。阅读和听解在信息处理方式上存在明显差异：阅读涉及在空间维度中处理静态的视觉信息，而听解则在时间维度中处理瞬时的声学符号。这两种信道的主要区别在于信息处理的控制权。阅读时，读者可以控制自己的处理速度，能够放慢阅读速度，随时停下来思考，或回顾已读内容以消除歧义。相比之下，听解时，听众的处理速度由说话者控制，因为口语信息是按顺序嵌入连续的语音流中的，语言单位只有在听众的记忆能够保留它们时才能被有效处理。这种信道特征的差异对信息处理和理解有重要影响：阅读提供了更大的灵活性和控制权，而听解则对听众的即时反应和记忆能力提出了更高的要求。理解这些差异对于语言学习、教育方法和信息传递策略的设计都有重要意义，可以帮助教育者和传播者更有效地利用不同的信息传递方式，以适应不同的学习和交流场景。

线索选择和信息重构是理解过程的重要组成部分。听者首先对语言输入元素进行初步识别，在这些元素基础上形成关于话语的抽象假设。然后，这些假设受制于语音规则，产生与话语的表面结构相对应的音素模式。接着，听者通过从信息中选择其他线索，将该表面结构与正在分析的模式进行比较。如果出现匹配，该模式就被提取出来以供更高级别的处理。语言的有序结构及其在语素、句法和语义层面的冗余使得熟练使用该语言的听众能够利用自己的语言知识对输入进行采样并重构预期的信息。

阅读也是一种接收语言的过程，因此线索选择和信息重构的原则也可以应用于对书面语的处理。古德曼（Goodman，1967）认为，阅读不是一个精确的过程，而是一个选择的过程，它涉及根据读者期望部分使用从感知输入中选择的可用的最小语言提示。在处理这部分信息的时候，初步结论被确认、拒绝或完善，进而完成阅读过程。此外，读者使用的不仅是印刷品中包含的视觉信息，在减少预期信息不确定性的过程中，还可以使用主题背景信息以及对语言系统的符号、句法和语义知识。瓦纳特（Wanat，1971）强调了读者期望对信息重构的重要作用。根据这一观点，读者会根据自身的期望和预设，对文本进行信息重构。具体来说，发展这些期望的结果是，只要书面材料符合读者的期望，读者就可以简单地对文本进行抽样和扫读，沿着文本从一个词向另一个词进一步证实自己的猜测，从而最终达成对文本的理解。

1.2　话语的模式

语言研究领域已经达成共识，研究不应局限于句子层面，而应在篇章层面研究交际中的语言。话语分析就是从不同角度去理解和认识人们如何使用语言，这对于口译中的话语理解具有切实的指导作用。话语一般具有语义连贯和衔接合理的特点，而话语理解实际上就是人们对话语意义的解构、建构以及重构的过程。

黄国文（2004）指出，作为交际单位的话语是按照一定思维模式（thought pattern）组织起来的。由于话语模式是语义内容的反映，所以不同话语模式便体现了不同语义内容。语义内容多种多样、千变万化，而话语模式却是有限的，思维模式也不是无穷尽的。可以说，一旦对于有限的话语模式，特别是口译中多见的话语模式有了深入了解之后，不论是理解还是重构类似的话语，就都会变得比较容易。即便构成话语的词汇等部分出现偏差，至少话语的表述结构和借由话语来表达的信息意图会整体地得到传达，也就是说，口译的基本任务可以得到完成。

学者们对于话语模式进行了丰富的研究，比较典型的有以下几种。

拉博夫（Labov，1972）总结的叙事话语的话语模式包括点题（abstract）、指向（orientation）、进展（complicating action）、结果或结局（result or resolution）、评价（evaluation）、回应（coda），这六个部分是叙事话语的典型模式。

温特（Winter）提出了三种主要模式（McCarthy & Carter，1994，转引自李美霞，2001）：问题—解决（problem-solution）型，即情景（situation）→问题（problem）→反应（response）→评价（evaluation），这种模式大多都以问题的解决而结束，但中间也有个别阶段会出现问题的解决被拒绝，从而导致更加复杂的模式：假设—真实（hypothetical-real）型，即先提出假设，后论证；一般—特殊（general-particular）型，即先概括，后详述。这三种模式既可以独立存在，又可以交叉存在于某一语篇中，对这三种模式的掌握能够促使读者更好地理解与生成语篇。

此外，刘和平和鲍刚（1994）总结了口译工作中常见的六种话语类型：叙述言语体、论证言语体、介绍言语体、礼仪言语体、鼓动演说言语体和对话言语体，并指出，熟悉口译工作语言中不同言语类的独特形式，无疑可以大大促进学生此类言语应用水平的提高。无论哪种话语语类，都具有某种"格式化"的问题，即存在某种独特的言语"套子"（鲍刚，1998）。口译特别是会议口译的服务场合大多为比较正式的会见或会议，礼仪祝词类口译语料是较为常见且具有较强规约性的口译话语，属于较为正式的演讲类篇章，其用词和句式往往较为正规，话语组织具备特定的套路。

下面，我们以此类口译中较为常见的话语类型为例，说明如何分析并掌握具体话语模式的特点。译员对其特点把握越精准，就越能更好地进行预测及传译。我们来看以下的例文。

Ladies and Gentlemen：

It is an honor for me to be here, on my first visit to your beautiful city. On behalf of all the members of my delegation, I

7

would like to take this opportunity to thank our hosts for the warm invitation and generous hospitality we have experienced since we set foot in this charming land.

I am **also** very pleased that this visit provides me with an excellent opportunity to convey to you and the people of Guangzhou the warm greetings and sincere good wishes of the government and people of my country. Although tens of thousands of miles lie between us, "long distances do not separate bosom friends," as one of your Tang poets said.

The whole world is watching with great interest the remarkable changes taking place in China and especially in Guangzhou. China is a country with the fastest growing economy in the world.

China's emergence as one of the strongest economies in the Asia-Pacific region has prompted a growing number of business and financial giants in our country to invest in China, particularly in a number of long-term projects in the Pearl River Delta. In recent years, there has been no other place than the Huangpu Development Zone that has so much appeal to our businessmen.

Knowing this, we have come here to look for better ways to promote our economic and financial cooperation. One of the goals of my mission is to sign our investment protection agreement. I am also looking for ways to establish advisory services for transnational companies in Guangzhou through a partnership with our Chinese counterparts.

Last but not least, I would like to extend our official invitation to the Mayor of Guangzhou personally. We would be delighted if he would visit the city of Frankfurt as soon as possible to give us the opportunity to reciprocate the warm welcome and hospitality we have experienced here.

I very much appreciate the close relations between **our two cities**. I also greatly appreciate the position we hold as one of your most important trading partners. Despite the global economic recession in recent years, our economic cooperation and trade volume have been growing steadily. It is our sincere wish that we continue to work closely together to strengthen our friendly relations and ensure sustainable growth in our economic, financial and trade cooperation.

On the occasion of this reception, I wish Mr. Mayor and all our Chinese friends who are here tonight good health! Thank you all.

概括版 1： We are grateful for the hospitality of the government and people of Guangzhou and are seeking to promote economic and financial cooperation with China, including signing an investment protection agreement and establishing advisory services. We wish Mr. Mayor and all Chinese friends good health and will continue to work together to expand our economic, financial and trade cooperation.

我们感谢广州政府和人民的热情款待，并寻求促进与中国的经济和金融合作，包括签署投资保护协议和建立咨询服务。我们祝市长先生和所有中国朋友身体健康，并将继续共同努力，扩大我们的经贸合作。

概括版 2： We are seeking to promote economic and financial cooperation with China, including signing an investment protection agreement and establishing advisory services.

我们寻求促进与中国的经济金融合作，包括签署投资保护协议和建立咨询服务。

这个篇章共由八段组成，是一篇典型的礼仪祝词讲稿，基本包括交代主宾、表达感谢、放眼世界、着眼当下、寻求合作、展望未来、祝福会议或来宾。所以，按照这样的脉络，可以大致复述整篇讲稿。第一段为表达感谢，代表谁对谁表示感谢，以及感谢的对象是什么（如代表团对主办方的邀请和款待）。

第二段为祝福语，代表谁向谁表达祝福（如我国人民向广州人民的祝福，或者吟诗祝福）。

第三段则是展望全球视野，指出中国发展最快。

第四段聚焦于中国，对从亚太到珠三角地区进行描述。

第五段提出合作需求，包括投资保护协议和咨询服务等目标。

第六段为邀请，如市长受邀回访法兰克福。

第七段则是强调两市关系的珍贵。

最后一段为祝福性结语，祝愿健康。

总的来说，这些常见的话语类型各有其特点，译员需要精准把握其内在逻辑和修辞特点，以提高预测和传译的能力。实际上，我们可以发现，这八个段落相互之间的联系非常紧密，位置不可以调换：第一段和第八段是典型的开头和结尾段落，其他段落，比如第二段的 also 与第一段相接，第三、四段为从宏观到微观的逻辑，第五段的 Knowing this 是对第四段的总结，第七段的 our two cities 是对第六段的延续。换句话说，我们可以边听边分辨段与段之间的连接方式，在总结话语模式的基础上，按照该模式进行口译中话语的重构。

礼仪祝词类演讲具有较为固定的模式，且可应用于不同语言中。我们来看一篇汉语的礼仪祝词例文。

各位代表，女士们，先生们：

十月北京，天高气爽，秋色宜人。世界旅游组织全体大会今天隆重开幕。我代表中国政府，向各位来宾表示诚挚的欢迎！向大会表示热烈的祝贺！

20世纪以来，现代旅游在世界范围迅速兴起，旅游人数不断增加，旅游产业规模持续扩大，旅游经济地位显著提高，旅游活动日益成为各国人民交流文化、增加友谊、扩大交往的重要渠道，对人类生活和社会进步产生越来越广泛影响。

新中国成立之后，特别是改革开放以来，中国政府高度重视旅游工作，旅游业持续快速发展，已经成为一个具有蓬勃活力和巨大潜力的新兴产业。目前，中国入境旅游人数和旅游外汇收入跃居世界前列，出境旅游人数迅速增加，已成为旅游大国。中国政府欢迎各国朋友到中国旅游观光，我们将全力保障广大旅游者的健康和安全，同时鼓励更多的中国人走向世界。我们愿与各国广泛开展合作，推动世界旅游业的发展。

我们相信，这次大会必将对实现全球旅游业的更大繁荣和发展起到重要的推动作用。祝世界旅游组织全体大会圆满成功！谢谢大家！

概括版：中国入境旅游人数和旅游外汇收入跃居世界前列。中国政府欢迎世界各国朋友来中国旅游，我们会全力保障游客的健康安全，同时鼓励更多的中国人走向世界。我们愿与各国广泛合作，促进世界旅游业的发展。

一篇典型的礼仪祝词基本包括交代主宾、表达感谢、放眼世界、着眼当下、寻求合作、展望未来、祝福会议或来宾等基本步骤。当然，这样的典型结构会随着会议主题场合的不同而有所变化，但大体是一样的。比如，上文关于旅游的会议演讲，第一段，交代主宾、表达感谢；第二段，放眼世界旅游发展及其带来的益处；第三段，着眼当下、寻求合作；第四段，展望未来、祝福会议。虽然基本囊括了礼仪祝词的典型部分，但个别部分并没有单独分段。同样，下文首先介绍了主宾关系，并对来宾表示欢迎；接着广泛地描述了新西兰；其次，聚焦于其旅游业的重要性和规模，具体提及了230多万游客数量和60多亿美元的游客消费收入，以及旅游业的特色项目，如文化和葡萄酒旅游；最后，对未来进行了展望。

早上好，欢迎参加新西兰旅游论坛。你们中的很多人长途跋涉来到这里，我们非常高兴你们能参加这次展示新西兰旅游业的盛会。我们要特别欢迎那些第一次来到新西兰的客人，并且希望你们今后再来。

我们希望你们可以借这次来新西兰的机会，体验新西兰这个旅游胜地的美丽风光及各种活动。与别国相比，我们的国土面积相对较小，但就景色和活动多样性来讲，我们比任何国家都毫不逊色。

旅游业是新西兰最大的出口产业，它对整个新西兰、对新西兰各个地区，以及新西兰的城镇，乃至于偏远地区的经济都起着至关重要的作用。我们每年接待游客人数超过230万，他们每年在我国的消费高达60多亿美元。近年来，本地区的旅游市场营销已经越来越富有创意。我们有很好的例子，比如一些地区充分发挥独特之处，推出文化旅游、葡萄酒旅游和其他活动来吸引游客。

你们带回美好的回忆和愉快的体验，并与他人分享，就是我们新西兰最好的使者。良好的口碑千金难买，而一次不愉快的经历则可能影响游客的整个假期。所以，我们的一个非常重要的目标就是，不断为游客带来更好的体验。

概括版： 旅游业是新西兰最大的出口产业，在经济中发挥重要作用。我们每年接待230多万游客，他们消费高达60多亿美元。近年来，我们的旅游营销已经变得越来越有创意，我们非常重要的目标就是不断为游客带来更好的体验。

此外，我们发现，在话语模式的基础上，有效辅助提升话语分析效果的因素还有话题及话题链。话题是会话中所谈论的事情，其基本话语功能就是"相关性"（aboutness）。话题链是共享话题的系列语句，把握话题链有助于提升听话人对语篇的理解。在语篇连贯的探讨中，传统的连贯方式一般包括衔接和词汇等，实际上，话题概念线索也可以构建连贯的语篇，促成对语篇的理解。在篇章中，话题的语义可以横向和纵向发展，形成不同长短和级别的话题链。有效利用话题和话题链，可以提高话语分析效果，帮助听众更好地理解和跟随话语。请大家看下面的例子，来体会话题和话题链如何帮助实现话题展开和语篇连贯。

　　我们今天要讨论的主题是"如何提高学生的学习效率"。**首先**，我们需要帮助学生建立正确的学习观念。学习不是为了考试，而是为了掌握知识和提高自己。**其次**，学生需要合理安排时间。每个学科都应分配一个合理的学习时间段，以避免时间重叠。**此外**，学生需要有效地利用课堂时间。上课时要积极参与互动，做好笔记，不要玩手机。**另外**，学生要掌握有效的学习方法。比如形成概括重点的习惯，多做练习，多与同学互相讨论。还要培养好学习动机，通过阅读有趣的书籍，参与有意义的活动来激发学习兴趣。**最后**，家长和学校也要给予支持。家长要关注孩子的学习进度，学校要提供有效的学习指导。**总的来说**，提高学习效率需要从多方面入手。正确的学习观念、合理的时间安排、有效的学习方法以及充足的动力和支持，共同推动学生的有效学习。

　　从以上段落中可以看到：话题是"如何提高学生的学习效率"。话题链的展开为"建立正确观念"→"安排时间"→"利用课堂时间"→"掌握学习方法"→"培养学习动机"→"家长和学校的支持"。话题链通过使用连词"首先""其次""此外"等实现连贯的表达。话题链从内因素到外因素，从个人因素到社会因素，实现了话题的纵向发展。通过把握话题链，读者可以更好地理解和跟随主题的展开。接下来，我们再来看几个例子。

例 1：The UN is divided into six <u>major groups</u>. <u>Each group</u> has an important job to do within the UN system. <u>They</u> are the General Assembly, the Security Council, the Secretariat, the Economic and Social Council, the International Court of Justice, and the Trusteeship Council.

例 2：Education is crucial to <u>your child</u>'s development, and as a parent, you want to make sure <u>your little ones</u> attend the best educational institutions available.

例 3：All <u>retirement homes</u> should be safe. <u>Some</u> are gated communities or have CCTV and/or are equipped with an intercom system. <u>Some villages</u> have 24-hour care staff, while in <u>others</u> a warden is on duty only during the day.

例 4：There are 45 million <u>Mexicans</u> living in poverty, and 15 million of them live in extreme poverty. Most of the time, garbage is their food, and on some days, they don't eat anything at all. The critical situation in <u>Mexico</u> is caused by individual, geographical and political factors. Nobody likes to see poor children eating out of garbage cans. Unless <u>the government</u> works on the causes of poverty, the problem is going to get worse.

这几个例子实现话题链的方式主要有以下几种。

例 1：通过分组实现话题链。主要话题链：大会→安全理事会→秘书处→经济与社会理事会→国际法院→托管理事会。

例 2：通过对比实现话题链。主要话题链：教育的重要性→你的孩子的发展→你想要的最好的教育机构。

例 3：通过列举实现话题链。主要话题链：所有养老院都应该安全→

有围栏社区或有监控和对讲机→有 24 小时看护人员或只有白天有值班员。

例 4：通过原因分析实现话题链。主要话题链：墨西哥贫困状况→有 4500 万贫困人口→1500 万人生活在极端贫困中→垃圾是他们的食物→有时他们一天都吃不上饭→贫困的原因，如个人原因、地理原因、政治原因→政府需要解决贫困的根本问题。

总结来看，找到话题链对口译至关重要。有助于理解源语，通过把握话题链，可以更好地理解源语的主题和逻辑，减少理解障碍；有助于跟随源语，随着话题链的展开，可以更好地跟随源语的话题变化和展开，减少跟丢情况；有助于产出连贯译语，可以根据话题链，产出相应的连贯译语，体现出译语之间的内在联系；有助于提高效率，随着话题链的展开，可以预测接下来的内容，提高口译效率；有助于提高准确性，可以根据话题链，验证产出的译语是否符合源语的主题和逻辑，提高译语准确性。

话题作为一个语篇成分，可以通过话题之间的语义关联来满足语篇连贯的外部和内部条件，从而实现语篇的连贯。不同的语言手段在实现语篇连贯方面发挥不同作用。下面我们来看几个结构清晰、条理清楚的语段，方便我们更好了解口译话语。大家可以尝试一次性听完或读完下面的语段，然后使用源语或目标语进行复述：

Washing Hands

It's generally best to wash your hands with soap and water. And there are **five simple steps** for you to follow：1）Wet your hands with running water；2）Apply liquid, bar or powder soap；3）Rub your hands vigorously for at least 20 seconds. Remember to scrub all surfaces, including the backs of your hands, wrists, between your fingers, and under your fingernails；4）Rinse well；5）Dry your hands with a clean towel, disposable towel, or air dryer.

此段讲的是如何洗手，开篇就说明了有五个步骤，可以说是按照"先概括，后详述"的模式来组织的，形成了清晰的话题链，实现了话题的展开。整个过程是从最初的准备工作（沾湿手），到添加清洁剂（加肥皂），再到清洗（擦手、漂洗）和最后的干燥（吹干或擦干），逐步完成整个洗手过程。由于人们对于洗手这件事非常熟悉，虽然步骤有五个之多，也不过是边听边验证，或边读边验证，与自己洗手的方法有何相同或不同之处，对于不同之处额外区分稍做记忆。这个语段的主要细节信息，甚至"20秒""手背、手腕、指缝、指甲"也依然可以记得，那么在复述或无笔记口译的过程中，只需要注意产出流利就可以了。本段相对简单，因为涉及的主题是大多数人的认知知识中都有的。我们再来看一个类似语段。

How to Get a Green Card?

Having a green card, or permanent residence status, gives you the ability to legally live and work in the United States, and it's a step toward becoming a US citizen. There are **three main ways** you can get permanent residency, or a green card. If you are coming to work in the US and you have a permanent job, then you can get an employer-based green card. In applying for this type of green card, your US employer must complete forms for you and both the Department of Labor and the Department of State must approve, and then you will be given an immigrant Visa Number. If you have family here who are citizens or already have a green card, then you can apply for a family-based green card. Finally, you can win a green card through the Diversity Visa Lottery program. 50,000 green cards are given away every year to people from countries with low immigration rates to the US.

段落的主题是"如何获得绿卡",话题链如下:获得绿卡可以在美国合法生活和工作,是成为美国公民的一步。有三种主要方式获得绿卡:①雇主推荐绿卡,如果有美国永久工作,雇主可以推荐你;②家庭推荐绿卡,如果有亲属已经是美国公民或绿卡持有者;③多样性签证抽签,每年有 5 万张绿卡通过抽签分配给申请人。雇主推荐绿卡需要雇主填写表格、劳工部和国务院批准、获得移民签证号码;家庭推荐绿卡需要由亲属申请;抽签申请需要申请人符合相关条件。

总的来说,通过时间顺序和逻辑顺序,将"如何获得绿卡"这个主题分解为三种方式和相应细节,形成清晰的话题链,实现了话题的展开。虽然涉及的主题并非是大多数人都有的认知知识,但每种绿卡类型提出之后,都有解释的语句帮助理解。只有最后一个类型,如果属于认知知识中完全缺失的内容,那么理解起来会存在较大困难。这也凸显了话语理解的真谛,也就是新输入的信息一定要与已有知识有效互动和融合,理解才能发生。

联合国和全球化

大家好!联合国和全球化都是非常重要的议题。今天,我就想以联合国框架下的全球化过程,来将这两个议题联系起来谈一谈。今天的全球化,是以欧洲近代文明为原点,逐步把世界纳入一个全人类认同的基本价值和行为规则的体系的过程。欧洲近代工业化文明,是在古代希腊、罗马文明的基础上发展起来的。恩格斯曾指出,没有希腊文化和罗马文化,也就没有现代的欧洲。联合国成立 70 多年来,它的六大机构以及下属机构,已经把全球事务纳入一体化的全球规则体系之中。为了世界经济的发展,在联合国的名义下,成立了国际货币基金组织、世界银行和世界贸易组织这三大经济组织。在世界上尚未有统一的货币和货币发行机构的情况下,为了稳定全球金融的运行,国际货币基金组织承担着稳定全球金融运行的功能。

为了帮助发展中国家的经济和社会发展，<u>世界银行负责在落后的国家进行援助性开发</u>。为了促进世界贸易的进行，建立<u>关贸总协定</u>，并于 1995 年起自动升格为<u>世界贸易组织</u>。

此段是按照"先背景，后详述"的模式来组织的，也集中凸显了背景知识对口译话语分析和理解的重要性。此段落的主题是"联合国和全球化"，话题链如下：首先概述了联合国和全球化的重要性。然后介绍了今天的全球化以欧洲文明为起点。联合国成立 70 多年来，其机构已经把全球事务纳入统一规则体系。为促进世界经济，联合国成立了国际货币基金组织、世界银行和世界贸易组织。国际货币基金组织负责稳定全球金融，世界银行负责援助落后国家发展，世界贸易组织负责促进世界贸易。总的来说，本段通过时间顺序和逻辑顺序，将"联合国和全球化"这个主题分解为联合国促进全球化的不同方面，形成清晰的话题链，实现了话题的展开。

在下面这个例子中，话语组织模式没有太大特殊性，但其详述分为三个方面，将"南极资源"这个主题分解为矿产资源、水资源和生物资源等方面，形成清晰的话题链，实现了话题的展开。需要在记住关键词的基础上，边理解边规划其话语展开脉络，为下一阶段的话语重述做好准备。

南极——地球上未被开发过的"宝库"

南极的资源诱惑太大了，这里不仅有重要的能源资源，如煤炭、石油、天然气等矿产资源，还有丰富的水资源、生物资源、土地资源、水力资源和风能资源。同时，还包括其他广泛的资源，如交通资源、军事资源、科学资源、环境资源、旅游资源和文化资源。<u>在矿产资源方面</u>，由于 95% 的南极大陆被厚厚的冰盖覆盖，地质调查非常困难，许多地方仍有待发现。在这里，除了铁矿，还有铜矿、锌矿、银矿、锡矿、金矿等等。根据多国的考察，南极估计有将近1000多处矿床。<u>在水资源方面</u>，南极储存着地球90%以上的冰雪和72%的淡水资源；此外，南极冰盖形成于数十万至数百万年前，未受污染，水质优良，即使是最好的"纯净水"也无法与之相比。世界各国一直在探索将冰山从南极拖到世界缺水地区，虽然技术上有很多困难，但总有一天，遥远的南极冰山会出现在人们面前，解决"渴"烧眉毛的问题。<u>在生物资源方面</u>，南极的磷虾是非常值得开发的生物资源。科学家指出，如果每年捕获磷虾1亿至1.5亿吨，海洋生态不会受到影响，这相当于世界渔业总捕获量的两倍。生活在南极高寒冷、高盐分、高辐射地区的生物，具备独特的生理结构及生活方式，使得南极成为地球的"基因库"，一些微生物甚至可能在火星上生存，这都对人类的发展具有重要价值。

通过以上例子的分析，我们发现，话题的展开依赖不同的语言变体和组织模式。不同的语言变体有不同的话题展开方式。比如，叙述性语言更多依赖时间顺序展开话题；论证性语言则更多依赖逻辑关系展开话题。提升对于话语模式、话题及话题链的敏感程度和理解能力，我们就可以在口译听解中更快分辨不同层次的话题布局，从而为口译话语的重述做出充分准备。

1.3　口笔译跨界

传统观点认为，笔译是书面语之间的转换，口译是口语之间的转换，源语和译语模态上的差异将笔译和口译区分开来。卡德（Kade，1968）批评了从源语和译语模态区分口笔译的观点，主要从翻译所用时间、源语的可及性、译语的可修改性三个方面阐释了笔译和口译的差异。从翻译用时上看，笔译时间更加充分，而口译需要即时完成；从源语可及性上看，笔译可以随时回访原文，而口译源语转瞬即逝；从译语可修改性上看，笔译译文可以多次修改，而口译的修改局限较多。近年来，不同的工作环境以及口笔译两种活动感知状态的差异受到了更多关注，但时间因素仍然被视为两者的主要差异之一。

此外，口笔译更加清晰的区分是随着口译独立地位的建立及翻译学科的确立相伴发展的。口译曾因"翻译等同于笔译"和"译员等同于译者"（Schäffner，2004）的认识被过度边缘化，但随着口译职业化进程的开启，1919年巴黎和会启用交替传译，1945~1946年纽伦堡审判启用同声传译，口译的独立地位得到了确立，使得口译在以"翻译"统称的整个学科中，获得了更多发展空间，开始与笔译比肩。口译以其独特的工作模式得到更多实践人员及实践型研究者的关注，系列口译手册式专著的出版也促进了口译职业化进程。芒迪（Munday，2001/2008）指出，口译的活动过程和技能要求都与笔译不同，更好的做法应该是将口译作为独立于笔译的过程来看待。这种区分不仅体现在实践层面，口笔译的差异在研究层面也比较明显：口译更多关注"当下即时"的翻译过程，而笔译更多关注翻译产品及其对文化系统的影响（Fraser，2004）。口笔译各自的研究对象和方法目的都不同，各自独立研究的成果可以为另一方提供借鉴（Gile，2004）。

实际上，虽然对于口笔译的传统划分与语言的口语和书面语特性相呼应，但随着交流方式更加趋向多模态，对口语和书面语的区分已被诟病且解构（Camitta，1993；Barton et al.，2008）。面对动态变化、多元复杂的翻译实践活动，仅依靠源语和译语模态差异对笔译和口译进行区分是不足够和过分简单的，甚至是局限的（Cronin，2002），传统的口笔译二分定义方法存在问题（Wurm，2014）。实践对于翻译产品产出速度的要求越来越高，翻译的机器参与度越来越高，这使得笔译更加趋向限时甚至即时翻译，因而笔译和口译更加接近了。

视译、口译与笔译。通常认为，笔译和口译是不同的过程，译者和译员所用技巧和策略差别也很大，而视译是介于笔译和口译之间的翻译形式。视译，顾名思义就是边看边译，是对书面文本的口头翻译（Agrifoglio，2004；Setton & Motta，2007）。视译可分为视阅口译（sight translation）和视听口译（sight interpreting），前者经常出现在使用交替传译并需对文本进行视译的场合，后者接近同声传译中的有稿同传（万宏瑜，2017）。吉尔（Gile，2004）认为，视译既非"纯笔译"，亦非"纯口译"，属于"过渡类型"，是笔译和口译的混合形式。但视译通常被认为更接近口译，特别是同声传译，因为两者的加工过程和所用策略比较相似（Mikkelson，1994）。一直以来，视译在口译实践和教学中都占有一席之地。

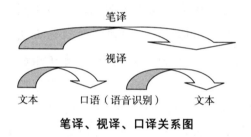

笔译、视译、口译关系图

随着翻译实践多样化发展，视译开始作为中介衔接笔译和口译。笔译实践中面临时间限制，有经验的译者产出笔译译文过程中停顿较少，甚至在计算机盲打达到一定水平的情况下，译者可以只看原文产出笔译译文，大大提升翻译速度，如果配合语音识别系统，则可提高速度产出经由音频转写出来的"笔译译文"。翻译实践中，采用口语模态进行笔译来"说出译文"，结合语音识别技术，已在更大范围内得到了应用，省时省力，且口语产出的译文质量没有受到较大影响（Dragsted & Hansen，2009），同时还能降低翻译成本（Gorszczynska，2010）。刘和平、雷中华（2017）调研发现，语言服务公司的部分笔译工作先由译员进行语音录入，再由译者进行译后编辑，这样做可以将"产量"提升50% 左右。

　　随着技术的发展，特别是自然语言处理和人工智能技术的进步，口头表达与书面写作之间的界限变得越来越模糊，口译与笔译的界限也越来越不清晰。网络交际形式使得交际从静态文本转移到电脑屏幕、手机短信、电子邮件再到各类同步文本与语音聊天，这导致翻译从语言文字转移到更为复杂的符号系统（Bassnett，2014；王洪林，2019）。不论在传统定位上，还是在技术辅助下的新用途上，视译都具有历久弥新的用武之地和重要作用。研究者建议，视译不应仅作为教学练习，而应独立成为一种教学方法（Lee，2012；Felberg & Nilsen，2017）。但学界针对视译的含义、视译如何使用、视译的变体等尚未达成共识（Li，2014），视译的教研和科研成果还比较有限。

　　跟读与视听翻译。跟读又叫影子跟读，就是用同种语言几乎同步跟随发言人的讲话，是同声传译的一种准备性练习方法，该训练的目的是培养译员的注意力分配和听说同步的技能。影子跟读与听力理解和注意力的集中有关，影子跟读类似鹦鹉学舌，跟读者紧接在发言人后面，保持几个词、半句话甚至一句话的距离，尝试边听边重复所听到的内容。但是，影子跟读又不完全是鹦鹉学舌，跟读者要保证在跟读的同时能够听懂源语意思，且发音清晰，音量适中，语句完整连贯。要做到耳朵在听（源语），嘴巴在说（同种语言复述），脑子在想（语言内容）。

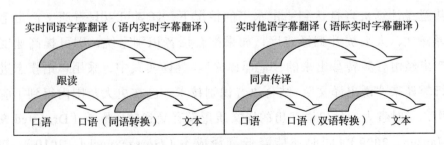

跟读、视听翻译、同声传译关系

　　视听翻译（audiovisual translation）于 20 世纪 90 年代成为一个独立的翻译实践及研究领域。视听翻译涉及语内（实时同语字幕翻译）、语际（实时他语字幕翻译／电视同声传译）、符际（画面及声音解说等）的界面转换。实时字幕翻译（live subtitling）是将视频画面中的话语转换为字幕的翻译形式，可分为语内和语际两种形式。语内实时字幕翻译近似跟读，语际实时字幕翻译近似同声传译，但实时字幕翻译需要在口语产出之后再进一步，通过语音识别系统将译员的口语输出转换为文本字幕，译员还应同时对字幕进行校对。实时字幕翻译中，信息由译员进行输入和输出，辅助画面及语音多模态之间的转换，直至以字幕的形式为观众所理解，整个过程受到翻译时间和字幕空间极大限制，对译员的翻译及技术水平要求较高。可以说，这种形式的翻译是跟读和同声传译的结合体，甚至是口译及笔译的结合体。

　　交替传译与同声传译。说到"译"的各种形式，它们之间必然有密不可分的联系。笔译和口译之间的异同已经为人所熟知和接受了。但口译的两种主要形式，交替传译和同声传译之间，到底是怎样的关系呢？人们似乎认为二者之间的差异是不言自明的，一个是边听边记笔记，然后再译，译语总在源语后；一个是边听边译，译语与源语几乎同步，少数情况还会出现经过预测，译语先于源语的情况。不同的口译模式决定了同声传译与交替传译在使用范围、译语与源语时差、译员运用记忆能力的方式、技术手段和工具、译语质量评估指标等诸多方面都存在较大差异。但是，从技能习得的角度看，交替传译和同声传译都要求学习者具备较好的双语水平、记忆能力、反应速度、应变策略。即便这样，对于二者差异的讨论远远多过对于二者相同点的考量。对于二者在口译教学中的先后顺序，业界早就有交替传译应该先于同声传译的论断。也有研究者认为，二者的教学和技能习得没必要分先后。对于二者哪个难度更大，业界也有诸多探讨，但仍未达成共识。

　　综上所述，对于交替传译和同声传译异同的探讨，更多集中于它们之间的差异，二者的相似点只是蜻蜓点水，可有可无。实际上，如果我们基于交替传译和同声传译的基本过程来看，二者并不是格格不入、截然分开的。我们可以将同声传译视为非常短小的"交替传译"，这里需要译员具备快速的双语反应能力。在这个基础上，同时需要译员掌握对信息预测、调整、补足的技巧。可以说，同声传译是几乎不需笔记的"超短迷你交替传译"。而针对交替传译的每个语段，我们可以说，交替传译译员在开口之前已经做过一遍"同声传译"了。下面，我们对交替传译的两个阶段进行详细说明。

在吉尔（Gile）提出的交替传译认知负荷模型（Effort Model）中，交替传译被分为两个阶段：①信息输入阶段 = 听力理解（Listening Comprehension）+ 短时记忆（Short-Term Memory）+ 口译笔记（Note-Taking）+ 协调（Coordination）；②信息输出阶段 = 记忆（Remembering）+ 阅读笔记（Note-Reading）+ 口译产出（Production）。从这个模型中我们可以看出，交替传译中的理解主要发生在信息输入阶段。信息输出阶段也可能对前一阶段的理解进行补充甚至重构，但更多是进行验证和夯实，并通过记忆对其进行保持和回溯。换句话说，在信息输出阶段，受到了话语产出的抑制和影响，理解的保持及记忆的回溯本身就是一个难点。成长中的译员，特别是口译初学者，往往会发现，明明已经听到并听懂的内容，在产出阶段就会在头脑中消失不见、无影无踪了。这都说明，交替传译中的理解实际上在信息输入阶段，也就是译员开口之前，基本已经达到了整个交替传译过程中理解程度上的最高峰。

口译中最重要的就是理解，交替传译中的理解是交替传译成功与否的关键。从这个意义上说，交替传译最难分析和研究的阶段就是信息输入阶段，这个阶段译员的头脑中发生了复杂的运作，是难以看清和解释的"黑盒子"。可以说，交替传译译员在听取源语的过程中，不论是否记笔记，都是要在头脑中对信息进行处理及转换的，而这种处理和转换的有效程度直接影响交替传译的最终效果。译员在有限的脑力精力范围内，信息输入阶段的信息转换进行得越有效，则产出阶段越从容；反之，信息输入阶段信息转换不够有效，则产出阶段的总体任务压力加大，势必在译语上显现出迟疑、反复、空白，而这些译语不流利现象正是大脑努力思索，甚至思索也不得解的直接表现。

交替传译的职业化历程早于同声传译，而对于前者的研究也相对较早。交替传译的信息输入阶段一直以来都是口译研究的重点和难点。研究者们发现，在交替传译中，信息输入和信息输出之间有一个中间地带，也就是在交替传译的第一环节有并行翻译过程的存在。而这个中间地带不仅只有信息处理那么简单，有一部分的信息输出在这个中间地带也已完成了，比如概念的理解和译语的转换等。也就是说，译员在开口翻译之前已经进行了语言和概念的转换，即与同声传译相似的信息听辨、理解、存储甚至转换，这个中间阶段被称为"并行翻译"（parallel translation）。而这个"并行翻译"阶段最有力的证明就是交替传译笔记的外显机制和更加深入的双语转换程度带来的译语质量的提升。

口译源语理解过程中的"并行翻译"可以在心理语言学中找到解释。心理语言学家把口译语言转换的在线过程作为研究对象，提出语言转换主要有串行与并行两种方式。在串行加工中，在用译语产出所构建的意义之前需要完全理解源语输入；而马西索和巴霍（Macizo & Bajo，2006）认为，在并行加工中，译语词汇单位在源语意义组块被完全理解并整合成话语表征之前，就以一种持续并行方式被激活、被检测。双语者倾向使用前面听到的语言结构来进行表达，这种倾向是无意识的。如果需要用到的核心词也是听到结构的核心词，这种倾向会增大（Pickering & Ferreira，2008），这就是词汇增强效应。可见，双语者在使用一种语言的过程中，同时激活另外一种语言的对应项目，是自然而然的无意识的心理加工。

金（Jin，2010）对交替传译中工作记忆是否运作以及如何运作进行了研究。结果显示，工作记忆在口译记忆保持和言语产出的语法编码阶段都发挥了作用。研究肯定了口译中语言转换并行加工方式的存在，即"并行翻译"的存在。研究还对被试的译语产出速度进行了考察，发现被试在源语理解阶段进行了"并行翻译",进而保障了其在译语产出阶段的流利表现。"并行翻译"可能作为一种策略来减少译语产出阶段的加工负担,而这种策略虽然是译员主动分析转换的结果,但受工作记忆容量和认知负荷的限制,是相对的和不完全的,其运用程度取决于译员能力(Zou & Guo,2024)。

延森(Jensen,2011)发现,学生译员和专家译员的注意力大多分布在源语上,虽然学生译员花费在译语上的时间比专家译员长,但两组译者中都发现了一定程度的"并行翻译"。"并行翻译"过程的深入程度可在一定程度上缓解译语产出的压力,进而可在其他条件不发生变化的情况下提升译语质量。冈萨雷斯(González,2012)还进一步针对初级口译学习者、高级口译学习者和职业译员进行了交替传译笔记的实证研究。研究发现,随着不同组别译员口译技能的提升,他们在笔记中会更多使用译语。这也说明,随着译员口译技能的提升,交替传译源语听解阶段会出现信息加工程度不断加深的情况。以上研究都验证了交替传译听解阶段"并行翻译"的存在。

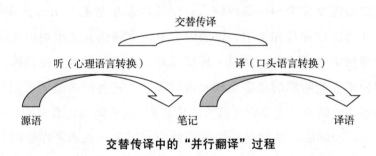

交替传译中的"并行翻译"过程

综合来看,关于交替传译和同声传译之间相互交织的关系,研究者们在理论和实践中都找到了一定的解释。因此,我们可以在口译训练中交叉使用这两种模式的训练方法。在传统口译教学中,交替传译的教学往往先于同声传译。学习者在学习同声传译的时候,基本上已经具备了一定程度的交替传译能力,对交替传译过程和技能有了较好的了解。这样，交替传译的技能可以指导并促进学习者同声传译的学习。那么，是否可以将同声传译技能训练融入交替传译的教学中呢？

比如，同声传译中双语快速转换的练习可以融入交替传译教学中，提升学习者交替传译第一阶段的信息转换速度和程度，可以保障并提升其交替传译的表现。具体来说，在同声传译中，为尽快熟悉具体会议的专有词汇，专业译员在会前的准备阶段，包括在会议开场之前的短时间内，往往会针对会议词汇进行快速双语转换的练习，俗称"乒乓练习"。练习希望达成的效果是，译员对会议具体词汇的双语转换可以像打乒乓球一样，连续保持较快速度，中→英→中→英，或者英→中→英→中。在交替传译中，可以引导学生通过"乒乓练习"的方法提升双语转换速度，辅助学生在交替传译的"并行翻译"中更快更好地进行双语转换，为其交替传译译语产出阶段做出更好的准备和铺垫。

另外，可以在交替传译教学中引入源语信息结构分析和新信息选择等练习方法，目的是训练学习者在有限时间内把握信息主干。在初始阶段，可以先进行书面练习，接着进行听音练习，要求学生不记笔记在源语时间内，或源语的一半时间内完成译语。这种主旨口译的训练方法可以引导学生"脱离源语语言外壳"，更主动地分析，增强源语输入阶段的信息处理程度，进而增强译语产出的质量和效率。

此外，同声传译顺句驱动的练习可以融入交替传译教学中，使学习者更好地理解并适应"脱离源语语言外壳"的理念，则其译语产出更加灵活。具体来说，在交替传译训练中加入视译的练习方法，可以训练学生在开口时尽量不重复，灵活流利地产出译语。与此类似，我们还可以让学生在训练中针对语段文本选择关键词，并最终根据关键词组织自己的话语。这样做的目的是让学生认识到，口译是基于意义的自我表达，源语的有效理解加上译员自身的演说能力，是实现较好口译效果的关键。

1.4 口译的话语

本章首先对口语和书面语进行了溯源，之后对话语的模式进行了探讨，接着从口笔译跨界的角度思考话语，最后探讨口译的话语。本节从两个方面展开：一是口语、书面语在语言特征上的异同；二是有译员参与建构的口译话语与一般话语的异同。在总结本章话语形式的基础上，为下一章话语的理解内容做铺垫。

大多数口语话语都是非常粗糙的"初稿"，通常被称为"未经计划的话语"（Ochs，1979），往往是即兴的，未经过多时间计划或准备的。与之相对的，"经过计划的话语"是经过加工的文本。通常，二者之间有着较大的差异，前者往往更多是突发奇想、第一反应、组织松散、语言不连贯、更多迟疑、同义语反复、词汇修复，甚至是语法不正确的句子（Hatch，1983）。当然，并不是说经过计划的话语就完全不存在以上问题，程度相对不同而已。

坦南（Tannen，1982/1985）指出，口语话语（oral text）和书面话语（literate text）在两个极端。口译话语位于这两个极端中间，可能是非常不正式的谈话，也可能是正式的书面稿件，由讲话人现场阅读。但是，由于口译是一种特殊的交流媒介，一旦有了译员的存在，讲话人清楚自己的话语需要借由他人转达才可以为对方所明白，那么往往都会适当地对自己所言有一定的计划和控制。所以，完全没有计划的源语在口译场合较少出现。另外，有时讲话人会阅读事先写好的稿子，即便如此，这样的源语也是与书面文本有差异的，信息转瞬即逝，不可复听，口语产出中的重复迟疑在文稿阅读时也不是可以完全避免的。可以说，口译场合的源语处于书面语和口语这两个极端中间，是可以无限接近两个极端，又不与两个极端完全重合的任一点。

口语和书面语的区别主要体现在语法复杂度，词汇密度，名词化，情境化，自发性，重复、犹豫和冗余等方面。语法复杂度方面，书面语在结构上比口语更复杂、更详尽。口语中的句子简短简单，而书面语中的句子更长更复杂。嵌入句更多是一种书面语特征，即句子中有从句。在口语中，从句又长又散，因此，口语话语在语法上也可能是复杂的。词汇密度方面，从句中实词（如名词、动词、形容词和副词）与语法功能词（如介词、冠词）的比率上看，口语的词汇密度低于书面语。实词往往分散在许多子句中，似乎被紧紧地塞进单个子句中。在某些类型的口语中，会发现大量实词，但与紧密排列的书面语相比，它们分散在不同的从句中。名词化方面，将动作和事件表示为名词而不是动词，书面语具有高度的名词化，即名词多于动词，书面语中较长的名词组往往更多，但有时口语也可能表现出更高水平的名词化，例如讲座和辩论。情境化方面，解释文本所需语境知识，写作比演讲更脱离语境，演讲比写作更依赖语境，因为演讲依赖于共同的情境和解释背景。自发性方面，相对来说口语自发性较高，进而缺乏组织性并且可能不合语法，而书面语是有组织的和符合语法的；不过，口语也可能是有组织的，只不过组织方式不同于书面语，比如当改变话题时，我们会说"顺便说一下……"，当打断别人时，我们会说"我不想打断，但是……"，这意味着我们知道有一个应该遵循的结构。重复、犹豫和冗余方面，口语包含更多的重复、犹豫和冗余，例如"en""er"和"you know"，因为它是实时产生的。

关于口语和书面语的异同到底如何，研究者们一直在进行探讨。麦卡锡（McCarthy，2001）主张一种连续统的观点，不是简单的一维差异，差异被视为连续统一体。比伯（Biber，2012）基于语料库的研究认为英语的口语和写作没有绝对的区别，不同类型的文本（即体裁）有不同的维度，即使在特定流派中，也可能会出现相当大的差异。所以，口译话语与一般话语相比而言，具备共通性，又不同于一般话语，译员的存在及其角色在其中发挥重要作用，使得口译话语具备一定特殊性，而对其进行分析及重构也是口译任务得以成功完成的首要条件和重要保障。译员既是口译话语的第一接收者，又是口译话语的共同构建者。因此，本书包括两个主要层面，一是通过探讨一般性话语及话语理解的共通性，提升我们对口译话语分析和重构机制的理解。二是通过分析口译话语及其理解的特殊性，增强我们对口译话语分析和重构的能力。

第二章　话语的理解

人类引以为傲的认知能力，多以语言为载体。认知科学就是关于心智研究的理论和学说。1975 年，美国斯隆基金会（Alfred P. Sloan Foundation）将哲学、心理学、语言学、人类学、计算机科学和神经科学 6 大学科整合在一起，研究人类如何获取、处理、存储和使用信息，以及这些过程背后的机制，于是产生了一个新兴学科——认知科学。对人类的认知和认知发展的研究一直是哲学家、数学家、心理学家和生理学家关注的中心话题，它不仅是人类认识自身的需要，还极大地影响着人类自身发展。一个系统不可能完全认识自身的运动，这是系统科学的一条基本定律。既然如此，人类为什么还要去认识自身呢？这是因为大多数科学家认为，人的思维能够指向自身——这就是自我意识。在所有动物中，人类和一些高级灵长类动物如大猩猩才具有自我意识。不仅如此，人还具有能够反映这种自我意识的、能够自指的语言。具有自我意识和能够自指的语言，是人类区别于其他动物的标志之一，所以，人类能够认识自身（蔡曙山，2007）。

人类的认知能力包括对世界进行概念化、结构化和预测推理等多种能力，这些能力与感知能力相对，通常以符号相互连接的某种图结构来表达。语言的理解其实就是要学习语言所指代的真实世界的概念，以及符号和符号之间所隐藏的人类认知的思维过程。人类认知以语言为基础，以思维和文化为特征。除了语言我们一无所知，除了语言我们一无所能——人类的存在，不过就是语言的存在（蔡曙山，2020）。但是，我们对于语言，特别是对于我们如何理解语言并使用语言进行沟通，所知依然非常有限。下文将从记忆与理解、信息与理解、最小的努力、模糊的痕迹等方面分析话语的理解，以帮助我们更加了解口译中的话语，进而在口译活动中对话语进行更有效的分析和重构。

2.1 记忆与理解

按照信息编码、存储、提取方式、存储时间长短的不同，记忆分为感觉记忆（sensory memory）、短时记忆（short-term memory）、长时记忆（long-term memory）。感觉记忆又叫瞬时记忆，是指外界刺激在极短时间内呈现后，信息被保留一瞬间的记忆。瞬时记忆保留的时间很短，如果对瞬时记忆中的信息加以注意，信息就被转入短时记忆。否则，没有注意到的信息过1秒钟便会消失，也就是遗忘了。短时记忆保持时间稍长，在15~30秒以内。长时记忆保持多年甚至终身，它的容量似乎是无限的。在短时记忆加工信息的时候，需要从长时记忆中提取已有的知识经验到短时记忆中来。因此，短时记忆中既有从瞬时记忆中转来的信息，也有从长时记忆中提取的信息，它们都是当前正在加工的信息，又叫工作记忆（working memory）。

工作记忆能力是公认的人类学习的决定因素。米勒（Miller et al., 1960）提出工作记忆的概念。阿特金森和希夫林（Atkinson & Shiffrin, 1968）在心理学研究中开始使用工作记忆的概念；直到1974年，巴德利等人在批判短时记忆的基础上，将工作记忆的概念引入认知心理学，用以说明短时性的存储与加工。巴德利和希契（Baddeley & Hitch, 1974）提出的三成分工作记忆模型包括：中央执行系统（central executive system）、语音回路（phonological articulatory loop）和视空间模板（visual-spatial sketchpad）。其中，中央执行系统是工作记忆模型的核心，负责各子系统之间以及它们与长时记忆之间的联系，还负责注意资源管理和策略选择；语音回路负责以声音为基础的信息存储与控制装置，它由两部分构成，一部分是语音储存，语音代码可以在此保持大约 2 秒，编码的内容随着时间推移逐渐衰退直至消失，另一部分是发音控制，通过默读复述防止语音表征的消退；视空间模板处理视觉空间信息，包括视觉元素和空间元素两部分（Baddeley，1990）。

工作记忆不仅与储存加工、关系整合、执行功能相关，也被认为与其他种类的记忆相关。考恩（Cowan，2001）认为工作记忆是长时记忆被激活的部分；巴德利（Baddeley，1986）把工作记忆视为长时记忆和短时记忆的界面。工作记忆要从长时记忆中提取相关信息进行处理，信息的内容经历动态的变化；工作记忆中的信息相互关联、相互作用，在信息被加工处理之后会产生新信息。

记忆的容量是有限的，所以我们会经常遗忘。实际上，关于"遗忘"的研究可以帮助我们更好地了解"记忆"。《自然》杂志 2021 年发表的关于"暂时遗忘的神经机制"的文章指出，心理学研究一直在深入研究大脑如何"记住"和"回想"，直到最近才更多关注"遗忘"。实际上，人类大部分的"遗忘"并不是神经连接断开或年龄相关的衰退造成的，而是一种重要的功能，是生存的必需（Sabandal et al.，2021）。如果将我们的头脑比作电脑的 CPU（中央处理器），每次执行认知相关任务时，CPU 会将外界的"输入"（外界的刺激包括视觉、听觉等感官刺激）和"硬盘"里面存储的某些信息（大脑的记忆包括经验、知识等）放进"缓存"里面进行相关运算。我们知道电脑的硬盘通常很大，但"缓存"通常比较小。工作记忆的容量也是同样的道理，这种限制很容易就能体会到，也就是我们很难同时进行多项认知任务，比如，很难边打电话边看书。

记忆对于人类的重要性不言而喻。培根说，一切知识不过是记忆而已。然而，对于如此重要的概念，人们对它的了解却不够深入和全面。更多的人认为记忆能力是天生的，不可后天改变，其实不然。诸多记忆大师都指出，记忆力是可以通过科学合理的训练而得到提升，甚至是大幅提升的。口译作为一种专家技能，可以保证译员在以记忆技能为主的口译任务中获得超常表现。不管一个人记忆力的基础如何，记忆力都能够在原有基础上通过训练得以提高，这方面的理论和实践由来已久。最早为记忆寻找物理基础的人是古希腊人，古希腊人非常崇尚记忆力，他们塑造了记忆女神——莫涅莫辛涅（Mnemosyne），现代的英语单词"记忆术"（mnemonics）就是由她的名字派生而来的（东尼·博赞，2014）。

定位记忆法。公元前477年，古希腊诗人西蒙尼德斯发明了名叫"定位记忆法"的记忆术，后来将其称为记忆宫殿。古罗马人是记忆技巧的伟大实践者，他们在记忆术上广为人知的贡献就是著名的"罗马房间法"，它是"定位记忆法"的一种变体，主要是将记忆内容与相关位置联系在一起，以便在需要时进行回溯。比如，我们需要记忆购物清单，可以将每个物品与家中的某个地点联系，如把鸡蛋和冰箱联系，大米和厨房联系，牙膏和浴室联系，回想时就可以快速浏览家中场景，依次想起需要购买的物品。"定位记忆法"是现代记忆术的核心记忆技巧，大多数记忆法都可以归结到"定位记忆法"。

思维导图法。思维导图就是极佳的记忆"路线图"，相比记忆成行的文字来说，记忆一幅图要容易得多（东尼·博赞，2005）。比如，我们需要记忆课文内容，可以在课文中找出关键词，利用这些关键词绘制思维导图。在思维导图中，用图画、颜色、符号等方式标注这些关键词，增加视觉效果。然后结合课文内容，在关键词周围添加一些简短的文字说明。这样可以更好地记住课文的框架和内容。举例来说，为演讲绘制一幅思维导图，我们可以把演讲题目写到纸中央，然后以此为中心，呈放射状标明自己想列出的关键图形或文字。绘制完思维导图之后，用数字标出我们需要讲解的各分支的次序，突出主要论点或分支间的主要联系，我们会发现，关键的词汇或图形若能发挥一分钟的话，对于半小时的演讲来说，一小幅思维导图就够用了。这个过程适用于演说者，更加适用于听取了源语之后进行口译的译员，只不过译员的"思维导图"是分析并理解源语之后由译员自行绘制的，在忠实于源语的基础上，方便译员重新产出"全景图"。

联想记忆法。联想记忆就是将抽象的、不熟悉的信息转化为具体的、较熟悉的信息，并结合自己已有的知识，这样就可以把需要记忆的信息转化为对我们来说更加容易理解的东西。视觉化是转化能力的一种重要体现，指的是将信息在脑海中转化为影像的能力，这是联想记忆法的核心技巧之一。这些影像越生动清晰越好。联想的方式越多样，画面越清晰具体，我们就越容易记忆。更进一步，联想的画面越夸张、越生动，给大脑的冲击力就越强，我们的记忆效率就越高（刘志华，2015）。

逻辑记忆法。逻辑记忆法是一种将想象和联想相结合并进行具体化的方法。与视觉化记忆不同的是，逻辑记忆法将需要记忆的信息转化为用逻辑可以解释的事情，这样的逻辑关系不一定是理性的、合理的，只要对个人来说是有逻辑的、有意义的，就可以了。例如：尝试记忆一个人的名字 John Bridge，我们只要想象一下他的鼻子上架着一座桥，那么下次再看到这张脸，我们首先会想起桥，进而想起他是姓 Bridge 的。例如 West-East（西 – 东），如果容易混淆这两个词，那么就可以记忆它们的首字母组合"WE"，"WE（我们）"这个词是成立的，而在方位图上是"左西右东"，这样就可以记住 West 是西，East 是东。

上文提到的这些记忆方法不是互不相关的，它们是互相联系、互为借鉴的。它们都基于同一个原则，那就是将需要记忆的内容变成自己更容易理解并回忆的内容。其实，对于所有人来说，无论大脑是否接受过记忆训练，都同样适用这样一条规则，那就是：想要记住任何新信息，就必须将这条信息与已经知道的信息联系起来，或者在它们之间建立起关系。这条规则是记忆的关键所在，是记忆力的基础。其实，人的一生都在使用联系这个方法去记忆，记忆力因此得以存在。有时，我们在听到或看到一些事物之后会似曾相识的感觉，我们正是在使用联系的方法。

每一件事都与另一件事有着这样或那样的联系。

不过问题是，大脑进行联系的过程大多是无意识的，而我们的目标是要有意识地将需要记住的信息与能够提醒我们想起它的信息联系起来。这个过程经过训练可以变成有意识的、可控制的（哈里·洛拉尼，2014）。口译记忆训练也是要将口译记忆变成有意识的、可控制的，以延长信息在短时记忆中持续有效保持的时间。这个时间并不是无限长，也不是要把所有翻译过的信息都转换为长时信息，只需要在口译中能够帮助译员完成当下信息语段的翻译，就可以了。

2.2　信息与理解

世界由物质组成，而物质之间相互作用，同时伴随着信息的传递。人类认识世界，有逻辑和信息两条路径。逻辑是基础，对应了必然性和理性，而信息用来处理偶然性和经验。人类的语言，就是信息传递的典型应用。语言具有表达情感和价值判断的功能，但语言的基本功能是传递信息。信息是有关情况、人物、事件、概念、数据等的事实、细节或知识，能够减少不确定性并帮助决策或理解。美国数学家兼通信工程师申农（Shannon）于 20 世纪中叶创立了研究信息处理的理论——信息论（information theory）。信息论是对信息的量化、存储和通信的研究，它将信息传递作为一种统计现象来考虑，在信息可以量度的基础上，研究有效并可靠传递信息的科学。如果句子的某一部分被漏听或由于噪声干扰被误听，听者应该仍可抓住句子的大概意思，因为语言存在一定冗余性，也就是所用语言符号数量超出了所需数量。信息论涉及信息量度、信息特性、信息传输速率、信道容量、干扰对信息传输的影响等方面的知识（曹雪虹，2009）。

在信息论中，信息被定义为一组可能的消息。其目标是通过有噪声的信道传输这些消息，并使接收者能够在存在信道噪声的情况下，以较低的错误概率重建原始消息（Shannon，1948）。人的任何行为、动作都是选择的结果。所谓选择，就是在多种可能性中进行比较，这个过程中"最"是一个离不开的字眼。即使在人工智能中，对"最"进行选择也是必需的过程。比如，阿尔法狗（AlphaGo）的围棋程序，它下出的每一步棋都是在多个可能性中，选择赢棋概率最大的一步。特征选择是模式识别和机器学习领域的重要研究课题之一。还比如，以 ChatGPT 为代表的人工智能产品也是对可以获取的大量文本样本进行深度学习（deep learning），最大限度地提取特征信息，去除无关特征和冗余特征，获得有助于分类的最优特征。

只有理解了的东西才更加容易记忆，这一点在口译中尤为重要，因为只有理解之后并有效保存在短时记忆中的信息才可能有效产出。因而，口译中的理解几乎等同于记忆的有效留存。短时记忆的研究告诉我们，短时记忆一般只持续 15~30 秒，但经过进一步的加工，留存时间可以延长，留存效果也可以加强。因此，即便在译语产出阶段受到由译员自身话语输出带来的"噪音"干扰，译员仍然能够保障译语的产出质量。

口译中需要的是"听解"，而不仅仅是"听到"。两者虽然都是心理过程，但对口译来说有着截然不同的作用。听解需要对声音赋予意义，并将其组织为可以理解的思维单位，而听到指的是声音从外部环境传输进大脑。由此可见，对于口译来说，理解不是自动的，是基于技巧之上的有意为之。口译过程中的理解涉及听解、消化、吸收、结合已有知识理解、储存等步骤。这些步骤同步进行，具有共时的特点。

在口译中，短时记忆需要结合长时记忆才能更好地发挥作用，或者说更好地进行理解。口译的理解需要各种关联（新知识与旧知识、前言与后语、言外与言内、形式与内容等），而关联的依据就是经验知识。长时记忆中的信息都是经验性的，是人们经验知识的总和，在需要的时候被加以提取。有越多的经验知识，口译时就越得心应手。概括地说，"短时记忆"是关键，"长时记忆"是基础。下面，我们结合实例对口译中的信息理解进行具体分析。

归类法。将相似或相近的信息片段整合，减少需要记忆的信息组块（chunk）的数量，也就是利用较少的组块囊括更多的信息总量。请看下面的例析。

Then actually how many people speak English as either a first or a second language? Some researchers suggested a few years ago that between 320 million to 380 million people spoke English as a first language, and anywhere between 250 million to 350 million as a second language. And of course, if we include people who are learning English as a foreign language all over the world, that number may increase dramatically.

1st ?	320-380m
2nd ?	250-350m
外语	more

针对这个例子，我们在听解的时候应该尽量寻找相似处。比如，数字单位都是 hundred million，即"亿"，当然，可以译为三亿两千万，或者 3.2 亿。而针对第一语言的一对数字，我们发现，它们都是三亿多，至于千万上的差异，可以通过记忆"二八定律""二八芳龄"等将其联系起来；针对第二语言的一对数字，我们发现 2.5 亿与 3.5 亿之间的差异是1 亿。这样记忆下来，本段落中最难记忆的数字就很容易把握，整个段落的回忆就成为可能。再看下面的例析。

Back in 1995, trade between our two nations was measured in the tens of billions of dollars. Today，it is counted in the hundreds of billions. Few people back then had cell phones, and almost no one had access to the Internet. Today，China has the world's largest mobile phone network and more Internet users than any other country on earth.

	1995	Today
Trade	10b	100b
Cell Phone	few	largest network
Internet	few/almost no one	more users

我们可以总结，本段落为 1995 年与现今在三个方面的数量规模上的对比。为了简便记忆，我们应尽量寻找相似处。比如，贸易量的比较都是以 billion（十亿）为单位，记忆为由 10b（百亿）增至 100b（千亿）；又如，互联网的使用者，记忆为 few，与上文手机的使用者相似，仅仅译出 few 也不算错误，同时可以大大减轻记听解负担。

构图法。琼斯（Jones，2008）指出，描写或叙述类源语往往包括事件、位置等具体信息，视觉化策略可将这样的源语信息整合成一幅图画。请看下面的例析。

If the fire alarm is activated, all staff should make their way to the main stairs unless it sounds at 11:00 a.m. on a Tuesday, in which case it is a test. Do not waste time picking up any bags or personal belongings. Once outside the building, staff should follow the fire marshals, who will direct them to the waiting area at the back of the building. Each department has an appointed fire safety officer who is responsible for checking all their staff have left the office. This person must then report any missing people to the fire safety manager. The fire safety manager will notify people when it is safe to return.

以上段落可以通过在头脑中想象这幅图画来有效地听解并回溯内容。我们可以对源语信息进行分条处理，按照条目出现的次序和内容进行记忆，也可以将源语中并未确切表达的内容分列成条目。不论怎样，都需要在各个条目之间建立联系，这样可以确保在回溯时克服话语产出的抑制干扰，按照信息原本顺序，有效回忆条目的内容，如同利用思维导图按图索骥一般，重新画一幅图，完成信息的回溯。

关键词法。我们可以将信息囊括在所列条目中，条目的数量远远少于整篇信息的句数或词数。因而，条目数量在 5 左右，或者一般不超过"神奇数字 7"的情况下，我们可以通过记忆条目的内容和顺序，将整篇信息通过条目的线条贯穿起来。下面所要说明的关键词法与此类似，但更加适合源语的逻辑条目不是特别清晰，需要译员自行理解并总结的情况。请看下面的例析。

There are lots of places for students around here. Firstly, if you go across the bridge over the river outside the campus and turn right, then you'll get to the bowling alley, which is popular at the weekends because it's so close to the campus. On Friday nights, they have a special discount for students. If you go down the road opposite the bowling alley and take the first right, then you'll get to the park. It's quite big and there's a lake in it. You can take a boat on it. The university rowing team practise there. If you like sport, you can join the rowing team. Apart from that, behind the sports center, they have a running track, and inside the sports center, you can find a badminton court, the swimming baths, and a leisure center, where you can get a student leisure card. So, you see, there is quite a lot to do in this town.

过桥右转：保龄（周末、周五）

保龄对面右转：公园（湖、船）

运动：船 + 中心（跑、球、游、闲）

采用罗列关键词的方式辅助我们进行复述，是非常好的方法。这一段的三个部分分别是"保龄、公园、运动"，它们之间利用关键词串联起来。以上最为简洁的几个关键词，可以帮助我们重构整个段落。这些关键词实际上就是口译笔记上需要出现的信息。这里需要注意的问题的是，关键词一定要体现最主要的意思，不能罗列过多词汇，数量太多就达不到一目了然地帮助回忆的目的。另外，这样的技能熟练了之后，加入笔记，我们就会习惯多听一些之后再记笔记，这样出现在笔记中的就是重要信息，或者是有必要记下的信息。

缩编法。整理并记忆关键词的方法可以帮助我们将更多信息串联起来，起到化零为整的作用。如果关键词之间的联系不大，比较任意，我们可以将关键词进行缩编。缩编法将需要记忆的材料的绝对数量尽量缩小，从而减轻大脑的记忆负担，进而通过记忆较少的内容而将更多的记忆材料囊括进来。比如，大家都比较熟悉的记忆《二十四节气歌》：春雨惊春清谷天，夏满芒夏暑相连；秋处露秋寒霜降，冬雪雪冬小大寒。代表的是立春、雨水、惊蛰、春分、清明、谷雨、立夏、小满、芒种、夏至、小暑、大暑、立秋、处暑、白露、秋分、寒露、霜降、立冬、小雪、大雪、冬至、小寒和大寒这二十四节气。请看下面的例析。

Today I'm going to talk about ways in which you can impress your boss and hopefully get the promotion. Well, obvious as it may sound, demonstrating leadership skills and the ability to work in a team are two of the main ways to get yourself noticed. Your manager will be impressed if you can collaborate with others on projects, especially if this maximises the company's profits or revenue. If you make sure your manager is aware of your strong points and the effort you have put into helping the company, you may be first in line for a promotion when your bosses decide to restructure a department or the company.

Another skill you should try to demonstrate to your boss is that of being able to resolve problems or difficult situations. Many people naturally shy away from problems. If you can tackle them head-on, you make yourself valuable to your manager.

Promotion（升职）

Leadership/team work → profits（领导力 / 团队合作→利益）

Problem-solving（解决问题）

Promotion（升职）

根据这些关键词，我们基本可以对段落进行复述或翻译，也就是说，产出的语言可以是源语，也可以是译语，因为信息框架是相同的。但如果不能够将关键词写下来，而是仅在头脑中储存，就需要在它们之间建立联系，以便在复述或翻译时能有效地进行重新访问。比如，我们可以记录英文关键词的首字母"PLPP"，或者中文关键词"升 / 领导 / 问题 / 升"。

灵活使用以上方法才能够真正发挥它们对口译话语分析及重构、口译质量提升等方面不可替代的作用。交替传译离不开对源语的理解和分析，因为不理解的内容是难以被有效记忆的，何况交替传译还要在保持记忆的情况下对内容进行回溯。因此，交替传译的话语分析和重构训练非常重要，只有当整个环节都能应对得比较自如，或者说一般长度的语段都可以在无笔记的情况下进行译述时，笔记才可以顺理成章真正地反映听解的成果，进而辅助我们完成交替传译任务。

2.3 最小努力

许多非凡的人类技能，例如阅读、掌握乐器或编写复杂的软件，都需要数千小时的练习和持续的认知努力。认知努力也是翻译过程研究的重要关注。随着笔译与口译的跨界融合发展，时间限制在交替传译、同声传译、视译、视听翻译、时间压力下的笔译等翻译活动中变得更为突出，而限时翻译活动的共性是译员需要采用更快、更大的信息整合、简译、直译、分译等决策，这使得翻译过程中努力与效果之间的权衡和互动变得更加重要。一方面，日常生活中即便没有外部奖励，人们也可能自愿付出努力，然而，流行科学理论认为，努力是令人不快的，人们会尽可能地避免它。另一方面，最近有研究者开始批判质疑认知努力是否总是令人厌恶，相反，他们认为挑战认知活动在某些情况下可以被体验为有益的和有价值的。也就是说，认知努力既是成本，也是奖励，其在翻译实践及研究中的作用还存在巨大的探索空间。

人们在日常生活中的体力和脑力活动中都会付出努力，努力是为了达到某种目的而付出的体力或心理活动，是一种能够被自身和他人观察到的外显行为（de Morree & Marcora，2010；易伟等，2019）。认知努力是人类有限认知资源的参与比例（Tyler et al.，1979）。认知努力与任务要求、任务负荷、任务绩效、认知需求、学习动机、专业能力、决策力、适应力、经验、意愿、年龄、环境等因素存在复杂的交互关系，共同对复杂任务中的个体表现及能力发展产生重要影响，因而逐渐在心理学、认知科学、神经科学等多个领域成为研究重点。

针对翻译过程的认知研究开始于 20 世纪 60~70 年代，延续到 80 年代翻译过程研究应运而生。早期研究者针对口译过程中认知资源（Gerver，1969）、认知负荷（Kirchhoff，1976）进行了探讨。古特（Gutt，1991/2000）通过斯珀伯和威尔逊（Sperber & Wilson，1986）的关联理论将认知加工努力的概念引入翻译理论。吉尔（Gile，1995/2009）提出口译的认知努力模型，关注译员在口译各项子任务中实际分配和协调的认知努力和精力，描述译员在口译过程中可能遭遇的认知能力局限，为解释译员口译表现欠佳的现象提供认知依据（苏雯超等，2021）。21 世纪以来，随着翻译认知研究不断发展，认知努力的研究成为翻译过程研究的重点关注。

但是，关于翻译过程中认知努力的研究还存在以下不足：第一，定义理解模糊，认知努力更多作为与翻译认知过程的任务难度、认知负荷、译员表现相伴相生的附属品，这给相关研究的变量控制及信度、效度带来挑战。第二，特质探讨不够，对认知努力的主体、条件、限度、变化、发展等特质关注不足，影响翻译认知过程中相关共时及历时因素的特质及共性研究。第三，测量方法单一，对认知努力的测量常与任务负荷等因素的测量方法混用，多元验证方法使用不足，影响研究设计及结果的解释力。第四，研究空间不足，翻译是更为复杂的语言认知活动，是人类语言研究及认知发展研究中不可或缺的领域。因此，翻译研究需借鉴语言及认知研究中的最新方法和成果，提升自身研究前沿性及可持续性的同时，为人类语言及认知研究作出贡献。努力需要消耗资源，个体倾向于避免付出努力，或者以最小的努力获取最大的效果，这体现了"努力是一种成本"的特性，认知科学和经济学的当代理论和实证研究均证实和强化了这一观点。

认知努力的成本观。首先，认知努力的内部成本体现在认知活动的完成者面临工作记忆容量有限的问题。工作记忆能力是公认的人类学习的决定因素。最早此方面的研究提出神奇数字 7，认为短时记忆广度为 7±2，即 5~9 之间，也就是在短时记忆任务中，人们可以记住大约七个组块的信息（Miller，1956）。之后的研究认为，神奇数字应为 4，短时记忆广度为 4±1，即 3~5 之间；年轻人一般可以记忆三到五个组块，儿童和老年人记忆得更少（Cowan，2001；Ayasse et al.，2021）。最近的研究指出，神奇数字为 4 的论断过于乐观，实际应为 2；个体的记忆力可以通过改变短时记忆中的组块大小来得到提升，而组块的数量对记忆力的影响不大（Gobet & Clarkson，2004）。总之，人类的认知资源是有限的，必须明智地分配。认知努力是昂贵的，人类被描述为"认知吝啬鬼"，只花费必要的努力做出令人满意的决定，并且尽可能使用捷径，而不是做出最好的决定。

其次，认知努力的内部成本体现在认知活动的完成者面临表征能力有限的问题。个体在一定时间内能表征的信息数量有限（Musslick et al.，2016），且在多任务认知活动中面临表征共享、分离和分配的问题，都会对具体认知任务的完成情况产生影响（Musslick & Cohen，2021）。布雷纳德和雷纳（Brainerd & Reyna，1990）提出的模糊痕迹理论（fuzzy-trace theory）被广泛应用于包括语言学在内的许多学科。该理论认为，精确与模糊的关系是辩证统一与矛盾的，两者之间没有不可逾越的鸿沟。在对信息意义的提取过程中，个体倾向于使用模糊痕迹来表征信息，因为它更容易获得，需要的认知努力较少；相比之下，精确痕迹更容易受到干扰，然后被遗忘。大多数人类认知活动并不准确，而是依赖模糊表征（感觉、模式等）。此外，语言理解的"足够好"表征（good-enough representation）也发现，针对给定的任务，语言理解系统创建的句法和语义表征只是"足够好"，而不是原有观点认为的，是说话者话语准确和详细的表征（Ferreira et al.，2002；Ferreira & Patson，2007）。对话中的话语信息很快接踵而至，因此系统没有时间考虑所有相关信息源，不会为每个信息源计算特定而详细的结构，以免落后于信息输入，使沟通受到影响。在时间压力和资源约束之下，应做最少工作来获得信息意义。

认知努力的奖励观。认知需求（need for cognition）被定义为"用有意义的整合方式组织相关情景、理解经验世界并使其合理化的需求"（Cohen et al.，1955）、"个体参与和享受思考的倾向"（Cacioppo & Petty，1982）。后者还开发了认知需求量表（need for cognition scale），可按量表得分将被试分为高认知需求者和低认知需求者，借以研究认知需求的个体差异及其对认知活动的影响和作用。研究发现，认知需求影响个体信息加工的努力程度。相比低认知需求者，高认知需求者更努力地投入到认知活动中，信息回忆表现得更好，认知任务完成得更好（徐洁、周宁，2010）。造成认知需求个体差异的原因尚不明确，但研究发现个人的学习经历、对挫折的包容度、文化相关因素等可能对个体的认知需求产生影响（Cacioppo et al., 1996; Inzlicht et al., 2018; Székely & Michael, 2020; Carruthers & Williams, 2022; Gado et al., 2023）。认知需求具备个体差异，不同个体对努力及其奖励的观点和认识不同。总结来看，认知需求更加凸显奖励观下认知努力的静态个体差异。

如果说认知需求更加凸显奖励观下认知努力的静态个体差异，那么，习得性勤奋（learned industriousness）则更多展现奖励观下认知努力的动态变化发展。习得性勤奋指的是"有回报的努力有助于形成个体在勤奋上的差异，且这种差异具备持久性"（Eisenberger, 1992）。一方面，个体通过条件学习形成努力的高价值体验之后，就会倾向于选择高努力行为（徐光国、张庆林，1996），增加高努力任务的价值（易伟等，2019; Clay et al., 2022）。另一方面，认知负荷与工作记忆一次可以保存的信息量有关（Sweller, 1988）。由于工作记忆容量有限，因此教学方法应避免因不直接有助于学习的额外活动而使工作记忆超载，也要避免超负荷，因为这两种情况都会阻碍学习进程（钟丽佳、盛群力，2017）。总结来看，适度的认知负荷及认知努力有助于习得性勤奋，习得性勤奋更多展现奖励观下认知努力的动态变化发展。

翻译中的认知努力。针对认知努力是一种成本，我们应充分认识到认知努力的"避重就轻"。行为学研究表明，人们选择进行高努力的意愿会随着所要付出努力的增加而降低，这一现象则是努力折扣（effort discounting）；当诱因较低或者难度过高时，个体的努力不会随着任务难度的增加而增加，二者可以分离（Kahneman, 1973; Brehm & Self, 1989; Richter et al., 2016）。翻译活动中，认知努力是努力与效果权衡之后的最优化；努力折扣现象可帮助我们优化翻译过程研究设计，同时也可成为新的研究点。总之，我们在翻译过程研究中应充分关注到认知努力与其他变量之间的交互作用，提升研究信效度的同时，注重对研究过程及结果进行多维度阐释。

在控制变量的基础上，我们应通过多元验证提升研究的信效度。任务难度被认为是努力的操作定义（Wang et al.，2017）。一般来说，任务难度越大，个体付出的努力越多；但是，努力是个体主动加工，难度是任务本身属性（曹思琪等，2022）。翻译活动中，被试在报告努力情况的同时会反映焦虑、压力、疲劳等感受，而这些相伴而行的感受不利于被试正常付出认知努力，可能触发努力折扣，这需要研究者在研究设计和过程中给予足够关注和考量。我们应避免认知努力及认知负荷测量方法的误用（Gile，2021），除了主观测量工具认知需求量表（NFC，need for cognition scale）之外，还可使用客观测量工具包括努力耗费奖励任务（effort expenditure for rewards task）、认知努力折扣范式（cognitive effort discounting paradigm）、认知动机状态量表（MFC，motivation for cognition state scale）等（Treadway et al.，2009；Westbrook et al.，2013；Westbrook & Braver，2015；Blaise et al.，2021）。

认知努力是一种奖励，我们需要关注认知努力的个体差异，并在研究设计及研究结果解读中充分考虑这种情况。努力是一种主动的、需要意志参与的过程。基于此，在翻译过程研究中，我们需要关注被试译员在认知努力上的群体及个体差异。根据认知需求个体差异及影响因素，如个人的学习经历、对挫折的包容度、文化相关因素等，我们可关注职业译员与学生译员在不同认知负荷下认知努力的付出情况，也可关注不同阶段的学生译员认知努力的发展情况。不同水平的译员能力不同，高水平译员所花费能力与产出效果之间投入产出比更高，低水平译员相反。研究发现，学习者可对自身判定其为更重要的信息投入更多努力，其任务表现也更好（Ariel & Castel，2014）。也可以说，能否更高效地运用认知努力，也是译员能力高低的一部分。

我们需要关注个体认知努力的变化及发展，并可对其与认知能力及翻译能力的协同变化和发展进行研究。以往的认知训练并没有在认知技能提升上达成泛在效果，习得性勤奋等相关认知训练可能是提升学习效果的突破口。通过设计可以展现最优化认知负荷的认知训练任务，调动符合技能习得一般规律及个性化发展的认知努力，最大限度地发挥认知努力本身的附加价值，进而通过发挥长期的、可持续的认知努力，提升个体的学习能力及学习效果。在这个过程中，应针对长期任务中的认知努力进行多次测量或重复测量，这样做可以有效跟踪认知努力的变化及发展情况，同时有助于更深入探究认知努力在反映认知负荷与任务表现之间交互复杂关系中的重要作用。

最小努力原则。选择一种努力任务往往意味着失去了完成其他任务的机会，因而认知努力表现为一种机会成本（Kurzban et al., 2013；易伟等，2019）。认知努力的机会成本主要从收益和成本权衡的角度解释努力成本，这可以追溯到"最小努力原则"（least effort principle），也就是人们执行最少劳动密集型的行为，完成特定任务，以最小化必要的努力（Zipf, 1949；Case, 2005）。自"最小努力原则"被提出之后，研究者将其与语言理解和信息加工结合进行研究，指出"最小努力原则"是理解语言行为真实本质的关键概念（Martinet, 1960）。决策者会一直寻找信息，直到找到解决方案，在很多情况下，人类在做出决定时不会考虑所有可用信息，在时间和认知资源有限的情况下尤其如此（Simon, 1956）；人类在时间和资源的限制下，对所有信息源都做出"最佳"决策在生物学上是不现实的（Gigerenzer et al., 1999）。寻找最佳解决方案以获得最大收益，这体现在翻译中就是译者付出最小的努力，达到最大的效果（Levý, 1967；Zou & Zhang, 2023）。

研究发现，翻译理解涉及的阅读和听解两个过程都展现"最小努力"的作用。大家看，下图展示的是眼动仪观测下人类的阅读过程：线条表示的是眼跳，圆点表示的是注视。基于眼动技术的阅读研究表明，读者的眼睛不是从左到右逐字阅读，这只是我们大脑产生的一种错觉。事实上，阅读中的注视时间只占大约60%（Rayner et al., 2011），大脑根据部分信息和印象，借助句法和语义规则，推断并获得整个信息。高效阅读者可以注视到每个实词，也就是名词、动词、形容词、数词、量词、代词等这类对于信息构建贡献更大的词汇；在每个注视词上所用时间更少，眼跳距离更大，很少回看。而低效阅读者注视到的不见得是实词，每个注视词所用时间更多，眼跳距离较小，而且经常回看。

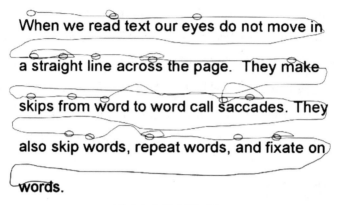

眼动仪下的阅读过程

此外，换位字母效应（transposed letter effect）也验证了这一点。只要单词的首尾字母位置正确，在单词中间随机化字母位置对高效阅读者理解文本几乎没有影响（Rawlinson，1976）。下面的语段表明，一个单词只要它的首字母和尾字母处在正确的位置上，其他字母顺序的变化对阅读的影响不大。尽管后来剑桥大学的教授证明，剑桥大学从未做过这个研究，但该语段却为此赢得了"剑桥大学效应"的名称（王军，2014）。

Aoccdrnig to a rscheearch at Cmabrigde Uinervtisy, it deosn t mttaer in waht oredr the ltteers in a wrod are, the olny iprmoetnt tihng is taht the frist and lsat ltteer be at the rghit pclae. The rset can be a toatl mses and you can sitll raed it wouthit porbelm. Tihs is bcuseae the huamn mnid deos not raed ervey lteter by istlef, but the wrod as a wlohe.

另外，限时翻译活动（口译、视译、视听翻译）涉及听和读。边听边读是双模态输入，相比单模态输入，更能够提升二语多种技能的发展，可以支持阅读理解以及阅读速度和流利度的发展（Chang & Millet，2015）。读和听被称为"接受技能"（receptive skill）或"被动技能"（passive skill）；说和写被称为"产出技能"（productive skill）。学习一种新语言时，学习者倾向于先发展接受技能，然后习得产出技能。研究发现，在听解过程中，听者对口语句子的理解并不总是源于对话语的单词和句法的全面分析；相反，听者可能会对信息进行肤浅分析，抽取单词，并使用假定合理性来理解句子含义（Ayasse et al.，2021）。

2.4 模糊痕迹

美国科学家扎德（Zadeh，1965）提出"模糊"（fuzzy）的概念，雷纳和布雷纳德（Brainerd & Reyna，1990；Reyna & Brainerd，1990）受到美国心理学家和认知科学家埃斯蒂斯（Estes，1980）的观点启发，即"人类的记忆在进行特殊目的计算和逻辑操作的时候还没有达到理想状态"，同时借鉴数学的基础理论和逻辑主义、形式主义、直觉主义三者之间的对照，摒弃传统认知观将思维看作计算或逻辑操作的观点，将直觉（intuition）认定为模糊痕迹理论的中心隐喻。精确表达是相对的，模糊表达同样是必不可少的。精确与模糊的关系是辩证统一的，又是矛盾的，它们之间并没有无法逾越的鸿沟。

模糊痕迹理论借用诺贝尔经济学奖获得者卡内曼（Kahneman）及其学生特沃斯基（Tversky）提出的框架效应（framing effect）来说明模糊加工偏好。框架效应的案例假设了一种罕见的亚洲疾病，预计该种疾病的发作将使得600人死亡。现有两种应对方案，假定对各方案产生后果的精确估算如下。

正面框架。

A 方案：200 人将生还。

B 方案：有 1/3 的机会 600 人将生还，而有 2/3 的机会无人能生还。

负面框架。

C 方案：400 人将死亡。

D 方案：有 1/3 的机会无人死亡，而有 2/3 的机会 600 人全部死亡。

特沃斯基和卡内曼（Tversky & Kahneman，1981）发现，正面框架下大部分人选 A，而负面框架下大部分人选 D，实际上 A 与 C、B 与 D 是等同的选项。人们在不同的框架下，产生了对于 A 和 D 的不同偏好，进而作出了不同的选择，这就是框架效应。模糊痕迹理论认为，成熟的推理者并不像大多数认知发展理论所认为的那样，采用逻辑定量方式解决问题；相反，他们根据直觉上未经加工的质的区别就产生了不同的偏好。框架效应反映了要点在推理中的重要作用。在高级认知加工活动中，人类对于信息意义的抽取分为两种形式：针对意义和模式进行的要义（gist）抽取和针对表面信息细节进行的逐字逐句（verbatim）编码；在心理语言学界早已达成共识，即记忆的细节痕迹比要义痕迹会更加迅速地消失。模糊加工偏好指的是人类记忆的信息在具体性上是不同的，范围从保存信息输入的原样、包含丰富的细节到仅仅保留原信息非常模糊的、语义的痕迹不等，要义和逐字逐句是这一连续体的两端（曾守锤、李其维，2004）。模糊加工偏好是推理的一个基本特点。人类大多数认知活动并非精确无误，而是依赖模糊表征（感觉、模式、主旨）；要义容易记忆，容易处理，信息编码过程中有能力提取要义模式，有能力在努力和精确之间进行权衡取舍，以最小努力获取最大精确，不做不必要的牺牲。

自模糊理论被提出以来，人们已经普遍认为，人的大部分知觉过程和思维过程都浸透着模糊性；语言描写就其本质而言是模糊的，因为这种描写通常是对复杂情况概括的描写。语言的古老性和语言的模糊性是成正比的。也就是说，语言中的词越往上追溯，其模糊性越发明显。甚至可以说，没有词的模糊性，在语义方面简直就无法进行词源探溯；比如，颜色词是典型的模糊词，颜色本身的界限就是模糊的，生理学研究表明，一个正常人能够区别光谱上大约七百万种不同的色彩，但任何一种语言中的常用颜色词却极其有限，因此，表达颜色的词在历史演变中明显地表现出模糊的特点（伍铁平，1986）。

人类所有的知识都来自对世界的感知、行为和情感体验，意识和语言已成为研究思维进化最流行的主题。语言不仅是一种行为现象，而且是人类用来感知世界的工具。人类语言不可或缺的部分是从口语和书面语中提取语义的能力，语义表征不受感觉模态的影响（Binder et al.，2009；Price，2012）。神经科学家发现，无论听到或看到信息，人类大脑的相同部分都会被激活。学习者在发展理解策略的过程中，可以通过推理来确定主要思想，这些策略适用于听解和阅读两种模态。在听觉输入中，语言外的线索如韵律信息可以有效地帮助听者断开信息，从而提升理解能力。说话人的重读和语调可以影响听话人对内容的理解，因此听解也是由框架和要点来驱动的。同时进行听和读，与自定步速阅读不同，可以避免逐字逐句的阅读方式，从而提高阅读的流利度。学习者可以根据自身的优势，选择听或读这两种模态中更加擅长的一种，以此来提升理解效果。听和读各自构建了理解的支架，因而可以促进理解；但由于阅读相比听解是一项较早习得的技能，所以在支架构建方面可能发挥更大的作用。不同模态下的信息理解过程与口译过程具有较高的相关性，研究这些过程有助于我们深入了解口译中听觉和视觉信息的独立输入或混合输入机制。

模糊痕迹理论与最小努力原则之间存在着密切的内在联系，这对口译研究具有重要启示：模糊痕迹理论认为，人类倾向于提取要义而非逐字记忆，这体现了最小努力原则。在口译中，译员也倾向于采用要点传译，而非逐字传译。模糊加工偏好是人类采用最小努力获取最大精确的表现，口译中译员同样需要在精确与努力之间求取平衡。口语语义本身就具有一定模糊性，口译传递的也是模糊语义信息，这要求译员进行模糊管理，而非追求绝对精确。听觉和视觉在理解中的作用不同，口译中译员需要合理运用两种感知模式，发挥各自优势。口译也存在框架效应，译员需要注意信息表达方式的影响，不能生搬硬套。口译需要处理不同语言间的语义对应问题，译员可以利用语义的模糊性进行转换，而非生硬地逐词翻译。模糊痕迹理论为口译的简化策略提供了认知基础，译员可保留要点，省略不必要细节。模糊痕迹理论为理解口译过程中的认知规律，特别是最小努力原则在口译中的作用提供了重要视角，这有助于我们更全面地认识口译活动的复杂性。

第三章　口译中的话语分析

胡壮麟（2001）认为，人们要研究语言问题，必然要把话语作为研究对象。话语分析重视和研究交际主体的心理认知因素和社会文化因素，以及交际场合等语境因素对话语生成和理解的影响，话语的生成和理解及语言交际都离不开对话语的语义分析。简单地说，话语分析就是解释话语中语言使用者对语言资源作出的种种选择。话语分析离不开对话语的理解，而理解实际上是话语与其接收者之间的对话。在口译操作层面上，话语的理解在很大程度上就是对源语的解释。

语言解释美学的创立者汉斯－格奥尔格·加达默（Hans-Georg Gadamer）认为，翻译是解释，也是理解的基础。但理解并非要求译者完全置身于作者的思想，或直接参与其内心活动。理解需要在尊重原作者思想和结合自身语境间找到平衡，适度诠释和表达，方能实现跨语言文化的真正交流。所谓的理解，本质上是在语言层面达成共识，而非完全进入他人的思维世界或亲身体验他人的感受。这种理解更多地体现为概念和观点的一致，而非情感或经历的完全共鸣。整个理解过程乃是一种语言过程，语言体现的是谈话双方相互了解并对某事取得一致意见的人的内心活动；因此，话语分析就是综合多方面的因素来解释说话人的意图，弥补交际鸿沟的过程（席晓青，2011）。

话语的生成是一个十分复杂的过程，涉及话语主体的思维方式态度、讲话的内容以及所处的语境等多方面因素。桂诗春（2005）将话语生成分为四个阶段：把意念转换成要传递的信息；把信息形成语言计划；执行语言计划；自我监察。从思维的角度考察话语生成主体如何将单句连接成篇，而生成的话语又是如何来体现话语作者的意识形态和对话语整体意义的构建，对话语理解至关重要。系统功能语言学的三大语言元功能（概念功能、人际功能、语篇功能）在社会语境中投射出三个相应的语域变量（register variables）：语场（field）、语旨（tenor）、语式（mode）。语场就是话语范围，指正在发生或谈论的事；语旨就是话语基调，是有关说话人的身份和他们之间的相互关系；语式就是话语方式，指语言是通过什么方式和渠道组织起来传达意义的。这三个语域变量组成了语境构型，决定语篇的意义范围，即语域（庞继贤，叶宁，2011）。

3.1 话语难度

我们将文本理解为一种交流行为，一种由其上下文定义的特定现象。只有在具体的交际语境中，词语、搭配和成语才能被信息接收者准确理解。因此，口译译语被认为是一种新型文本，是交际事件中的自主文本。值得注意的是，口译与语言学研究的其他形式的交流不同，因为它涉及至少一个既不是消息的发起者也不是消息的接收者的参与者（Setton，1999），这种复杂的交流对译员造成了挑战。"输入变量"对口译质量的影响一直都是口译研究的重要关注点，诸多"输入变量"可使口译任务变得困难（Pöchhacker，2004）。与讲者特征和工作条件相关的因素包括源语的输入速度、语调和背景噪音等，而与源语材料特征相关的因素包括信息密度、句法复杂度和词汇难度等（Kintsch & Miller，1984；Liu & Chiu，2009）。相对来说，源语的输入速度、语调和背景噪音等因素容易控制，而源语材料的内在因素很难控制，因为它们受多方面因素影响，而且评估语料难度具有较大的主观性。复杂的文本并不一定难翻，翻译起来是否困难取决于译者的翻译技巧、专业知识等多方面因素。下文将从问题触发点和话语可听性两个角度探讨口译中的话语难度。

3.1.1　问题触发点

吉尔（Gile，1995/2009）认为，任何会增加译员处理能力要求的事情，比如需要在听觉/理解、短时记忆或产出上付出更多努力，或增加信号脆弱性，都可能是口译过程中的问题触发点。以往，我们并没有使用通用概念框架来分析口译中的问题触发因素，也没有对其复杂性进行分析。吉尔（Gile，1990）列出了一系列参数，这些参数对口译表现的影响得到了专业人士的验证，源语、速度、风格、演讲专业化程度、演讲者发音、环境噪音、展位温度、演讲者和会议室的能见度、主题的先验知识、译员的精神状况和身体状况、经验、才能、诚实、团队成员之间个人关系、会议代表人数以及组织者和代表对译员的态度等。比如，研究表明，在远程口译中，译员虽然认为某些技术方面如音质、图像和屏幕显示仍有改进空间，但这些并非决定与会者是否接受远程口译的关键因素。相反，最重要的影响因素似乎是译员与会议现场的物理和心理距离。由于无法更直接地参与会议室内的活动，译员往往会产生一种"置身事外"的感觉，这种疏离感才是影响远程口译接受度的主要原因（Moser-Mercer，2003；Mankauskienė，2016）。

如果按照不同类别来划分，问题触发点可能包括以下方面的难点。

信息处理能力需求增加带来的问题：比如面临源语密度高、语速快、信息内容密集的情况，这些任务的复杂性和难度可能导致问题的出现。译员需要在听、理解、记忆和输出等方面投入大量精力，同时会出现理解源语的困难、记忆信息的挑战以及在压力下进行准确、快速翻译的挑战等。

外部因素带来的问题：比如面临音质变差、口音浓重、语言风格、推理风格异常等情况，这些因素可能导致译员难以集中注意力，从而影响他们的翻译质量。

未知术语带来的问题：比如面临源语和译语在结构上非常不同、源语可预见性低、言语产出的差异、特定文化等情况，这些因素可能会增加译员的压力，从而影响他们的翻译质量。

技术因素带来的问题：比如在远程口译中，技术设备（如音频和视频设备）的质量也可能成为问题触发点。如果设备质量差，可能会导致译员难以听清或看清源语，从而影响他们的翻译质量。

下面，我们来看一个例子，相似的信息内容分别采用口语体和书面体展示出来，对比一下即兴发言与读稿发言的差异及其可能给口译带来的影响。

口语体	书面体
空间太阳能发电站的概念其实挺酷的。想象一下，我们在地球轨道上建立一个巨大的太阳能电站，这个电站能收集太阳能，然后把这些能量以无线的方式传输回地面。这就意味着我们可以在任何地方、任何时间都能获得清洁的电力供应，不论是白天还是夜晚，不论是晴天还是阴天。 但是，虽然这个想法听起来很棒，但要实现它还有很长的路要走。首先，需要解决一些技术问题。比如，我们如何在太空环境中安装和维护这些电池和设备？又如何把收集到的能量有效地传输回地面？这些都是我们需要解决的问题。其次，建设空间太阳能电站的成本非常高。我们需要投入大量资金来购买和安装设备，以及运送这些设备到太空中。目前还没有国家成功地建造出一个完整的空间太阳能电站。再者，我们还需要考虑到一些政策和法律问题。比如，这个项目可能涉及国家安全和国际法律问题，可能会受到一些政策限制。 所以，虽然空间太阳能发电站的概念很吸引人，但要实现它还需要克服很多挑战。但我相信，随着科技的发展和我们对太空的了解越来越深入，这个梦想终有一天会变为现实。	空间太阳能发电站的构想是建立地球轨道上的太阳能电站，利用太阳能并以无线能量传输的方式供应到地面。空间太阳能发电站有望解决能源需求并大幅降低对传统能源的依赖。它可布置大规模太阳能电池阵列并利用微波或激光将电能传输回地球，实现清洁能源供应。此技术前沿性与潜力巨大，一旦实现将根本改变现有能源格局并拥有广阔的应用前景。 然而，空间太阳能技术目前仍面临诸多严峻挑战，包括技术难题、高昂成本、安全风险以及政策限制。例如，需要解决太空环境对电池与设备的影响以及如何将收集到的能量有效传输回地面等问题。此外，空间太阳能电站建造成本居高不下，需要大量资金投入。同时，由于涉及国家安全与国际法律问题，政策限制可能成为制约因素。 总的来说，尽管空间太阳能技术的发展仍面临诸多挑战，但其潜力与前景却更为可观。随着技术不断进步与成本进一步降低，相信此技术最终会从科幻走入现实，为人类带来更为清洁可持续的能源供应。

口语体更加注重表达自然流畅，使用简洁直接的句子结构和口语化的词汇，而书面体则更注重句子的复杂性和修辞手法，使用更正式和规范的词汇和句式。比如，在以上例子中，两种表达方式在内容上是相似的，但口语体更加口语化、生动自然，书面体则更加正式、严谨。译员需要根据目标受众和场合的不同选择合适的表达方式，并在口译过程中灵活转换语体，以确保信息准确传达。我们再来看一个英文的例子，相似的信息内容分别采用口语体和书面体展示出来，对比一下即兴发言与读稿发言的差异及其可能给口译带来的影响。

Spoken Text	Written Text
So, on the whole, the Green and White Papers are successful because they show that the government cares about equity towards the unemployed. They have also made recommendations that are practical. By this I mean that their recommendations are likely to solve the problem of mass unemployment. For example, they have recommended the training wage, which is a good way to solve the problem of unemployment.	In general, the Green and White Papers successfully underline the government's well-placed concern for equity towards the unemployed and propose practical recommendations that are likely to reduce the problem of mass unemployment, such as the training wage.
General Description	
Longer	Shorter
3 shorter sentences	1 long sentence
Less formal language e.g. "show" "cares about"	Formal language e.g. "highlight" "concern"
Uses the first person occasionally	Written in the third person only
Uses more sentence connectors	
Uses repetition to aid understanding	
ATOS for Text Analyzer Results	
ATOS Level:10.0	ATOS Level:11.0
Word Count:70	Word Count:38
Average Word Length:5.1	Average Word Length:5.7
Average Sentence Length:23.3	Average Sentence Length:38
Average Vocabulary Level:3.5	Average Vocabulary Level:4.6

总结来看，这两种交流方式在表面语言特征和难度系数上都显示出差异。口语体更加简洁、口语化，使用了较少的长句和正式语言，而书面体则更加正式、详细，使用了更多的长句和高级词汇。这些差异不仅体现在语言的表面特征上，如语言的长度、形式和人称使用，还在更深层次的语言难度上，如文本难度指标（ATOS，Accelerated Reader Text Complexity Measurement）的分析结果所示。译员需要处理的信息量增加，源语和目标语之间的结构差异，以及特定语言和文化相关问题等都是需要面对的挑战。因此，对于译员来说，理解和适应这些差异是至关重要的。

3.1.2　话语可听性

口语语域特征和书面语语域特征可以看作是语域特征的连续体，两者之间的关系密不可分。口语包含书面语语域的特征，书面语包含口语语域的特征。两者是互利共生的连体关系，问题的关键在于把握度，例如如何达到最佳的交际效果（肖福寿，2013）。由于缺乏可量化的方法，语料库难度的测量是翻译研究领域（包括口译研究）中的一个困难的实验变量。坎贝尔（Campbell，1999）指出，源语难度是非常复杂的因素，翻译研究中缺乏适用的模型来确定源语难度，这阻碍了翻译教师将难度因素纳入翻译课程测试。然而，研究人员对话语难度的测量一直保持兴趣，如对话语可听性的讨论。

关于话语可听性的讨论，首先要从话语可读性的讨论开始。文本的复杂性、熟悉度、易读性和排版都会影响文本的可读性，可读性衡量一段文本的易读性，通常，低可读性分数意味着文本不易于阅读，高可读性分数意味着文本易于阅读。可读性作为语料难度的测量方法之一，近年来吸引了更多研究者的关注（Liu & Chiu，2009）。虽然口语早于书面语，但关于可听性的研究是在可读性之后。可听性是指信息以减轻听众面临的特定认知负担的语言和修辞结构为特征的程度（Rubin，2012）。很多研究认为可听性和可读性是密切相关的。可听性的早期工作实际是使用可读性分数来衡量可听性，但这种方法从那时起就受到质疑并被要求改进。

可读性对于语料难度的测量较为可靠。根据弗莱施（Flesch，1948）的可读性计算公式，语料的可读性 =206.835–（1.015 × ASL）–（84.6 × ASW）。其中 ASL = Average Sentence Length（如 the number of words divided by the number of sentences）；ASW = Average number of syllables per word（如 the number of syllables divided by the number of words）。该公式的解读指标如下：可读性得分在 0~30 分之间为"非常困难"，30~50 分之间为"困难"，50~60 分之间为"比较困难"，60~70 分之间为"标准"，70~80 分之间为"比较简单"，80~90 分之间为"简单"，90~100 分之间为"非常简单"。

可听性的研究之所以困难，是因为它由学习者的主观判断决定，还受到学习者各自偏见的影响。自可读性计算公式诞生以来，鉴于口语和书面语具有共通的语言特征，例如词汇和语法，研究者们一度认为，获得了可读性公式，那么合理预测口语文本可听性是有希望和可能的，无须考虑口语的声学特征。然而，口语特有的语言特征如语速、不流畅特征和语音现象导致口语文本处理上的困难，这些语言特征为感知理解提出了挑战（Anderson，2005）。

最近的研究显示，话语可听性或可听话语是指信息以减轻听众认知负担为目标，采用简洁流畅的语言和恰当的修辞手法来表达（Rubin，2012）。无论文本最初是编写之后大声朗读的，还是口述之后转录的，话语可听性与文本紧密相关。无论是设计用于阅读还是听力的，一段话可能或多或少显得口语化，这取决于典型口语特征的密度，口头表达是任何话语都具备的特征。比如，研究发现，视觉材料呈现数字对译员是有益的，但材料的阅读模式和译员的眼球运动可能被源文本的传递速度所改变；专业译员整合视觉和听觉数据的水平高于学生译员，或者说前者更擅长口译中多模态信息的处理（Korpal & Stachowiak-Szymczak，2020）。而且，当信息同时通过视觉模式和听觉模式进行传输的时候，信息的难度和理解过程就会变得更加复杂。视觉信息提供与听觉信息直接对应的背景知识时，会促进理解；视觉信息与听觉信息不对应时，会产生分散理解力的认知负荷。同时接收不同的信息会导致认知成本过高，从而阻碍信息的理解。

此外，研究者关注到了纸张和印刷品的大小、形状、颜色和质地对阅读理解的影响。比如，我们会发现使用排版可以引起人们对要点的注意，格式化、粗体、带下划线的单词、数字或项目符号列表都有助于增强内容的可读性，副标题也是提高可读性的好方法。也就是说，信息展现方式的差异会影响信息提取的路径和效率。

我们来看一个例子，大家感受一下，话语的可读性是如何构建起来的，其对口译听解的重要性是怎样的。

人类曾濒临灭绝的新理论遭到质疑，这揭示了探寻人类自身故事面临的挑战。新研究认为，人类祖先在大约 90 万年前曾经历严重的种群瓶颈，仅有 1000 个繁殖个体存活。然而，这一理论遭到了质疑。**首先**，这项研究主要依赖于对现代人类基因组的分析，但基因组数据有其局限性，无法准确推断当时的种群数量。**此外**，研究使用的种群遗传学模型和假设存在缺陷，可能影响结果的可靠性。**其次**，目前缺乏考古和化石证据证实 90 万年前人类曾大幅减少种群数量。90 万年是一个漫长的时间跨度，仅通过基因组分析很难准确推断当时的种群状况。**最后**，人类基因组中的模式还可以有其他解释，不一定意味着曾发生严重的种群瓶颈事件。总的来说，探寻人类演化历史面临诸多挑战，需要综合运用多学科知识和方法，才有可能逐步解开人类物种故事中的谜团。

人类曾濒临灭绝的新理论为何遭到质疑？

研究提出，人类祖先曾在大约 90 万年前经历了一个严重的种群瓶颈，种群数量仅剩下 1000 个繁殖个体。但这一理论也遭到质疑，主要有以下几个方面的原因：

1. 证据有限。这项研究主要基于对现代人类基因组的分析，但基因组数据存在局限性，不能准确推断出当时种群数量。

2. 模型和假设存在问题。这项研究使用的种群遗传学模型和假设存在缺陷，可能影响结果的可靠性。

3. 缺乏考古和化石证据。目前尚无考古或化石证据证实人类曾在 90 万年前经历严重的种群减少。

4. 时间跨度过大。90 万年是一个极其漫长的时间跨度，很难仅通过基因组数据准确推断出当时人类种群状况。

5. 其他解释存在。人类基因组中的模式也可以有其他解释，不一定说明曾发生严重的种群瓶颈。

探寻人类演化历史仍然面临诸多挑战，需要综合运用多学科知识和方法，才有可能逐步解开人类物种故事中的谜团。

我们再来看一个例子。

There are a number of good reasons for immigrating to Finland. **First,** everyone speaks English *(though they're not very talkative).* **Second,** Finland has a superior, free health system *(if you don't mind the long lines)* and all education is free *(and you get what you pay for).* **In addition,** most public transport is free *(except if you get caught).* **A third <u>reason</u> is that** Finns are friendly, outgoing people *(when they're intoxicated).* Finns **also** value equality between the sexes *(so, no opening of doors for the fairer sex).* **Finally,** where else except in Finland can you swim outside in winter *(through a hole in the ice).*

There are a number of good reasons for immigrating to Finland:

1.All Finns speak English (though they're not very talkative).

2.Finland has a superior, free health system (if you don't mind the long lines) and all education is free (and you get what you pay for). In addition, most public transport is free (except if you get caught).

3.Finns are friendly, outgoing people (when they're intoxicated).

4.Finns also value equality between the sexes (so, no opening of doors for the fairer sex).

5.Where else except in Finland can you swim outside in winter (through a hole in the ice).

以上例子中，上框和下框内的信息相同，不过是采用了不同的展示方式。上框中的下划线和粗体等方式有助于读者快速把握重点信息，而下框中的分行排版方式更能凸显信息层次，一目了然，这对信息的可听性也有启发。研究者关注了响度、音调、速率、短语、强调、重音和发音对听力理解的影响。虽然这些元素的可视化比较困难，但我们可以参考可读性的元素分析，更多了解可听性及其对口译话语分析和重构的重要性。一方面，我们要对源语的可听性有足够认识，对影响源语可听性的元素有足够了解和预期，从辅助讲话人和自身努力熟悉主题知识的角度，都可以适当把控好源语的可听性。另一方面，我们要对译语可听性有足够认识，通过调整响度、音调、速率、短语、强调、重音和发音等元素，辅以可视化材料、表情、手势等多模态信息，提升译语可听性，产出"听众友好型"译语。

3.2　信息权重

权重是指某一因素或指标相对于某一事物的重要程度，其不同于一般的比重，体现的不仅仅是某一因素或指标所占的百分比，强调的是因素或指标的相对重要程度，倾向于贡献度或重要性。口译中不同的信息具有不同的权重，这体现在他们的相对重要程度上。译员需要根据信息的权重进行选择和取舍，尽量传译重要信息，舍弃次要信息。译员需要根据信息的权重进行合理取舍，并在译语产出过程中不断监控和修正信息，确保重要信息得到准确传达。接下来，我们举例分析，请从以下小段中挑选出四个最重要的词或词组，用于支撑段落的主要意义。

例 1：We are all aware how damaging fossil fuels are to the environment, so some people in recent years have considered buying an electric car and I'd like to briefly run through the pros and cons of electric cars, to try and reach a conclusion about whether this is a good buy. First advantage of electric cars obviously is that a fully electric car rather than a hybrid does not burn petrol as fuel, it runs on electricity which we think is much cleaner. Second advantage of electric cars is that it's very easy to recharge them. Third advantage of electric cars, they are very quiet, you don't have so much engine noise, which is a welcome relief in town where we're surrounded with the noise of buses and cars and taxis and planes. Fourth advantage of an electric car is that it is cheap to recharge it.

electricity cleaner; easy to recharge; quiet to drive; cheap to recharge

例 2：Guangdong faces some new challenges, which to some extent are a result of this success. So, I see three key challenges that Guangdong is facing. One concerns rising production costs. Wages have been rising, which is…which is good for the workers. Many natural resource and material prices are going up in the world. So, there is a lot of cost pressure on Guangdong industries. Also land prices are going up. So, the success has generated some rise in production cost, which creates a challenge for the industries in Guangdong. At the same time, there are a lot of environmental issues. Guangdong's rapid growth has caused some problems for the environment. And I'm happy to say that we see quite a bit of improvement.

challenges brought by success; rising production cost; rising land price; environmental issues

例 3：My first tip for saving money when you live in Switzerland concerns shopping, as is everything in Switzerland grocery shopping can be very expensive. That being said, if you go to budget supermarkets like Diner, or Aldi, or Lidl, you can save a lot of money, instead of going to the two larger more expensive Swiss supermarkets, micro and co-op. Another tip, if you're moving to Switzerland is to try to go vegetarian meat in Switzerland is very expensive, so taking the time to try some new vegetarian recipes will be a good way to help you save money. What can you do to save money, in terms of housing here? There aren't a lot of options, but if you are a student or a young professional, I suggest you look into the possibility of special intergenerational housing programs. What can you do in terms of health care? If you're unfamiliar with Switzerland's health care system, it is like everything else here, very expensive. That being said, there are affordable options out there, again if you're moving to Switzerland as a student, I highly suggest that you look into whether or not the canton you live in offers a special health insurance for foreign students. My last tip, transportation is very expensive in Switzerland as is everything on my list, especially if you need to take the train. So, what I suggest you do is buy or rent a bike, um it's a healthy way to get around, it's usually very affordable in Geneva.

go to budget supermarkets; special intergenerational housing programs; special health insurance for foreign students; buy or rent a bike

例 4：Why should we read more translated literature? To answer this, we quickly need to discuss why we read literature at all. In fact, studies have proven that reading literature increases our capacity for empathy. We have the potential to become kinder, more patient, and more inquisitive through our reading of good books. So then, why is translated literature so special? Why should we be reading more of that, specifically? There are a lot of answers to this question, so let's start with the most enticing: exploring the unknown. Reading translated literature means gaining access to the stories, culture, traditions, lands, philosophies, politics, and methods of storytelling from far-flung nations. What's more, readers of translated literature enjoy creative and exciting styles of writing, as translators routinely find their command of English stretched to its limits in the process of finding a style that recreates that of the original. Translators are never invisible, nor should they be. Because you will be reading some of the best writing from another language and culture, and a good translation is itself a work of art. Some prestigious literary prizes have come to recognize this. Last but not least, translated literature help us explore new genres. And to give a more recent example, there is a new wave of Chinese sci-fi available in translation. *The Three Body Problem* by Liu Cixin (translated by Ken Liu) won the Hugo Award for Best Novel in 2015 and has gone a long way to popularizing Chinese sci-fi and fantasy writing.

exploring the unknown; creative writing style; work of art itself; explore new genres

例5：Supermarkets do a few things to make consumers spend more money. They put freshly baked goods such as bread, as they smell lovely, near the entrance to make us feel hungry, and hungry shoppers spend more. They also rearrange things and put them in different places; this makes us spend more time in the store and that means spending more money. They put sweets and chocolate near the checkout, so it is easy to add bars of chocolate to our basket or trolley while we are waiting in the queue. And they put the most expensive items on the middle shelves where you are more likely to see them. Loyalty cards have their advantages, without a doubt. But deep down the store is probably benefiting more than the loyalty card holder. But who can resist a discount or money off? So, while a loyalty card will give you money off, the main reason a supermarket wants you to use it is so they can track your spending habits and learn more about what you buy and when. And be careful of special offers, for example, three for the price of two, buy one get one free. People often buy more than they need and throw away half of it. So, every part of the supermarket from entrance to checkout counter is designed to make you spend more money and buy more things than you need. There's a reason your mother told you to make a grocery list and stick to it.

baked goods smell lovely; rearrange things; loyalty cards; special offers

对口译中的信息进行权重判断、取舍、转换、监控，是口译过程的重要环节。这在源语听解阶段体现在将听辨信息与长时记忆所存储的信息进行比对、对不同信息的权重进行衡量和取舍、听记和笔记有效互动等方面；在译语产出阶段，则体现在信息回忆与产出的有效互动，产出语速的松弛有度，词汇及信息选择的有效程度及修正频率等方面。下文将从信息冗余和信息密度两个角度探讨口译话语中的信息权重。

3.2.1　信息冗余

美国数学家申农（Shannon）于 20 世纪中叶创立了研究信息处理的理论——信息论（information theory）。冗余（redundancy）是信息论的重要组成部分，指的是信号中与信息内容无关的因素（Reza，2012）。信息论认为，从信息发出者发出信息，到信息接收者收到信息，信息在这个传递过程中会发生各种变化，主要是由曲解、无关信息的干扰、信息减弱造成的损失等引起的，这些因素统称为"噪音"（noise）（潘文国，

2002）。由于噪音的存在，信息接收者得到的信息与信息发出者发送的信息可能会产生不等值现象。而信息发出者为了确保信息正确有效地传递，需要采取补偿手段如重复、拉长或重叠等，以弥补信息上的不等值，这些补偿手段就构成了语言交际过程中的冗余信息。冗余的存在可以减少噪音对信息传递的负面影响，提高信息传递的准确性和有效性，避免不必要的误解。

信息论应用于语言学领域，便提出了语言的冗余问题。冗余信息与有效信息并存于语言中，是语言的重要属性。冗余同时也是人类语言的一个重要特征，克鲁斯（Cruse，2002）认为语言中的冗余占了50%。与现代语言相比，古语或文言文的冗余度较低。语言学中的冗余简而言之就是指多次重复的信息。在语言学范畴内，冗余信息是指并不增加信息内容，却有助于语言构建、达意和理解的因素。不同语言在语言结构和文化背景上存在巨大差异，冗余程度和标准也不尽相同，冗余表现方式也各具特点，这些决定了语言之间的转换是有难度的。

语言的高度冗余这一特性表现为在语言中往往存在许多线索可以帮助听话人理解说话人的意图，这些线索包括语音、语法、语义、语用等多个方面。例如，在语音方面，说话人的语调、重音、停顿等都能为听话人提供理解语义的线索；在语法方面，词性、语序、虚词等能够帮助听话人把握语义结构；在语义方面，词汇的选择、搭配等能够提示说话人要表达的意思；在语用方面，语境、身份、场合等因素也能影响听话人对语义的理解。总之，语言中的冗余成分能够为听话人提供多种线索，帮助其准确把握说话人的意图，使交际得以顺利进行。但由于口语实时发生的特性，往往不能够复听，这样就会产生两种结果：其一，听话人加工话语的速度需要视说话人的话语产出速度而定，往往后者比较快；其二，听话人不能够重听，对于刚刚听到的内容只能留下些许记忆，通常是不完美的记忆。

对于了解一门语言的听话人来说，由于对该语言的句法规律和冗余表达比较熟悉，往往可对其进行语法甚至语用上的预测，这种预测能力可以衡量一个人对某种语言的掌握程度。在口语转瞬即逝的过程中，听话人能否在有限时间内迅速把握信息主干，是决定其是否能理解源语的关键。如果能对源语的规律进行预测，对话语中的冗余信息进行甄别并忽略，对话语中的新信息进行识别并记忆，就可以大幅提升对源语的理解速度和程度。

冗余通常体现在语言的多个层面：词法上的多重一致特征，音系学中的多重分辨特征，以及修辞中使用多个词汇表达同一意思。这种冗余往往在语言中自然产生，但也可以被刻意使用以达到特定效果，或为了更清晰地表达某个概念，避免误解。冗余的最主要功能是提高信息的可预测性，从而降低接收者理解信息的难度。

Well, distinguished faculty, students, it is a pleasure to be *on any university campus*, but to be *on a university site* with so many students in such a large university is indeed a pleasure. Today I want to briefly talk about the world as a whole and then come down and talk a little bit about China, and then a little bit about university and then a little bit about you as students and what you might expect going forward.

这段英文比较容易理解，因为冗余部分较多，体现为同义语反复比较多，使听者有足够时间消化和理解重要信息。请看上段中标注的部分：下划线的两个部分是一对同义语反复；斜体的两个部分是一对同义语反复。也就是说，标注的地方虽然反复了多次，但只要理解一次就够了。需要特别注意的仅仅是其他与之不同的部分，也就是新信息部分。如果上段同样的意思以下面这种方式说出来，冗余程度就会大大降低。请看下面这段英文。

Well, distinguished faculty, students, it's a pleasure to be on a university site with so many students. Today I want to talk about the world, China, university and you as students and what you might expect going forward.

我们发现，这段的篇幅简短了一半，同样数量的主要命题由较短的句子且较少的词数来囊括，则用来表达单位命题的词数较少，说明信息更加集中出现，也就是信息密度上升了，理解和记忆的难度也随之上升。正是因为信息往往具有不同程度的冗余，所以需要我们在听解过程中尽快判断哪些部分是冗余的。如果针对冗余信息费了很长时间去听，或者记在笔记上，反而忽略掉或者听不到非冗余信息，就得不偿失了。另外，对于冗余信息，我们也可以根据口译场景的情况和需要，在译语中相应进行缩减，以提升口译效率。请看下面这段英文。

She opened the envelope, which **contained** a confidential document **inside**. After reading it with **close scrutiny**, she discovered it was written in the **exact same** handwriting as the mysterious note she'd received before; the **reason** she knew this was **because** of handwriting studies in her **past history**.

句子短语中加粗的部分是重复的，它们使句子显得多余和冗长。如果上段同样的意思以下面这种方式说出来，冗余程度就会大大降低。请看下面这段英文。

She opened the envelope, which contained a confidential document. After reading it with scrutiny, she discovered it was written in the same handwriting as the mysterious note she'd received before; she knew this because of handwriting studies in her past.

此外，我们应该知道，虽然冗余是语言的普遍特性，也是提升语言理解度的必要手段，但超过一定程度的冗余可能成为过度冗余，影响语言表达的效率和质量。过度冗余具体表现在以下几个方面。

1. 句式冗长：过于复杂、啰唆的句子结构，使得语言表达不够简洁明了，难以理解。

2. 同义语反复过多：过度使用同义词或近义词，导致表达重复累赘，缺乏新意。

3. 逻辑松懈：语言表达缺乏逻辑性和条理性，前后矛盾或缺乏连贯性，使得语义模糊不清。

4. 信息冗余：在语言表达中加入过多无关或不必要的信息，干扰了主要信息的传递，分散了听话人的注意力。

5. 语义空泛：使用过于笼统、抽象或泛化的词语，缺乏具体、明确的语义内容，使得表达缺乏实质内容。

对于这样的口译源语，译员可以在保留主要信息的基础上，整合逻辑和表达方式，使译语在可理解度上有所提升。请看下面这个例子。

The Finnish higher education system consists of universities and polytechnics. The universities stress the connection between research and teaching. The basic purpose of the universities is to carry out scientific research and to provide teaching in related subjects. Students at universities may take a lower (Bachelor's) or higher (Master's) academic degree, as well as academic further education, consisting of licentiate and doctoral degrees. Universities also arrange further education and open university courses. In contrast, universities of applied sciences emphasise links with working life and the degrees offered are higher education degrees with a vocational focus. Universities and universities of applied sciences are spread throughout Finland and are designed to ensure that all prospective students have the same study opportunities regardless of where they live.

如果上段同样的意思以下面这种方式说出来，冗余程度则会大大降低。

The Finnish higher education system consists of universities and universities of applied sciences. The former focus on research and teaching, while the latter focus on working life and offer higher education degrees with a vocational focus.

通过以上的说明，我们知道译员应充分利用冗余信息增强自己对源语信息的理解。同时，也要注意到译语产出中一定程度的冗余是增强译语可理解度的必要手段。但也要避免过度冗余带来的负面影响，口译过程中理解、记忆、转换几乎同时发生，记忆压力可能随着各种因素的发生而加大，过度冗余的信息可能造成记忆负载过重，就会出现信息缺失。

3.2.2　信息密度

信息的冗余程度越高，信息密度越低。信息密度最常见的衡量方式就是话语的词汇密度。尤尔（Ure，1971）最早提出词汇密度的概念以及计算词汇密度的方法，即实词数量占所有词数的比重。通过研究，她得出口语中的词汇密度低于40%，而书面语中的词汇密度高于40%这一结论。韩礼德（Halliday，1985）指出，词汇并不能单独表达信息，信息是被"打包"（pack）在语法结构中的。因此他认为，更加精确地计算词汇密度的方式是看实词数量与小句之比，即每小句中的平均词汇信息的数量，并根据词汇项（实词）打包在语法结构中的紧密程度来衡量话语信息密度。他还对不同话语的词汇密度进行了比较，并指出口语的词汇密度相对较小，比较典型的是口语每小句中含有两个词语；语言越正式，词汇密度越高。书面语的词汇密度大于口语的词汇密度，书面语一般可以达到每小句含有 4~6 个词语；在科技类文体的书面话语中，词汇密度可以高达每小句含有 10~13 个词语。

此外，有的研究者认为，如果基于词汇对信息密度进行判定，那么不能忽视词汇难度的作用，词汇难度可以通过平均音节数（average number of syllables）和高频词汇出现率（occurrence of high-frequency words）等指标计算（Davison & Green, 1988）。另外，还有的研究者认为，平均句长（average sentence length）也可作为衡量文本信息密度的一个指标（Dam, 2001）。这一观点基于以下推理：句子越长，通常包含的从句就越多，句子结构也随之变得更加复杂。这种复杂性往往意味着更高的信息含量。因此，平均句长可以在一定程度上反映文本的信息密度。这种方法为评估文本复杂性和信息量提供了一个相对简单且直观的量化指标。

在信息密度判定中，研究者们早已发现了命题在其中发挥的作用。命题是最小的意义单元（Solso, 1998）。一个典型的命题包括谓语（predicate）和一个或多个论元（arguments），其中谓语的作用是表明论元之间的关系（Kintsch & van Dijk, 1978）。有研究发现，对于词数相同的文本来说，含有命题数更多的文本的阅读时间更长（Kintsch & Keenan, 1973; Kintsch et al., 1975）。也就是说，话语的平均命题数可以作为其信息密度的一个衡量指标。

学习和分辨命题并以其为单位进行信息转换，对于口译教学和实践都具有重要意义。口译中需要做到的不仅仅是转换源语字词的信息，更重要的是获取这些字词组合所表达的语义信息。言语记忆主要采取以命题为单位进行意义存储的方式（桂诗春，1998）。译员在记忆时对信息进行条块化处理，使之成为以命题为单位的意义模块，因为意义记忆比机械记忆效果好。如果笔记不是分析理解后的内容提示，而是源语信息的字词翻译，译语表达将是相当困难的（刘和平，2001）。

将命题应用于口译研究是与口译的翻译单位研究紧密相关的。孙海琴（2012）提到，量化命题需要找到相关语言符号间的"述谓关系"，完成"逻辑分句"的划分。同时，根据英语语言中的"名物化"和"主谓关系"，可以找出可操作的命题单位，即带有述谓关系的逻辑成分（包括非谓语动词结构、名词化成分、独立主格结构等）和带有主谓结构的分句。

句子表征的命题模型认为，命题是能够单独对之进行判断真或假的最小意义单元，它包括两个词项，即主项（arguments）和表示它们关系的关系项（relation）。一个命题表示一个完整意念，例如：大家去饭堂。一个句子可以包括不止一个命题，"大家去饭堂吃午饭"这句话就有两个命题。

又如：John got into an argument with Bill, hit him, and then left the bar.

在这个英文例句中，一共有3个命题：Initiated（John, Bill, argument）；Hit（John, Bill）；Left（John, bar）。此外，同一命题的句子形式可以不一样（桂诗春，2005），比如：John hit bill；Bill was hit by John；It was Bill who was hit by John；The one who hit Bill was John。

上文已经指出，单词数量一致的文本中，命题数量可以区分文本的难度和可理解度。另外，在单词数和命题数得到控制的情况下，文本所含新概念（也就是新的论元）数量越多，所需阅读时间越长，且回忆效果越差（Kintsch et al.，1975）。这里可能涉及类符（type）和形符（token）的统计，也就是说类符/形符比（type/token ratio）可以是衡量信息密度的标准之一。然而，传统的类符/形符比的区分如何与命题或新概念相结合，仍是需要研究的课题。

在口译中，讲者使用信息密度较高的书面文稿或者译员使用书面译稿的情况也是有的，其中前者的情况多于后者。但是，口译中源语和译语更多情况下趋向口语体，译员更多情况下作为现场演说的译语产出者，为听众提供口语文体的译文。口语信息转瞬即逝，为了帮助交际顺利有效地进行，人们在口语表达中往往遵循一定的原则。不论从译员产出译语的角度，还是从听众理解译语的角度来看，口译应该将源语中密度较高的句子或话语进行适当拆解，以降低译员的产出负担，同时增强译语的可理解度。

综上所述，信息密度的判定可以遵循一些指标，但是口译源语的信息密度和难度还要综合考虑已知信息和新信息对于信息听解的影响和辅助。下面我们比较以下两个段落，它们篇幅相当，我们先来看看它们在信息密度上是否存在差异？对它们进行口译，难度上的差异如何？然后思考，我们在应对高密度信息口译源语的时候，可以采用什么样的策略？

例 1：Josh works for a company that makes furniture. He does not work in the factory where the furniture is made, but in the offices across the street. His job involves a lot of paperwork. He types letters to different companies, sends invoices to customers and emails. He also has to organise visits to other companies, make appointments for his boss and sometimes he shows visitors around the factory. Occasionally he has to attend meetings with his boss, but one of Josh's most important tasks is to organise the office party every year. Josh is having a bad day today. The photocopier is broken, the computer does not work, and the printer has run out of paper.	例 2：One of the biggest obstacles to developing culturally appropriate user interfaces is the elusive nature of culture. In anthropology, the term culture has been described many times without an accepted definition or common understanding of the concept. As a result, many anthropologists have turned to the question of how to understand culture and how it is affected by the dynamics of globalisation. As technological innovations combined with mobility and telecommunications have led to international cooperation, worldwide communication and migration, this new dynamic has led to an exchange of people, ideas, and resources.
ATOS for Text Analyzer Results	
ATOS Level:7.2	ATOS Level:13.2
Word Count:116	Word Count:92
Average Word Length:4.6	Average Word Length:5.7
Average Sentence Length:14.5	Average Sentence Length:23
Average Vocabulary Level:2.8	Average Vocabulary Level:5.8

例 2 与例 1 篇幅相近，但是对比来看，例 2 的平均句长更长，句子总数更少，每个小句中实词数量更多，词汇难度更高，具备较高信息密度的特点。不考虑主题、语速等因素的话，例 2 的信息密度更高，其口

译难度也就高于例 1。在应对高密度口译源语的时候，译员除了进行译前准备，还应该在听解过程中集中理解命题之间的关系，以听懂作为记忆的前提，防止为了在笔记上记下某个难词，而忽略信息层次的情况。

3.3　信息结构

在系统功能语言学理论框架中，主述位结构和信息结构是两个重要的子系统。通过研究这两个结构，我们可以了解和掌握新信息在话语中的分布情况，从而更好地理解话语。主位（theme）和述位（rheme）的概念最早由布拉格学派的代表人物马泰休斯（Mathesius）提出，用于描述句子的信息结构。他认为，句首的成分在交际过程中有着特殊作用，即引出话题，这类引出话题的成分称为主位，其他成分称为述位（胡壮麟等，1989）。主位和述位对交际发展发挥不同作用：主位通常负载已知信息，是叙述的出发点、对象和基础，而述位则通常负载新信息，是对主位的叙述、描写和说明，是叙述的核心内容（张德禄等，2005）。之后，系统功能学派代表人物韩礼德（Halliday）和汤普森（Thompson）对主位结构做了详尽探讨。韩礼德（Halliday，2000）指出，主位总是在述位前面出现，这是由主位的起点功能决定的。一般来说，主位通常传递交际双方已熟悉或有所闻的内容，即已知信息，述位则通常传达受话者未知的内容，即新信息。

主位和述位传递不同的信息，这就涉及信息结构（information structure）的问题。对于信息结构的研究开始于布拉格学派，并通过韩礼德在欧洲得以传播。韩礼德（Halliday，1967）将信息定义为已知和可以预测的和新的或不可预测的两者之间相互作用的过程。在语言学意义上，信息是由新旧交替产生的。每个信息单位都是由已知信息（given information）和新信息（new information）组成的。信息结构指的是把语言组织成信息单位的结构，信息单位是信息交流的基本成分，而信息交流即为言语活动过程中已知信息与新信息的相互作用。信息结构就是已知信息与新信息相互作用从而构成信息单位的结构（胡壮麟等，2005）。

主述位结构和信息结构都主张，信息是在已知信息和新信息的互动中产生的，这一点对于话语理解特别重要。如果能够准确快速把握新信息，就能跟进话语的发展，进而更好理解其意义。这对于信息转瞬即逝的口语话语来说格外重要，是口译听解中需要强调的非常重要的分支技能。我们对已知信息和新信息的认识更加清晰了之后，就可能对其进行迅速分辨和甄别。在话语发展中，新信息必不可少，否则信息单位就是不完整的、没有意义的、不能成立的，或者会因为已知信息过多而使话语变得乏味；而新信息过多也是不可取的，这样会降低其可及度（availability），从而加大话语的理解难度，甚至变得不能理解（邹德艳，2016）。

韩礼德（Halliday，2000）认为，句子的信息结构一般都是从已知信息到新信息。已知信息在前，新信息在后，前一句的新信息又可以成为下一句的已知信息，这是符合听话人心理认知过程的最理想的信息处理方式。已知信息是听话人已经知道的，或根据语境可以断定的信息；新信息是听话人还不知道的，或根据语境难以断定的信息。韩礼德认为新信息指说话人要听话人格外留心注意的信息，它可能以前没被提到过，或可能与预想的不符，或需要对它加以强调。通过分析各个信息结构的新信息部分，就可以把握整个话语的要旨。

关于信息结构，一般已经达成的共识是，人们传达信息所使用的表层句子是传递信息的中间环节，句子的形式和意义都不完全等同于信息内容，说话人和听话人对于句子的形式很容易忘却，而只对信息内容进行处理和存储。在说话人说话和听话人听话的过程中，涉及信息编码和解码两个过程。编码过程是说话人用头脑中的信息构建信息结构，再生成表层句子的过程（刘文翠、崔桂华，2005）；而听话人的解码过程是相反的。用信息结构来解释话语产出和接受的过程，如果从口译的角度加以考虑，就是译员经历抛却句子表层结构，获得信息结构，并在此基础上，用另外一种工作语言重建句子表层结构的过程。释意理论中"源语语言外壳"被抛却之后，剩下需要重组进行表达的也是信息结构。所以说，信息结构是以读者或听话人定位的信息体系，下文将从新旧信息和可知信息两个角度探讨口译话语的信息结构。

3.3.1 新旧信息

研究者在口语非流利现象研究中，使用新语义内容来判定口语产出者对于话题内容和相关语言的把握能力。口译中的听解反其道而行之，有效分辨话语中的新语义内容，忽略旧语义内容，抑制无关语义内容，从而将有限的认知容量用于新语义的理解、记忆和回溯。具体来说，研究者通过计算语料中包含的有效的、完整的、有意义的语义内容的音节数与总音节数之比来判定话语中的新语义内容比重。如在语句"…Yeah, we should…we should care…just as it is, we should care about what we said. It's very important. We can't tell…we can't tell…we can't talk about some personal things."中，包含新语义内容为"we should care about what we said""it's very important""we can't tell about some personal things"，新语义的音节数与总音节数之比约为 62.5%（高莹等，2014）。分辨和提取新语义内容对口译源语理解至关重要，这个占比也说明，新语义内容的比重会对话语的可理解度造成较大影响，新语义比重越高，话语难度越大。

研究者对话语中新旧信息的表现形式作出总结，屈承熹、潘文国（2006）把汉语中的已知信息及其表征具体分为五类：上文出现的实体；上文出现的实体所指的语义场；使用回指代词或指示代词；周围的实际环境，零回指；上文出现或暗含的谓语。新信息一般分为三种情况：通过话语或其他手段都不能推导的信息；跟某个预设或陈述选择项对立的信息；替换预设问题中疑问词的信息（刘文翠、崔桂华，2005）。英语信息结构中常用于表达已知信息的语法形式包括以下几种。

1. 带定冠词的名词短语。I bought a new shirt yesterday. The shirt is very cheap.

2. 上下义词。I bought some flowers yesterday. The roses are very beautiful.

3. 前指某一个名词的代词。What were the children doing? They were playing football.

4. 外指的代词。(Two friends are watching a football match, and one player misses an obvious goal opportunity) "I can't believe he missed that!"

在标识旧信息的语法形式中，代词和带定冠词的名词短语最为重要。一般认为，在同一语境下，这两种形式可以相互替换，无论使用哪一个都是恰当的。这意味着，在特定语境中，代词和带定冠词的名词短语在指代已知信息时具有等价性，使用者可以根据语体、语义重复程度等因素进行选择，以达到语言表达的连贯和自然。例如，以下例句中 B 句的代词 they 可以用 A 句中的 the flowers 替代。

A. The flowers in the garden are very beautiful.

B. They were grown by the gardener.

C. The flowers were grown by the gardener.

但是，显而易见，C 句重复了前文中带定冠词的名词短语，所包含的信息自然要比 B 句更多（鞠玉梅，2003）。唐纳伦（Donnelan，1978）列举过以下例子来说明这个问题。

A1. A man came to the office today carrying a huge suitcase.

A2. The suitcase contained an encyclopaedia.

B1. A man came to the office today carrying a huge suitcase.

B2. The huge suitcase carried by the man who came to the office today contained an encyclopaedia.

唐纳伦认为，类似于 A2 和 B2 的带定冠词短语的重复，在通常情况下是不应该出现的，因为一般来说，说话人不必过多重复旧信息，这种做法只在某些文体或体裁中出现，例如儿童初级阅读材料等，否则，这样的语言运用就是笨拙的（鞠玉梅，2003）。我们看下面的例子。

例 1：I was born in Cardiff. Cardiff is the largest city in Wales.

例 2：I was born in Cardiff. The largest city in Wales is Cardiff.

这两个例子在语法上都是正确的，但例 1 在英语中更受欢迎，因为它遵循 new → given → new 的模式。在这种模式下，已知或旧信息"卡迪夫"首先被介绍，然后是新信息"卡迪夫是威尔士最大的城市"。这种顺序允许读者或听者在引入新信息之前建立上下文或熟悉的参考点。它符合在引入新信息之前呈现旧信息或已知信息的原则，有助于更顺畅地理解和处理句子。另外，例 2 被认为是有问题的，因为它遵循 new → new → given 的模式。在这种模式下，首先介绍新信息"威尔士最大的城市"，然后是其他新信息"卡迪夫"，最后提供已知信息"我出生在卡迪夫"。这种顺序可能会破坏读者或听者的理解流程，因为它在提供上下文或已知信息之前引入了多个新信息。我们再多看几个例子。

new→given→new	new→new→given
My favorite movie is *Titanic*. It was directed by James Cameron.	*Titanic* was directed by James Cameron. My favorite movie is *Titanic*.
My favorite animal is a panda. Pandas are native to China.	Pandas are native to China. My favorite animal is a panda.

new→given→new	new→new→given
I love to travel. My favorite destination is Japan.	Japan is my favorite destination. I love to travel.
My favorite color is green. It reminds me of nature.	Green reminds me of nature. My favorite color is green.
I enjoy playing tennis. Wimbledon is my favorite tournament.	Wimbledon is my favorite tournament. I enjoy playing tennis.
My favorite season is autumn. I love the colorful leaves and cool weather. It's also the season of my birthday.	Autumn is the season of my birthday. I love the colorful leaves and cool weather. My favorite season is autumn.
I am a big fan of *Harry Potter*. The books were written by J.K. Rowling, and the movies were a huge success.	The books were written by J.K. Rowling, and the movies were a huge success. I am a big fan of *Harry Potter*.
I love to cook. My specialty is Italian cuisine, and my lasagna recipe is always a hit among my friends and family.	Italian cuisine is my specialty, and my lasagna recipe is always a hit among my friends and family. I love to cook, and it's one of my passions.
I am a teacher. I specialize in teaching English as a second language. It's a rewarding job that allows me to help people from all over the world.	Teaching English as a second language is a rewarding job that allows me to help people from all over the world. I am a teacher who specializes in it.
My favorite hobby is photography. I enjoy capturing beautiful moments and landscapes. My dream is to become a professional photographer someday.	Capturing beautiful moments and landscapes is what I enjoy doing in photography. My dream is to become a professional photographer someday. Photography is my favorite hobby.

新旧语义的辨别对于话语理解至关重要，其中的难点就在于如何分辨，如何更快地分辨。新语义是听解中需要格外关注的信息，那么试想一下，如果我们可以对话语中的旧语义更加敏感，可以做到不受其干扰，那么新语义自然而然就会如同浮雕一样凸出，变得更加清晰可辨。那么，旧信息或旧语义在话语中的显现方式主要有哪些呢？

读者希望任何新信息都能在他们熟悉的内容中呈现。熟悉的信息包括两种类型：一是最近在上文中提到的信息（即使用词不完全相同）；二是读者根据其对文本主题的一般或专业知识所了解的信息。这意味着，优秀的作者通常会将熟悉的信息（或至少是他们认为读者熟悉的信息）置于句中新信息之前。这种"先旧后新"的排序方式使读者更容易理解新信息如何与已知信息相融合。正如学生希望在学习"量子物理学"之前先修"物理学概论"一样，读者也希望作者在引入未知内容之前先为他们提供一个熟悉的话题基础。如果作者以新信息开始句子，读者可能难以把握文本的真正含义，也无法将新信息与之前的内容或已有知识关联起来。因此，我们必须深入理解"先旧后新"原则的运作机制。换言之，已知信息通常置于句首，因为这样更有助于读者理解。

例1：

The application of science to the creation of useful devices to meet the needs of society is called mechanical engineering.

The design, manufacture, operation and maintenance of a wide variety of machinery are the focus of a mechanical engineer's work.

Jet engines and minute instruments for use in medicine are amongst the products designed by mechanical engineers.

Engineering drawings of the devices which are to be produced are created by mechanical engineers. Manual work was the normal means of creating drawings before the late 20th century, but computer-aided design (CAD) programs have been used to create drawings and designs since the use of computers became widespread.

Three-dimensional models can be used directly for manufacturing the devices thanks to modern CAD programs.

例2：

Mechanical engineering is the application of science to the creation of useful devices to meet the needs of society.

Mechanical engineers focus on the design, manufacture, operation and maintenance of a wide variety of machinery.

The products of their work range from jet engines to minute instruments for use in medicine.

Mechanical engineers usually create engineering drawings of the devices which are to be produced.

Before the late 20th century, drawings were usually made manually, but the widespread use of computers has now enabled the creation of drawings and designs using computer-aided design (CAD) programs.

Modern CAD programs allow engineers to produce three-dimensional models, which can be used directly in the manufacture of the devices depicted.

续表

ATOS for Text Analyzer Results	
ATOS Level:10.9	ATOS Level:10.9
Word Count:122	Word Count:117
Average Word Length:5.3	Average Word Length:5.4
Average Sentence Length:20.3	Average Sentence Length:19.5
Average Vocabulary Level:4.2	Average Vocabulary Level:4.4

上面两段文本的内容差异不大，难度差异不大，但例2更容易阅读，为什么呢？尽管两个文本都介绍了相同的信息，但信息呈现的顺序不同。例2更有效，因为每个句子（除了第一个）都以已经提到的内容开头，或者以其他方式为读者熟悉（"给定"信息）。在本文中，新信息位于句子末尾。这种"先旧后新"的顺序让读者更容易看到每条新信息如何融入他们已经知道的内容。因此，"给定"信息提供了帮助我们理解新事物的背景。我们再看下面的段落。

下划线处为"已知信息"	
1.During the second half of the 1970s and early 1980s, the steel industries of the developed world operated with considerable excess capacity.	1. 作者假设钢铁行业的概念是一个给定主题，读者可从文章标题中预测理解它。
2.The situation was particularly acute in the UK where, in 1980, effective capacity was some 2.3 times greater than production.	2. 这与上一句中讨论的内容直接相关。此处指的是英国和1980年，指的是已经提到的那个时期。
3.This was the result of an ambitious investment programme（of about £3000m at 1972 prices）aimed at boosting capacity from 27 million tons in 1973 to 35 million tons by the end of the 1970s and some 38 million tons by the mid 1980s.	3. 同样，这与生产能力有关。
4.Most of this investment was to be concentrated at the five heritage sites—especially at South Teesside.	4. 指上一句的投资主题。
5.Absent from this programme was a detailed analysis of future steel requirements and, when the mid-1970s depression deepened, projected profits turned into substantial losses（£268m in 1975-76 and £1784m in 1980-81）.	5. 指上一句的投资主题。在这里，作者假设读者知道70年代出现了萧条。前面提到的投资的目的是为该行业产生未来的利润。

通过以上的例子，我们将话语分析中新旧信息的分辨与具体的口译话语相结合，这个过程体现了真实话语环境中的信息结构及其复杂性。已知信息被说话人看作能从前文或语境中恢复的信息，新信息是焦点，即说话人认为无法从前文恢复的信息。但是，信息已知与否并不能仅通过看其是否在话语中已经被提及来加以确定，我们还需要考虑预设的因素。预设是关于言语活动的预设，是说话人对自己所说语句的预设，表示的是说话人认为自己与听话人所共有的信息，即交际双方共同接受的已知信息。在言语交际中，说话人往往根据预设对语句进行编码，以突出所要表达的新信息。预设常常可以通过语调、副词和句型表现出来，这些语音与句法和词汇方面的选择是有效反映说话人心理预设和突出新信息的聚焦手段。英语中有一类副词，例如 only，even，also 等，具有反映说话人预设、标明语句信息焦点的作用，这类副词被张今和张克定（1998）称为聚焦副词（focusing adverb）。这类副词在语句中比较灵活，即使在同一语句中，也可以出现在不同的位置上，从而引起信息焦点的变化（鞠玉梅，2003）。我们需要对这类词提升敏感度，按图索骥，帮助我们分析口译话语。

下划线处为"已知信息"

1. A pressure screen is a piece of equipment used for fibre fractionation to produce pulp of a high, uniform quality. 2. A typical pressure screen consists of a cylindrical casing, containing a screen basket and a rotor. 3. The pulp is fed into the screen basket, where the feed flow is separated into two fractions with different fibre lengths. 4. The short fibre fraction passes through the basket and out the accept port at the side of the screen. 5. The long fibre fraction, which contains debris, remains within the basket and is removed from the screen through the reject port at the foot of the basket. 6. The motion of the rotor prevents the plugging and blinding of the screen.

我们发现，话语的推进是以"旧信息＋新信息"的方式螺旋推进的。如果前者占比过大，则冗余信息过多；如果后者占比过大，则话语的可理解度大大降低。在话语发展过程中，可以通过熟悉并掌握旧信息出现

的一般方式，进而更快搜索出新信息。在口译相关整段话语中，新旧信息的推进往往更加复杂。那么，在口译的源语语段中，如果我们对旧信息出现的方式更加敏感，就可以更快分析出信息层次，分离出新信息，更快更有效构建话语主干。在听解过程中，可以迅速将精力从较为相似的信息身上移开，着重听取不一致的、不可预测的信息。如果精力不允许，可以将这些相近意思的表达用相似的译语产出；如果精力允许，可以在细节描述上再进行细致区分。听解过程中的信息获取应该是有主有次、有轻有重的，而不是毫无区别地对待所有信息。

综上所述，我们可以推断，对于译员来说，口译话语中的已知信息比重越大，话语听解难度越小。对于不同译员来说，针对不同主题话语，已知信息比重不尽相同。适当的、有效的话语分析训练可以帮助译员提升分辨新旧信息的能力，而此能力的提升至少可以从以下两个方面着手：一是分析和总结语言层面的相关规律；二是储备和增加世界知识，即长时记忆。语言层面的原语重复、同义语反复、上下义词的反复使用、相似表达的多次出现、语法结构的辅助、语用功能的达成等，都可以帮助我们甄别话语中的已知信息，这也是经过练习可以得到较快提升的口译技能。但是，相对比来说，世界知识即长时记忆的储备和增加更加费时费力。而且，因为口译主题千差万别，所需知识包罗万象，这可能给人无从下手的感觉。这就需要我们对此加以重视，培养自己对多种知识的好奇心和学习兴趣。一旦所听话语的主题知识是我们熟悉的，那么已知信息，包括可以通过长时记忆推断进而理解的信息的比重就会大大增加，最终辅助我们完成整篇话语的理解和口译（邹德艳，2016）。

3.3.2 可知信息

桑福德和加罗德（Sanford & Garrod，1981）提出了框架（scenario）的概念，指出框架是一个基于过去经验的处理模式，是一个过去经验的固定轮廓。在他们看来，已知信息即是框架中被语言激活的那一部分，例如，在"教学"的框架下，"课程"就应被看作是已知信息，因为它是这一框架的一部分。桑福德和加罗德还提出课文理解的情景模型。按照这种模型，一篇文章的记忆表征可以分为三个部分：明示焦点、隐含焦点与长时记忆。明示焦点包含了当前语句中明显提到的项目，如主人公，其内容处于前景，往往可用代词来提及。处于隐含焦点的项目是那些来自长时记忆中的与明示焦点有关的内容，这往往包括主人公的特征、与情景相关的信息，以及一般背景知识的相关信息。新接收的信息与明示焦点及隐含焦点中的信息的联系，主要通过一个消极的激活过程来实现（王穗苹，2001）。

已知信息是在言语交际中已经提到过的信息和说话人假定在他说话时存在于听话人背景知识之中的信息，包括由这种信息可以推导出的可推知信息。已知信息应包含两个方面，一个是在前文中明显提到过的信息，它是一种显性的已知信息，听话人可以在语言语境中找到这种已知信息；另外一种已知信息包含于非语言语境中，主要指说话人在发话时认定某种信息存在于听话人的背景知识之中，听话人可以根据自己的背景知识推导出这种已知信息，这种已知信息是隐性的，不能从话语表层中找到，藏于语境之中（鞠玉梅，2003）。这就为"已知信息到底包括什么？"提供了多种可能性和巨大的探讨空间，进而产生了可推知信息的概念。

听话人的背景知识可用于确定信息状态的维度。储存于交际者头脑中的知识是一种潜在的已知信息，但它又不同于确定的已知信息，这类信息介于已知信息和新信息之间。在具体的语境中，听话人的背景知识框架可以被激活，从而产生可推知信息。可推知信息在推导过程中会在联想意义、内涵意义、感情意义、文体意义等方面有所增减（徐盛桓，1996）。确定信息状态不仅要依赖于交际过程中产生的文本，还应考虑语境因素的作用，因为任何交际都不是在真空中进行的，它必然发生在特定语境中。此外，文本中的信息状态也不是一成不变的，而是动态发展的（鞠玉梅，2003）。我们来看下面的例子。

There are a few things that are just not right with drinking **bottled water**. The first is the bottle itself is made from plastic. Did you know that most plastics are made from petroleum? Yes, you heard me right. One of the biggest consumers of oil is plastic itself. The next thing that I find wrong about bottled water is its price. When compared to **tap water** the cost is more than 500% higher. The same money you spend on one gallon of bottled water can get you roughly 500 gallons of tap water. Of course, it all depends on where you live and what your water company charges.

If you are a bottled water drinker, here are some things, you can do today to help. For one, go to Walmart or Kmart or whatever and purchase a reusable plastic sport drink bottle. Then, while at the store, purchase a pure water filter that either attaches to the faucet itself or to the water supply line. Then, when you want some fresh bottled water to turn your sink faucet on and fill up your reusable plastic bottle and immediately you will have clean, **filtered bottled water**.

If the average person drinks just one bottle of water per week, with 302 million Americans in the country, it will reduce the use of over 15 million petroleum-based plastic bottles. That is huge savings on the need for oil, reduced landfill space, and of course savings in your wallet. Make the change today away from bottled water and toward the more economical and environmentally correct option of reusable bottles and water filters or in the Chinese case, boiled water.

这段英文讲的主题是"瓶装水之过"。在这个主题之下，我们可以通过头脑风暴想到还可以喝什么水、用什么喝、怎么喝等问题。实际上，媒体报道早有涉及相关知识，比如："有些瓶装水装的就是自来水""有些发达国家的自来水可以直接饮用""国人保健意识增强，纷纷购买净水器提升生活品质""中国人习惯喝热水，西方人习惯喝冷水，在更多中国人出国游的今天，西方酒店特别为中国游客准备热水壶以增加服务品质"。如果这些信息都熟悉的话，那么我们在听到"bottled water"之后提及的"tap water""filtered water"甚至中国人最熟悉的"boilded water"时，它们就像是我们久别重逢的"故人"，或者像是出现了我们期盼已久的"朋友"，构建了我们想要构建的场景，就像是译员感觉自己变成了讲者。

综上所述，语言层面的分析和长时记忆的参与可以极大帮助我们清楚分辨已知和未知信息，提升我们对于口译话语的理解程度。下面我们基于较为复杂的语篇进行综合分析。

If you look at the world, I think there are **two major changes** that have taken place in the last ten years and have influenced all of our futures. **The first** is that practically every country in the world now is part of the world free economic system, part of the world free trade system as others say, easy interchange of goods and services between most countries. And this is a major change from where we were only a few years ago. About half of the world's population has joined the free economic system in the last ten years, China is included, India, Russia, and Eastern Europe, some of Latin America. So, there has been a major change in the world free economic structure, which means that if you are in any one country, you can deal with any other country, especially in goods and services and ideas which are knowledge-based. **The other change** that has taken place in the last ten years is associated with technology and the Internet. Today it's very easy to communicate between any two spots on the earth. It is very inexpensive to do so, such as you can transfer knowledge, transfer information and communicate anywhere in the world today for almost nothing.	过去十年 两大变革 1. 自由经济体系 2. 互联网技术
And if you take these two major changes together, what it means is, eh, there's great opportunity in the world as well as great competition. And the competition is what drives us the opportunity is what drives us. And so, every country must accommodate this change. Every country must accommodate in its economy this new competition and this new	国家三件事 1. 良好教育

opportunity. So, if you look at what **countries** can do, eh, they can only **do three things** for their citizens to make them more competitive going forward. **One of the things** they can do is the reason you are here at this university. They can provide you good education, and generally standard of living goes directly with education level, so the higher the educational level within the country, the greater the opportunity for standard of living, the greater the opportunity for economic competitiveness. So, providing an education to the whole citizenry is very important.	
The second thing that any country can do is in fact to invest in research and development. Research and development create ideas for the future. And ideas create new products, new services, new companies. So, we need to invest in research and development and just as the standard of living of any country is directly related to the education level of the workforce, refine the standard of living and the economic competitiveness of any country is usually related to its investment in research and development. And obviously China has recognized both characteristics with a great emphasis on education is the last decade, and the more recent emphasis on increasing the expanding the research and development.	2. 投资研发
The third thing that any country can do is in fact to create an environment that allows smart people, well-educated people to come together with smart ideas, generated from research and development and create new products, new companies, new services, new economic growth. So, the government, the central government of any country can focus on education, research and development in creating an environment to allow people to be successful and an environment that allows entrepreneurs to succeed. And increasingly we see this sort of entrepreneurial spirit here in China. My company happens to be the largest high-tech venture capital investor in the world. And increasingly we see more and more high-tech venture capital investments made here in China. It used to be ten years ago those investments were predominantly made in the United States. Now only about 50% of those investments are made in the United States. About 50% are made here in Asia. So those are the three things that any country can do: education, research and development and setting the environment.	3. 有利环境

续表

Companies are not much different than countries. If you look at our company, the **three things** that we focus on to be successful: hiring the best and brightest in the world, well-educated people, investing a large amount of money in research and development for our researchers to be successful, to bring their ideas into the marketplace.	企业三件事

　　这篇文章探讨了过去十年中两大变革对世界未来的影响，并提出国家和企业应对全球化挑战的策略。全球化的两大变革：世界自由经济体系的形成，促进了国际商品、服务和思想的交流；互联网技术的发展使全球沟通变得便捷廉价。国家提升竞争力的三项措施：提供良好教育，提高国民素质；投资研发，鼓励创新；营造有利环境，促进创业。企业应对全球化挑战的策略：招聘优秀人才；大力投资研发；推动创意进入市场。这篇文章提到，国家和企业在应对全球化挑战时采取的策略是相似的，都涉及三个方面：重视人才，国家要提供良好教育，提高国民素质，企业要招聘优秀人才；鼓励创新，国家要投资研发，鼓励创新，企业要大力投资研发；优化环境，国家要营造有利环境，促进创业，企业要推动创意进入市场。这种相似性使得文章的内容更加紧凑，也更容易理解和记忆。

　　在理解语言时，要将单个词语的含义与整个语段的意义有效连接起来，通常需要经过句法分析的过程。这一过程帮助我们理解词语在句子结构中的位置和功能，从而更准确地把握整体语义。通常来说，听话人建构一个信息单元，然后就会遗忘具体的字词和句法，只剩意义的概要或总结，然后每个信息单元的概要与其他信息单元的概要结合在一起，就成为整个语段的意义概要。通过这种方式，整个语段的摘要也就建构起来了。这个过程帮助建构话语各部分的关系，最终得出谁做了什么、对谁、用什么方式等重要信息。

　　通过跟随承载新信息的关键词，迅速并瞬时地找到源语的语义分布，并将其以关键词串的形式存储于工作记忆中。要使这个过程快捷有效，关键是要能够迅速辨识已知信息。此外，对于已知和未知信息的迅速甄别还能够提升笔记记录的有效性。安德烈斯（Andres，2002）在笔记记录方面提到了采用替代形式（pro-form）来记录已知信息。这些替代形式可以包括更加简洁地记录相似信息的方式，也包括使用最为广泛和便捷的回指箭头（recall line），不仅是回指已经提及的概念，而且可以包括整个意义单位、整个段落或一系列的事件。下面的两个例子可以较好说明回指箭头的重要性，我们在以下两个段落的加粗部分都可以使用回指箭头来记录笔记，以替代已经提到的已知信息。

So how are we to meet this challenge? In a globalized world, Europe needs to modernize and reform if it is to remain competitive. **It was for this reason** that the Heads of State and Government of the European Union agreed in Lisbon in 2000 a series of ambitious goals.

And the key thing to remember about climate change is that it is a cumulative process. If the rate and magnitude of climate change are not slowed down by a reduction in greenhouse gas emissions, any beneficial effects are expected to diminish while the costs and risks continue to increase. The negative effects predominate in the long term. **This is why** New Zealand can't afford to ignore climate change, and why we can't refuse to play our part, however small, in trying to do something about it.

综上所述，可知信息指在言语交际中已经提到过的信息以及说话人认为听话人已熟悉的信息，包括显性的已知信息和隐性的可推知信息。可知信息主要来自语言层面和世界知识层面。语言层面上，重复出现的词汇、短语、上下义词、代词等语言特征可以帮助我们快速识别可知信息。世界知识层面上，与主题相关的背景知识和长时记忆可以激活框架，帮助我们推断可知信息。

新信息主要指话语中无法从前文或语境中推导出的信息，是话语推进的动力，是口译产出的重点。区分新旧信息有助于分析信息结构，突出新信息，提高理解效率。长期进行区分新旧信息的训练可以提高我们识别语言特征的能力，同时还需要主动学习积累世界知识。丰富的可知信息可以帮助我们更好地理解和分析源语话语，扩展我们的理解框架，有利于分辨新信息，实现更高效的口译产出。

3.4　信息推进

上文讲到信息结构中的新旧信息和可知信息，它们是口译话语构建、分析、理解及重构的核心内容。然而，信息内容并非是相互独立、互不干扰的个体。这些信息单元需要通过语法规则和语义关联作为"黏合剂"，按照特定的方式组合起来。只有这样，才能够完整地表达预期的话语含义，并最终达成特定的交际目的。这种组合过程不仅赋予了单个信息单元更丰富的意义，也使整体信息结构更加连贯和有效。话语标记和启承结构在这中间发挥重要作用，下文将从话语标记和启承结构两个角度探讨口译话语的信息推进。

3.4.1　话语标记

话语的衔接（cohesion）是指存在于话语内部、能使全文形成语义连贯的各种意义关系成分（Halliday & Hasan，1976）。衔接是通过词汇和语法将句子连接成篇的手段，借此达到话语连贯的目的。韩礼德和哈桑指出，当话语中某一成分的解释依赖于另一成分的解释时，便会产生衔接。因此，任何表达话语内部语义关系的语言特征，如词汇、语法等，都可视为衔接手段。

衔接可分为显性衔接手段和隐性衔接手段。显性衔接手段包括词汇、语法和音系（篇内衔接）。词汇层面上的衔接表现为词汇复现、同义词、反义词、下义词、局部关系词和词汇搭配等方面；语法衔接主要表现为照应、省略、替代和连接等语法手段。隐性衔接手段包括情景省略和背景省略，隐性衔接手段中省略部分无法在上下文中找到，但可由听话人根据情景语境和文化语境推测出来。话语连贯必须依靠参与者运用丰富的世界知识来达成，因此，语言形式不连贯的语段，在意义上可能是连贯的。

理解并重建话语的基础是辨识观点，但与观点同样重要的是衔接，衔接是说话人指引听话人将新旧信息联系在一起的信号（Baker，1992）。一篇演讲最重要的两个要素就是观点和联结观点的衔接信号。在辨识新信息，将新旧信息结合起来进行理解的同时，衔接信号对整个话语框架的构建非常重要，也是重构话语信息的重要工具。因此，不论是否记笔记，对衔接信号的辨识和记忆都是口译训练的重要一环，衔接信号可以分为显性的和隐性的（Gillies，2009）。

话语标记语是实现话语连贯的重要因素。话语标记语作为衔接手段反映的是作者或说话者的思维模式，在译文中反映的是译者的思维模式，而把这两种思维模式联系到一起的则是译者的准确理解和等效表达（陈明瑶，2005）。语言信息的获取和记忆是口译的重要环节。译员有效获取源语信息，有效将其加以记忆和存储，能够有效保障其译语的产出，有助于提高口译效率。译语话语的连贯性和逻辑性对口译质量至关重要，而话语标记语虽是语言表层成分，却能够增强话语深层的连贯性和逻辑性，因而在译语话语构建中发挥重要的作用。美国学者弗雷泽（Fraser，1999）根据语用功能把话语标记语分成四类（转引自陈明瑶，2005）。

1. 对比性标记语（contrastive markers），如 though…but, contrary to，however, on the other hand, whereas, in comparison; in contrast, yet, still 等；

2. 阐发性标记语（elaborative markers），如 and, in addition, moreover, what is more, for another thing, furthermore 等；

3. 推导性标记语（inferential markers），如 as a consequence，as a result，so then，therefore，because of，accordingly，all things considered 等；

4. 主题变化标记语（topic change markers），如 by the way，incidentally，speaking of，just to update you，to return to my point，back to the original point 等。

对话语标记语在听力理解中的作用，学者进行了研究。肖德龙和理查兹（Chaudron & Richards，1986）的实验表明，宏观标记语有助于听力理解，而微观标记语的作用不明显。弗劳尔迪和陶罗扎（Flowerdew & Tauroza，1995）的实验也表明话语标记语有助于听力理解。勒博尔（Lebauber，2006）将话语标记语称为"重要的线索词"，它们是说话者有效组织语言并借助语言表达思想、观点和意图的重要工具，这样的线索词有如下功能：引出话题、提出话语结构、引出结论、指出以下信息为重复、引出解释或例证、指出以下信息为偏题等。杨承淑（2005）认为，这类词汇的数量虽然有限，但出现的频度却非常高，担负前后句之间的信息与逻辑的转折功能。考虑到话语标记语在信息传递中的关键作用及其高频使用特性，口译课程应当加大对这一语言要素的教学力度。这不仅能提升学生的口译技能，还能增强他们对源语言结构和意图的把握能力。

总结来看，我们可以知道，经过加工的信息更加容易被记忆并复述出来，而有意识地记忆"话语衔接词"和"重要线索词"，有助于听者更好把握讲者的话语含义（徐然，2010）。多数情况下，这些词是意义的引领者。换句话说，正是因为有了这些词，它们所衔接的上下文才可以顺利地被回忆或复述出来。下面的英文段落中，加粗部分都是话语标记，如果缺少了这些标记，段落的可理解度会大幅降低。

The birth rate in Finland, as in all developed countries, has been very low for a long time. **As a result**, the age structure is much more heavily weighted towards older age groups. **Unfortunately**, it seems that the situation may not get better in the near future. **Consequently**, labour markets will face a serious shortage of people of working age. Two possible solutions to this problem are being widely discussed: attracting labour from foreign countries and raising the retirement age. **However**, there are objections to both of these proposals. **Firstly**, importing foreign labour can cause social tensions, **and secondly**, many people feel it is unfair that they should be obliged to continue working beyond the retirement age.

再看下面的例文，话语展开和概念联系采用了话语标记，请关注右列的内容标识，结合由话语标记支撑起来的大框架，再对全篇进行主旨口译，我们会发现，话语标记在话语构建中发挥了重要作用。在口译听辨中，我们应该对话语标记多加注意，这样会帮助我们更好地进行话语分析和重构。

So, what is holding back the development of solar power after all that energy is free and a hundred percent renewable so as long as we have the technology to harness it? What is holding back the development of solar power?	采访者提问
Well in a way you can't actually say it isn't being held back because the cost of producing solar panels has fallen so significantly that it's been possible to roll out solar panels in very large areas, not just of the developed world, but also in the developing world. **The most obvious** challenge that it faces is its seasonal nature. You don't get as much sunlight year-round in fact here in Yorkshire I don't think we've had any sunlight since October. It's been raining non-stop but more seriously. There is very obviously a seasonal effect and there is **also a problem** with uneven distribution of sunlight around the world, to take an extreme example in countries that lie in very northern latitudes, for example, let's say northern Sweden or Norway or Finland. There are whole months in the year when the sun only rises for about three or four hours in the middle of the day, and the rest of the time is just night. This leads to obvious difficulties in generating electricity from sunlight.	被访者回答 同意 挑战 1 挑战 2

So, there are two major intrinsic challenges faced by solar power, seasonality and uneven distribution across the globe.	承上启下
And there is **another factor** that has to do with recent economic developments, namely that the price of oil has dropped massively because new resources have been found in certain countries so that they are less dependent on imports, because fracking has taken place and a number of other factors have led to the price of oil dropping significantly, and this has had a major impact on other energy sources, not just solar energy, by the way.	因素 3＝ 挑战 3
So, I would like to briefly explain **some of the things** that solar energy needs in order to become a more competitive energy source. **One of the things** that solar energy needs is better electricity storage, similar to wind energy. The wind turbines do not spin all the time, and you would need some kind of battery storage to shop the energy from solar energy overnight. **Another thing** that solar energy needs is a better grid infrastructure. The national grids are designed for relatively constant power generation and struggle with the fluctuations of solar and wind energy. The national grids are adapting, but slowly, and the infrastructure investment required is huge. **The other thing** that solar energy desperately needs is better transport. I have already talked about the uneven distribution of solar energy as a resource. So ideally, what you need is a cheap, reliable and safe way to transport solar energy from one country to another, from those countries that are blessed with constant sunshine to those that are not.	**解决方法：** 方法 1：储存 方法 2：基础设施 方法 3：运输

　　下面我们来看几个现场问答的例子，在话语转换更加频繁的现场问答活动中，话语标记是如何帮助组织话语的。

Journalist: Mr Prime Minister, we have had a great deal in the last few months how **deceit** has caused the problems that we are now facing globally. Are you being **totally honest** with the people of the world to say that there has been **genuine agreement** here when we know there have been a number of splits among the G20, and also there is a one-size-fits-all agreement for twenty countries who are at different points in the economic cycle and different points in the global recession as well?

Prime Minister: **Isn't that what is remarkable**, that you can have countries that would never even have sat round the table a few years ago coming round a table and coming to agreement? **The reason** we've got to meet and come to agreement is that **unlike a few years ago** when you could run national financial systems without thinking about what was happening in the rest of the world, every bank affects every other bank, and a bad bank in one country affects good banks in every country. **That is why** we must come together, **so that we have** rules and supervision on financial institutions that are global; **we have** that cross-border regulation that is necessary; **we have** the international regulators coming together **so that** we know what is happening not only on one continent but on all continents.

I believe people are **encouraged by the fact** that China and India and Japan and many countries from Asia, Latin America, Brazil, and Argentina, Mexico, Africa, South Africa, and the African Union, and the European countries, Russia as well, and of course the United States of America, we have all been able to come together in a way we could never have done even a year or two ago to decide quite detailed proposals that will reshape the global financial system for a long time to come. **I must say** that I have been putting forward some of these proposals for ten years. We have achieved more in ten weeks because people have recognized the need for change in the international financial system.

提问：**The Prime Minister must be honest with the people of the world.**

回答：**We are encouraged by the fact that countries have come together to agree on proposals that will reshape the global financial system for a long time.**

Journalist: Mr Prime Minister, **I heard** you say that you will help the poorest countries. **I was wondering** if you will also save countries like Greece from bankruptcy, and **if so**, to what extent, unlimited or not?

Prime Minister: **I think it is true to say** that interest rates have been coming down in the Eurozone area, of which Greece is a part, **and that** there has been a major stimulus to both economies within the Eurozone economy and trade, **as a result of** what has been agreed within the European Union. **I believe** that the measures we are taking collectively right across the world will also help the Greek economy, **because if we can** restore financial confidence in our banking system, then every country will benefit. **If we can** channel more international resources into economies, then it is not only emerging or developing countries that benefit, but all of us.

Look at the Marshall Plan after the Second World War. Money was spent in America, sent to Europe to invest in the reconstruction of Europe. The beneficiaries of that were **not just** the European countries who got the money, **but** the trade that then flowed between Europe and America. There is an injection of resources, this time internationally, and **it will** have a benefit to all countries, **whether you are** developing countries, emerging markets, **or whether you are** industrialized countries, like Greece as part of the European Union.

提问：Prime Minister promised to help the poorest countries, but it is unclear if this will be unlimited or not.

回答：The interest rates have decreased in the Eurozone, which will help Greece's economy as well. If we can restore financial confidence in the banking system, it will benefit all.

Journalist: Mr Prime Minister, you have made an important announcement today about the future of tax havens and I warmly welcome it, but the criteria being used is that of the OECD, which focuses upon private tax evasion. Of course, we know that tax avoidance by major corporations around the world is just as important, and we know that the developing countries of the world have so far been excluded from the OECD information exchange process. Is this the start of the end of tax havens, or is this the end of the end of tax havens?

Prime Minister: **This is** the start of the end **because** country after country is now signing up to the principles that have been set forward internationally. **The principle** is that you've got to be prepared to exchange information about tax on request. **In the past few days**, we have had a lot of other countries who have been prepared to sign up to this. **Now** I think you are going to find other countries wanting to join this group.

It is an announcement today of a list of countries that are not abiding by the rules. **There are** countries that have signed up to the principles, **but** we say they have yet to agree bilateral deals, and **then**

---

there are those countries who have signed up to none of the principles and have no bilateral deals. **This is** a comprehensive attempt with other initiatives to follow, initiatives that we agreed today to go outside the range of OECD countries **as well later**, to clean up this problem and to try to solve it once and for all. **Of course**, there will be people who try to avoid taxes, **but** we are taking all the legitimate legislative measures to close these loopholes.

提问：The OECD's focus on private tax evasion is important, but the exclusion of developing countries from the OECD information exchange process raises questions about the future of tax havens.

回答：We have announced a list of countries that are not abiding by the principles of exchange of information about tax on request. This is part of a comprehensive attempt to close loopholes and solve/address the problem.

Journalist: Mr Prime Minister, you said you were confident that countries would do whatever was necessary to get growth. How can you be so confident? Are there any sanctions in this communiqué? Are you hoping the IMF names and shames those countries that don't? A lot of them didn't sound very keen on doing anything else.

Prime Minister: I am pleased you've asked that question because we say specifically in our communiqué that **not only will we** do whatever it takes, but **we will also** ask the International Monetary Fund to assess the action that has been taken and the global action that is then required. **We will** meet again in the autumn **to look at** what countries have done, **to review** the progress we have made, **to take** whatever action that is necessary on top of that.

Do not forget this: we are in the middle of the biggest fiscal injection, the biggest injection of resources into our economies in history. $5 trillion is a huge sum of money, **but** it means that **not just one** country but almost **every country** is trying to get their economy moving by putting more resources into it. That is the sensible thing to do when banks fail, and markets fail. That is what we are doing. **But** people have signed up to a declaration that allows what is being done to be assessed, and **we will** report back of course in the autumn about what is being done. **But** the International Monetary Fund will regularly assess the progress that is being made. **So**, I have some confidence that this money is not only going to be put into the economy, **but** it is going to be put to good use in saving or creating jobs. Thank you all very much.

提问：**Mr Prime Minister is confident that countries will do whatever is necessary to get growth, but there are no sanctions in the communiqué.**

回答：**We are in the middle of the biggest fiscal injection of resources in history, with $5 trillion being put into the economy. The IMF will assess the progress and report back in the autumn. I have confidence that this money will be put to good use in saving or creating jobs.**

从以上分析我们可以看出，话语标记对话语展开和理解具有重要作用，是口译听解中不可忽视的环节。在口译教学中，我们可以专门针对这部分进行训练，这有助于学生更好地分辨信息层次和功能。同时，在交替传译训练中加入笔记之后，我们会发现，口译源语中的话语标记往往也是需要在笔记中记下的重要元素。

3.4.2 启承结构

话语的推进结构包括信息结构、主述结构、话述结构和启承结构，其中启承结构是《现代汉语篇章语言学》提出的新的篇章结构。这种篇章结构分为两个部分：前一部分称为"启后语"，其特点是具有启后性；后一部分称为"承前语"，其特点是具有承前性。两个部分加起来，构成启承结构；启后语与承前语中"语"的概念，是广义的，这个"语"可能是小句，可能是复句，也可能是比复句更大的语言单位。启后性有两个种类，一类是由语言成分表现出来的启后性，如词汇和标点符号，这种启后性主要是由语义，或者说由语义和语用表现出来的现象，暂且称为有标记启后性；另一类没有明确的语言成分，没有固定表现形式，是由听话人自己推断出来的启后性，主要属于语用现象，暂且称为无标记启后性（徐赳赳，2010）。虽然关于启承结构的分析和说明主要针对书面语，但其对口语的启后及承前的话语功能的分析有启示作用，对口译中的源语分析及译语组织具有重要意义。本节从启承结构的角度分析口语中的启后和承前的功能，并结合实例分析启承结构对口译话语分析及理解的重要作用。

根据徐赳赳的分析，篇章中的一些关键词可以给读者理解语篇提供启后的作用，这些词就是"启后词"，与其相对应的就是"承前词"，属于有标记的"启后承前"现象。比如，汉语中的"虽然，但是""不仅，而且""因为，所以""不是，而是""首先，其次"都是启后并承前的关键词对。也就是说，我们看到或听到前一个词，就会预测到下一个词的出现。而一旦下一个词不出现，或距离前一个词比较远，都会影响篇章的连贯性和可理解性。以下例句还可体现其他类似"启后承前"的结构。

1. 中文的"危机"由两个字组成，**一个意味着危险，另外一个意味着机会。**

2. **以前**，日记是写给自己看的，然而**现在**更多的年轻人喜欢把自己的日记放到网站上，希望和更多的人交流。

3. 我对现在的这份工作还比较满意。**首先**，我学的就是这个专业；**其次**，同事们都很喜欢我；**另外**，工资还算可以，有奖金，收入不错。

4. 国家建设需要大批人才，**唯有**广开才路，任人唯贤，**才能**使其发挥所长，为国家做最大的贡献。

5. 虚荣心强的人，**与其说**是为了脱颖而出，**不如说**是由于自以为出类拔萃，因而不惜耍弄欺瞒、谋略的手段，使虚荣心获得最大的满足。

6. "太阳花"这个名字的来源十分有趣，**为什么**叫它"太阳花"呢？可能是**因为**只要太阳出来，它便会绽开一朵朵五颜六色的小花朵。太阳花还有一个特别之处，它就像向日葵一样，阳光从哪边照射，它的头就往哪边转。

7. 从根本上改革学制，是一项极其艰巨的工作。**没有**教育家的抱负、政策制定者的决心，以及所有相关者——包括家长、学生、教师、院校、纳税人以及社会上每个人的充分支持，这项工作**决不能完成**。

8. 从全球钢铁行业来看，总体仍然面临较大压力。**一方面**，国际市场钢材价格有所反弹，但上涨乏力，市场价格总体处于低位向上调整状态；**另一方面**，由于燃料价格上升，钢铁生产成本增加，钢铁企业的经营和生产面临更大的成本压力。

9. 世上除了生死，都是小事。世界微笑日，从今天开始，每天微笑吧，**不管**遇到什么烦心事，**都不要**自己为难自己；**无论**发生多么糟糕的事，**都不要**感到悲伤。今天是你往后日子里最年轻的一天，因为有明天，今天永远只是起跑线。记住一句话：越努力，越幸运。

10.**除非所有人都获得自由，否则没有一个人能够是完全自由的，除非所有人都有道德，否则没有一个人能被称为完全是有道德的；除非所有人都过得快活，否则没有一个人能够称为是完全快乐的。**

汉语中"启后承前"关键词的概念比较好理解，实际上，在英文中，我们同样可以遇到很多类似"启后承前"的关键词及概念。尽管英语是我们的外语，我们对其敏感度有限，但我们应该多储备英语中"启后"及"承前"的关键词，以提升语感，最终提高我们在中英互译口译活动中的话语理解能力和解释能力。比如，在"**Hardly any major global issue today can be resolved** without US-China cooperation and understanding."这句话中，我们在听到加粗的前半句时，就应该可以预测到后半句应该有 without 或者 if not 等否定表达，并引出达成前半句结果的条件。如果前半句的结果是 A，后半句的条件是 B 的话，则整句的译语结构也就出来了："想要 A 就需要 B；只有 B 才能够 A"等类似的表达。以下例句还可体现其他英语中类似"启后承前"的结构。

1. It **isn't** that I'm stupid; **it's** mainly that I don't work overly hard.

2. **Just because** it's not happening right now **doesn't mean** it never will.

3. **For one thing**, you will earn money; **for another**, it is good to work with others in a team; **finally**, it is a good chance of finding a suitable job.

4. **Unless** the Mexican government works on the causes of poverty, the problem is going to **get worse**.

5. Let's put it this way: Mr. Denton was **a new teacher**, and **new teachers** are impressionable; I wanted his **impression** of me to be a good one.

6. As you can see, there are many reasons why young North Americans get tattoos. A tattoo **can be** part of a group's uniform. It can be a sign of fashion. It **can be** an expression of individuality. The decision to get a tattoo is most often a result of the influence of friends or media, or the desire to express oneself.

7. China will make sustained efforts to fulfill the development goals of the UN Millennium Declaration and contribute to the early control of HIV/AIDS epidemics worldwide. **For that**, the Chinese government has pledged US$10 million to the Global Fund to Fight AIDS, Tuberculosis and Malaria in support of HIV/AIDS prevention and treatment efforts in developing countries.

8. Throughout our long history, we have always looked **outwards, not inward**. We have used the seas that surround our shores **not to** close ourselves off from the world, **but to** reach out to it, to carry our trade to all corners of the earth. And **with that trade have come people**, companies, jobs, and investment. We have always understood that our national greatness is based on **openness**.

9. Sometimes misunderstandings occur between **people from different cultures, even when they can communicate in a common language**. And these misunderstandings can even lead to the breakdown of intercultural communication.

10. If we talk about the influence of the weather on our feelings, why do people say they feel more **cheerful** when the sun shines, and **miserable** when it's raining? Why do some people suffer from SAD (seasonal affective disorder), which makes them **depressed** during long dark winters? Can the weather **really influence** our mood, or do we **just imagine it**?

相对比来说，另一种"启后承前"关系并没有明确的语言成分来构成，也就是说没有固定的表现形式，而是由听话人自己来进行推断，主要属于语用现象。这样无标记的"启后承前"现象只能通过小句或者更大的语言结构来表现整体意义（徐赳赳，2010）。比如，在以下例句中，虽然没有明显的启后承前的关键词，启后承前的关系仍可以通过上下文推导出来。

1.**不过**，至少还有一点令奥迪值得欣慰，**因为**即便增幅放缓，**但**奥迪仍占据了中国高档轿车销售市场份额的 70%。

2.（在他看来，）评判一个企业，**不能**仅看其营业额，**还要**看它是否有为社会做贡献的行动。

3.他期中考试受挫，持续努力了半个学期，**也**没有在期末考试中获得好成绩。

4.**为了**宣传中国旅游业，吸引更多海外旅游者，中国文化和旅游部全面开展旅游宣传促销工作。**如今**，在世界各国主流媒体上都能看到中国旅游业的广告。

5.中国去年新增了 9500 万网民，其中 60% 以上都是具有高中学历以下的人，**也就是**说年轻人正在成为互联网真正的主流。**那么**，年轻人成为主流，直接带来的效应就是互联网在更快、更大程度上向着娱乐化的方向去发展。

6.We've got a **cleaner** who **does a lot of the housework**, and that includes doing my **laundry**. But I **still** have to make **my bed** and do some of **my ironing**, and I sometimes do the **shopping with my mother**.

7.As languages such as English, Spanish, and Mandarin become more widely spoken, there is a fear that **many minority languages might die out**. Therefore, some countries have taken steps to **protect minority languages by promoting the use** of these languages.

8.I have coffee and cereal for **breakfast**, then have a light **lunch**, maybe a sandwich and an apple, and a snack in the **afternoon**. We have our main meal in the **evening**. If Mum's late home from work, she doesn't bother to cook; we just get a **takeaway** instead.

9.**Some** students go to university because they enjoy studying, **others** just want a qualification. No matter what, you have to get good grades in the **entrance exams** to get a place at a university. You can then study for **a degree or a certificate**.

10.The government says that the GDP target this year will be set around 7.5%. Can we reach the target? Actually, the economy is a very **complex** thing. Nobody can predict what the growth rate is going to be this year. You could ask the 100 greatest economists in the world, and they would have estimates all over the place. So, it **doesn't make sense** to create expectations that the growth rate will be exactly 7.5%. It could end up being **more than 8, or less than 7**. Given all the **difficulties** that exist at the present time, it's possible that more bad news will come out during the year, and there will be some undershooting of the target. But, as I said, the world is a complex place, and some **things might tip in favor** of the country, and it might come out higher. There are other forces that cannot be predicted or cannot be identified.

从以上分析可以看出，启承结构作为构建语篇的重要方式，无论采用有标记还是无标记的形式，都在口译过程中发挥着关键作用。这种结构不仅有助于话语分析，还对译语的准确产出具有重要意义。

有标记的启承结构可以帮助译员在听取标记关键词的同时，记录关键词，并把握上下文的逻辑关系，这样可以帮助译员在翻译过程中保持准确性和连贯性。

然而，当遇到无标记的启承结构时，译员需要依赖自己的语感和语言能力来分辨并理解多层次的关系，这要求译员具备较高的语言敏感度和理解能力。在这种情况下，译员需要更多的思考和推理来准确捕捉到源语中的启承结构，并在译语中进行适当的显化，以增强译语的可理解度。

启承结构分析在口译过程中扮演着关键角色，它不仅有助于译员准确理解源语内容，还能促进流畅、精准的译语表达。为提升对语言启承结构的敏感度，尤其是对外语结构的把握能力，译员可采取多种策略。首先，广泛接触目标语言材料，包括新闻报道、学术文章、影视作品等多元化资源。这种沉浸式学习有助于熟悉目标语的句法结构和表达习惯。其次，系统性地学习语言学知识也不可或缺，深入了解语言的结构特征和语法规则，能够帮助译员更透彻地理解启承结构的功能。与目标语的母语者进行深入交流是另一种有效方法。通过这种互动，译员可以更准确地把握目标语中的启承结构，并了解当地的语言习惯。在日常学习中，译员还应培养对语言细节的敏锐观察力，特别是在处理复杂句式时，要关注其结构特点。最后，理论学习与实践应用的结合至关重要。译员应在日常口译训练中有意识地运用启承结构分析，通过不断实践和总结，持续提升口译质量。这些系统化的学习和实践方法将帮助译员逐步提高对语言启承结构的敏感度，从而更好地完成口译任务。

第四章 口译中的话语重构

口译中的话语分析不是随着源语的结束而戛然而止的，相反，话语分析是否成功有效，必须由记忆的回溯或者译语的产出来体现。经常听到学习口译的学生反映，明明听懂了源语，可是到了译语产出阶段就几乎不记得什么信息，也不知从何说起，或者说这句时就忘了那句。这里当然有源语听解不充分的原因，但也不排除译语的产出对口译学习者的干扰作用。如果译员对信息的选取、信息的产出方式、问题信息的应对等不能做出果断有效的决策，那么，即便是已经听懂甚至已经有效记忆的信息，也可能由于过多干扰的出现或回忆时间过长而产生遗忘或混淆的情况。所以说，译语产出阶段的话语重构是口译不可或缺的重要环节，训练译员在有效分析话语的基础上做到相应程度的有效产出，是口译训练的必备步骤。本章我们将从话语生成、话语整合、口译脱壳、口译分脑四个方面讨论口译中的话语重构。

4.1 话语生成

语言生成的理论和实践对口译至关重要，其重要性主要体现在两个方面：译员如何理解源语和如何生成译语。大多数人可能认同这样一个看似朴素的观点，即译员生成译语必然比说话人生成源语更容易，因为译员无需自行构思内容，只需"鹦鹉学舌"，重复说话人的话语即可。这种观点既对也不对。之所以说对，是因为上述原因；之所以说不对，是因为即使是重复源语，难度也会因主题熟悉程度和话语长度不同而有所差异。更何况，口译是两种语言之间的转换，如果译员没有"脱离源语语言外壳"，而是亦步亦趋地跟随源语，那么译语产出不可避免地会带有源语的句法和词汇特点，听起来就不像地道的译语。如果译员要"脱离源语语言外壳"，就需要用新的语言外壳来承载源语意义。这就要求译员在成功分析源语的基础上，依靠自身较强的语言生成能力来产出译语。从这个意义上说，译员本身也需要是优秀的演说者。

既然译员不是仅在"鹦鹉学舌"，那么其自身"说话的能力"对其口译表现来说就是非常重要的。一个人的说话能力是否是天生的？后天的训练是否可以使其得到提高？在口译教学中我们发现，有的同学生怕译不好、译不全，对源语进行"字对字"的翻译，进而会因为个别词不会译而百般纠结。训练时间加长也不会改善这种情况，因为总是有不会译的词，最终只能得出结论，"口译太难了，我不是那块料啊"。如果我们退一步思考这个问题，假设因为某个词不会译，就无法进行口译的话，那么这个世界上应该没有几个人可以胜任口译这项工作了吧？须知不会译的词永远存在，不明白的概念永远存在。除了增加自己的知识储备和专题词汇，并在口译任务之前进行大量有针对性的准备之外，现场应对也是译员的必备能力。这种能力实际上至少包含两个层面——心理调节、语言应对。

首先，我们来看心理调节层面。不能因为个别词不会译，就在面部表情和语言组织上表露无遗。这种情况在学生译员身上表现较为明显，一旦遇到不会的概念或词汇，他们往往会不自主地表现出不一样的表情，比如吐舌头、挠头、咧嘴笑、眨眼睛等。此外，他们的语言组织马上就会出现速度下降、零散混乱的现象。然而，经过训练或有丰富经验的译员往往不会出现上述情况，主要原因在于他们深知采用应对策略的重要性，并且能够较为从容、有效地进行心理调节。至少在保障口译质量的同时，他们不会让听众察觉到译员在哪些地方是完全有把握的，而在哪些地方采用了应对策略。

其次，我们来看语言应对层面。译员能够保证在心理调节方面表现如常的话，那么面对不会的概念或词汇，如果是非常关键的，可以采用现场问的方法，向讲者提问，当然也不适合问"What is the Chinese meaning of …you just mentioned?"这种问题，但可以尝试让讲者更多解释一下某个部分，如"Could you elaborate on…?""By…, do you mean…?""What do you mean by…?"等，讲者解释了之后，就可能解决了问题；倘若还是不行，如果足够幸运，听众中的双语人士可能提供解决方案。当然，现场提问的方法并不适宜频繁使用。除此之外，还可以采用上义词的方式，先应对一下，期望接下来的语段可以再次涉及甚至着重解释这个概念。实际上，很多情况下，并不一定所有词都要译出，也不必完全按照其字典里的意思译出。请看下面关于亚洲就业情况的一篇访谈。

Are enough jobs being created?

The latest ILO report notes that unemployment has risen by 5 million, and about half of that increase is here in East and South Asia. And this is affecting young people, young job seekers coming into the labour market. But another important finding is that the quality of jobs in developing countries in the region is still very low. Nearly 600 million workers still earn too little to escape $2-a-day poverty. This is hindering consumer demand and stifling prospects for business expansion in the region.

这段展现的是亚洲就业的两个主要特点。

1. 新增失业 500 万人，其中一半来自东亚和南亚，主要影响年轻人；

2. 就业质量比较有限，6 亿人每天所得不足 2 美元。

　　基于以上两个特点，最后一句总结：这阻碍了消费者需求并抑制了该地区业务扩张的前景（This is hindering consumer demand and stifling prospects for business expansion in the region.）。即便不知道 hinder 和 stifle 的确切意思，或者因为语速等原因没有听到这两个词，都不影响意义的获取。前面提到两个较为负面的特点，一定是"影响""妨碍""阻滞"消费需求和商业发展。这里有了上下文的帮助，大胆推测和抓大放小的策略就显得非常重要，这也是译员需要练就的话语分析和重构能力。上下文或语境是口译的源语理解和译语产出必须要依赖的因素。所以我们说，短句不见得好翻，长段也不见得难翻。但是，由长入短易，由短入长难。所以，口译练习不应局限于半句或整句的转换，应以段落或篇章练习为主。

　　段落和篇章练习最接近口译，特别是交替传译真实场景。在段落和篇章即兴演讲过程中，讲者首先产生演讲计划，详列交流意图并选择意欲表达的信息，可能包括在长时记忆中寻找相关信息，比如描述从 A 位置到 B 位置的行程（Levelt，1989）。但是，即便讲者正在进行这样的信息搜索，这种搜索也要受制于交流目的，且讲话中包含的内容也是不固定的。对于译员来说，他们演讲计划的来源就是储存在长时工作记忆中的话语记忆，当然要看选择哪一个框架。一旦话语题目对译员来说是熟悉的，那么其长时记忆中就出现很多支持因素，不仅辅助理解，还可以在长时工作记忆中帮助构建连贯的表征和提取结构。但是，如果话语是不熟悉的或者不连贯的，那么新命题与译员已有知识相结合的可能性就大大降低，结果就是，表征是不连贯的，可能较少被提取到。在工作记忆框架中，不连贯的表征可能随时被重写，并不大可能被强化成为长时记忆的一部分。所以，即兴演讲和话语口译之间的区别可能就在于信息的提取位置不同。

　　输出干扰（output interference）是指在自由回忆过程中产生的噪音会影响对细节痕迹的提取。同样地，口译过程中的回忆也会显著影响源语信息中细节痕迹的提取。译语的组织和表达占用了工作记忆资源，对源语信息的记忆提取产生噪音，起到输出干扰的作用，使得记忆提取过程，尤其是细节痕迹的提取变得更加复杂和困难。接下来，本节将从自动化和不流利两个层面，对译语产出的特点和规律进行阐述。

4.1.1　自动化

口译现场中，译员在承受巨大心理压力的情况下，需要做出迅速、及时、准确的反应。因此，口译对迅速理解源语要求极高，译员必须在短时间内抓住说话人的意图，逐层梳理话语的层次结构，这样才能在口译时使译语富有条理性、逻辑性和可理解度。在这个过程中，信息分析及听辨能力发挥重要作用。还有一个因素也非常重要，却常常被人忽视，那就是语言转换速度。

经典言语产出模型（Levelt，1989）主要由三个部分组成：概念形成器（conceptualizer）、构成器（formulator）和发音器（articulator）。对于口译更加重要的是语言经过复杂的理解及产出过程，最终以译语的语言形式出现。也就是说，口译中的概念在两种工作语言中的转换越快、越精准，就越能够辅助口译过程的多任务协调，保障口译质量。转码（transcoding）在其中起到重要作用，指的是将源语的字、词、短句在语言层面上转换成译语。甚至有研究者（Gile，1991）认为，转码速度和能力是职业译员的标志。工作记忆中的语音回路可在 2 秒之内存储语音及视觉信息，方便译员进行转换。也就是说，译员将输入信息进行快速转换，可以提升信息理解和传译效率，进而保障口译整体质量。

20 世纪 80 年代，美国语言学家克拉申（Krashen，1985）提出了语言输入假说（input hypothesis），指出学习者必须接受可理解性输入、包含已知的语言成分、略高于已知语言水平的成分这三个方面的输入，语言习得才有可能发生。输入理论是二语习得研究领域中对语言输入在学习过程中所起作用进行的探讨，对二语习得具有重要的指导意义。但学界对输入理论的局限性也多有探讨，认为语言输入假说过分强调理解新语言，而忽视了产出该语言的重要性，即语言输出的重要性。针对语言输入假说的不足，二语习得研究者斯温（Swain，1985）对加拿大法语沉浸教学法进行了调查，发现"可理解输入"在二语习得过程中固然起很大作用，但不足以使二语学习者获得语言使用的流利性和准确性。如果习得者要使第二语言既流利又准确，不仅需要"可理解输入"，更需要"可理解输出"，这就是输出假说（output hypothesis）。

语言学习是一个动态的循环过程，语言输入是语言学习的前提条件，经过加工的语言输入只有在输出过程中被加以运用和尝试，才能使学习者真正习得语言。输入和输出理论解释了语言习得的重要特征，对外语学习的听、说、读、写、译各方面都具有指导意义。输出理论注重的是为二语习得者提供表达语言和获得反馈的机会，让学习者注意到自身的语言问题。在对二语输出质量进行评价之外，输出理论能够有效提高学习者二语的流利度。输出理论对口译实践及教学的贡献在于它指出输出能够提高语言表达的自动化（automaticity）。心理语言学认为，语用过程是自动性（automatic）和控制性（controlled）两种过程的混合（Carroll，1999）。语言在表达过程中占用的注意力资源越少，其自动化程度越高，反之亦然。

口译中译语输出的熟练程度可通过练习获得提高，如果双语转换可以脱口而出，这就达到了输出自动化。在这个过程中，译员的长时记忆被激发，成为口译工作记忆的一部分；译员的被动词汇被转化，成为不同口译任务中的主动词汇。输出自动化在口译中不仅指二语或 B 语的输出，听到、理解 B 语之后用 A 语表达源语的意思，同样检验的是译员对 B 语语义的掌握和熟练程度。语言表达自动化是口译至关重要的能力，双语之间迅速转换的能力是口译的要旨（邹德艳，2011b）。英国学者贝尔（Bell，2005）指出，绝大多数语言学家承认，语言产生的心理语言模式需包含一个"常用结构存储"机制，即存储在记忆里的单个词汇、短语和句子能够直接访问。该机制在翻译过程中能够瞬间将意义与词汇连接起来，减轻短时记忆存储负担。由此可见，语义与词汇的瞬间连接是口译的必要前提。

很多研究表明，预先习得对应的词语、术语、短语的表达，会使口译过程中部分译语的输出做到自动化，译员可以节省出精力专注于理解源语、组织译语等任务。理想的翻译方式必须包括自动化地运用文字来表达意义的过程。意大利学者法布罗和格兰（Fabbro & Gran，1997）指出，在翻译过程中，翻译与理解可以出现"分离"现象，在某些情况下，语言的输出可以不需要意识理解体系的介入。没有译语输出的自动化，持续地投入精力于每一环节，将对总体的口译临场表现具有破坏性。

人的大脑是一个处理能力有限的系统。认知过程自动化程度越低，需要占用的工作记忆容量越大；认知过程自动化程度越高，需要占用的工作记忆容量越小。大量的对应词汇、表达以随时待命的状态存在于译员的大脑中，以自动化的形式被传译表达出来，这不仅有效减缓口译现场的时间压力，同时减轻译员的工作记忆负担，有效利用译员大脑有限的处理能力（邹德艳，2011b）。

输出自动化对口译教学和实践都具有指导意义，加强口译中的输出自动化对提高口译质量至关重要。那么，如何能够有的放矢地加强口译中的输出自动化呢？一方面，应该在口译中强调块语与范例的积累。这样，在有限交际时间的压力下，译员能够很快从记忆中提取语言资源，满足即时交际的需要。另一方面，块语和范例的积累需要以双语形式进行转换强化，这样才能确保在将块语和范例以双语形式进行表达的过程中，译员能够做到准确、流利（邹德艳，2011b）。

在口译教学中，输出自动化的难点更多来自学生二语运用能力的局限。二语水平有限，则理解二语（英到中口译）和表达二语（中到英口译）这两个方面都可能出现输出自动化程度低的情况，进而影响整体的口译效果。因此，在口译教学中提高输出自动化，离不开工作语言的有效输入及转换。这里需要注意的是，母语的信息输入同样重要，由于往往因为是母语而被忽视，反而显得更加重要。主要是因为，口译中的话语通常并非我们熟悉的生活语言，具备特殊的话语特征，因而需要通过"刻意练习"（deliberate practice）进行输入，然后是双语转换。有了工作语言的有效输入和转换，口译中的输出自动化才成为可能。

在口译的话语产出方面，不论是 A 语还是 B 语，对于没有接触过的，甚至概念都是陌生的事物，期望学生可以使用地道的 A 语或 B 语进行表达是不切实际的。在口译中结合技巧进行专题口译练习时，可以按专题为学生提供各个专题所涉及的专有概念、固定词汇及表达法，要求学生对这些内容进行双语快速转换。根据语言习得领域对于输入、输出理论的探讨，只输入不输出，或者只记忆不运用，不利于语言输出自动化及流利度。因而，在学生熟悉了特有概念和表达法之后，可以在口译课堂上针对不同专题进行口译练习。根据哈默（Harmer，1981）的说法，输出分为两种：第一种是操练性输出，第二种是交际性输出。带句型操练或翻译就是典型的操练性输出，这种输出很难提高学生实际运用语言进行交际的能力。相比之下，交际性输出更加适合口译教学的需要。针对不同的专题设计模拟口译场景进行训练，既能够调动口译学生的输出积极性，又能从实质上提高学生的输出自动化，进而提高他们的口译交际水平。

另外，口译中的双语转换涉及方方面面，专题训练不能一劳永逸地解决所有问题，也不是提高口译学生输出自动化的万用良方。在口译教学中，可以随时进行双语转换练习，既能够活跃课堂，又可以增强学生的输出自动化能力，至少可以让学生更深刻认识到输出自动化对于口译的重要性。比如，可将学生分成两组，一组提供 A 语词汇，一组提供 B 语词汇，两组互相提供相应的译语输出。对于数字转换这类口译重点技巧训练，可以采用随时随地进行游戏式或竞赛式的转换训练方式。这样的练习不必要求学生事先准备，学生需要时刻感受口译的"即时性"和"瞬时性"，这能够为学生从事口译职业打下良好基础（邹德艳，2011b）。

通过同声传译中的"乒乓练习"方式可以加强交替传译中的平行翻译过程的转换速度和程度，可以从根本上提升交替传译的整体效果。这种练习可以增强口译输出自动化程度，口译学习者平日遇到任何概念或词汇，都可以尝试这样的"乒乓练习"，而这些概念和词汇将慢慢由不熟悉到熟悉，它们的转换也会逐步提速，最终可以达到脱口而出的程度。在口译教学中，教师也可以根据教学内容和目标，将"乒乓练习"加入课堂教学，在提高学生们对陌生词汇双语转换速度的同时，提升他们对该种练习和习惯的重视程度，并使之成为同学们课后口译练习的一个必要组成部分。在课堂上，教师可以在具体练习内容中抽取陌生词汇，作为译前准备活动，让学生们采用"乒乓练习"的方法尽量熟悉这些陌生词汇，这样势必对接下来的实际训练起到较好的铺垫作用。比如下表所列出的双语词汇。

Breast cancer	乳腺癌
Climate change	气候变化
European Union conference	欧盟会议
Exchange of views	交换意见
Externally oriented economy	外向型经济
Film and television industry	影视业
Foreign secretary	外交部长
Greenhouse gas emission	温室气体排放
Intergovernmental relationship	政府间关系
Medical insurance	医疗保险
Monetary policy	货币政策
Multilateral trading system	多边贸易体系
Panama Canal	巴拿马运河
Protectionism and discrimination	保护主义和歧视
Regional and international issues	地区和国际问题
Trade liberalization	贸易自由化

　　教师可以首先扮演主考官的角色，教师朗读词汇，学生们将词汇转换为译语，并记录整个过程所需的时间；然后让学生们自行熟悉词汇，之后再以两人为一组进行练习，一人朗读词汇，另一人进行译语转换。通过对比练习前后的表现，可以评估学生在双语转换的准确度和速度上是否取得了明显进步。语言基础扎实、语速较快的学生可以将速度提高一倍，即在第一次转换所用时间的一半内完成任务。这种练习方式不仅能够提高特定词汇的转换速度和准确度，还能够延伸到其他相关词汇的学习。例如，上表中的词组可以被拆分，并与其他词汇重新组合，形成新的词组。通过这种方式，口译常用词汇的习得范围就会逐步扩大，由点及面，由面及片。

　　此外，教师还可以根据准备练习的话语进行关键词抽取，随后采用"乒乓练习"的方法让学生熟悉关键词的转换，然后让学生采用母语或外语将这些关键词作为基本词汇串词成篇。同学们可以根据词语之间的联系，加入自己的推测、预判和推理，势必需要添加很多内容，才可以产出具备一定可理解度的话语。然后比一比，谁的产出听起来合理、流利、丰富。这可以让同学们充分体会，更大限度地"脱离源语语言外壳"是一种什么状态，译员自身的公共演讲能力在口译中发挥着何等重要的作用。最后，将需要练习的话语整体展现给同学们，对比仅靠关键词组织的话语与讲者的话语区别到底在哪里。这样，同学们较大距离远离源语，可以更加清晰地看到关键词和讲者的组篇方式是口译听辨中更应该把握的因素，具体的字词，特别是不关键的词语不应占用过多的转换精力和时间。

　　同时，这样的关键词组篇练习可以提高学生理解口译话语的能力，因为学生自我组篇能力的提升可以增强其理解讲话人话语的能力。这样的练习还可针对口译源语进行更深程度的信息处理。译员对源语的信息处理程度越深，理解越透彻，记忆越持久，表达也就越完整、清晰和准确。超前的逻辑推导会随着言语链的发布和接收得到印证，并为随后的信息分析提供更为可靠的语境和认知环境基础（刘和平，2001）。下面我们通过例子对此加以说明。

关于一个语段，只给出以下关键词：students，abroad，thousands of pounds，travel and accommodation，save money，online，Internet and emails，advantages，future，home/computer。译员基于这些关键词，结合自己认知语境中有关"留学"的主题知识，对讲话人想要传达的信息做如下推断："学生出国留学花费较大，但网课可以解决一部分问题，可能是未来发展趋势。"实际上，本段的英语源语如下。

Every year, many students travel abroad to study at universities. Most of them spend thousands of pounds on their courses. The cost of travel and accommodation significantly adds to their expenses. However, they could save a lot of money by taking their courses online via the Internet and emails. More and more universities are offering courses over the Internet, and this has many advantages for students. In the future, most students will probably stay at home and study in front of a computer.

我们发现，在给出关键词的前提下，结合自身的世界知识和主题知识，我们可以将关键词连词成篇，而具体使用何种语言，采用什么字词和句式，都不会影响主要意思的表达。实际上，同样的一组关键词，还可以连词成篇为下面这样一段话。

Thousands of students studying abroad are now able to save thousands of pounds on travel and accommodation by taking advantage of the benefits offered by the Internet and emails. With the convenience of online platforms, students can easily search for affordable options and make arrangements from the comfort of their own homes or computers. This not only allows them to save money but also provides them with the flexibility and convenience they need for their future endeavors. The accessibility of the Internet and emails has revolutionized the way students plan their study abroad experiences, making it more cost-effective and efficient.

以上两段话都是根据所给关键词构建出来的话语，虽然在具体用词和句式上有所差异，但两段话都强调留学生可以通过利用互联网和电子邮件的优势在旅行和住宿方面节省费用，它们还提到了在线平台在搜索经济实惠的选择和在家中或电脑上进行安排方面的便利性。也就是说，这两段话都强调了在线学习对留学生节省费用的好处，这是信息的关键点和段落的中心思想。我们再来看几个例子，随着主题的扩展，大家可能会发现，主题知识的缺乏会极大影响组词成篇的效果。

Taking Notes in Lectures	
taking notes in lectures vital skill not a dictation use abbreviations keep pace active listener predict know about the topic	Let me first give you some advice on taking notes in lectures. Taking notes in lectures is an important skill. The most important thing is that you should not try to take notes on everything. A lecture is not dictation. You have to decide what is important and what is not. Secondly, when you take notes, do not write everything down in full. Use abbreviations, symbols, numbers, anything that helps you keep the pace. Also, try to be an active listener. By this I mean that you should try to predict what the speaker is going to say. Before the lecture, ask yourself what you already know about the topic, and during the lecture, think about what the lecture might lead up to.
China's Economic Growth	
China's economic growth the last decades geopolitical reform in the 1970s 10% growth rate global manufacturing output population resource large market	Well, most people would agree that the massive economic growth China has experienced in recent decades is perhaps the most significant geopolitical event of the 21st century. It started with economic reforms in the late 1970s, when China's economy was still largely rural. Since the 1970s, China's economy has grown by an average of 10% per year. Since 2001, China has doubled its share of global manufacturing output. In fact, China is second only to the US, and most forecasts predict that it will overtake the American economy

China's Economic Growth	
large workforce the growing middle class	within the next decade. China's vast population resources not only mean that China is the world's largest market, but they also underpin the main reason for the country's economic rise: a large labour force. Many would also argue that the growing middle class is the backbone of China's success.

Tech to Help Tackle Ikea Flat Packs	
Ikea flat packs furniture giant teamed up with a start-up scan a product code smartphone instruction video assemble and co-create with Ikea motto of the company collaborating local presence social good	If you have ever opened an Ikea package and felt helpless, there may soon be a simple solution. Furniture giant Ikea has teamed up with a London-based start-up that could allow people to scan a product code with their smartphone and access information, such as how-to videos that show step-by-step how to assemble or set up a bed. The idea behind the app is to work with Ikea to make its services more accessible. Ikea believes that such a service has great potential to make everyday life at home better for everyone, in line with the company's vision. This case is a successful example of how large companies can gain a competitive advantage by working with start-ups to achieve a better local presence and greater social benefit.

Gardening Tips	
gardening tips wellbeing mental health grow herbs hanging baskets one-pot containers	A wealth of research suggests that gardening has a positive impact on wellbeing and mental health. We are delighted to share with you some of the best gardening tips for small outdoor spaces. 1. Grow herbs. Herbs are the perfect plant for a balcony, patio or even in a window box. Not only are they relatively easy to grow, but they can also liven up your kitchen and add flavour. 2. Hanging baskets. Hanging baskets are a great way to make the most of limited space and add some variety and colour to your balcony or terrace. Make sure you use a good quality food material for your basket. 3. One-pot container vegetable gardens. There are a variety of different one-pot containers that you can use to create your own mini garden in a small space. You can grow salad plants, chilli plants or herbs in a steel tub or wooden planter. Tomato bags are also a practical solution that allows you to easily grow your own tomatoes. String beans and pumpkins are also easy to grow in pots and containers. Do you have a small garden or just a balcony? Let us know what you grow.

在这个练习中，学生需要利用所给的关键词自行组织篇章。起初可能会感到无所适从，特别是因为所给的关键词多为主题专有词汇。然而，在各自的认知知识范围内，学生可以自由地利用这些关键词来组织篇章，并尽可能使其更具说服力和内容丰富。这个过程可以锻炼学生的逻辑组织和语言表达能力。如果学生能够将自己的篇章录音，并与真实语段进行比较，那将更加有益。这样做可以帮助学生更深入地理解关键词的含义以及整个语篇的组织模式，并进一步提升练习的效果。通过这样的练习，学生不仅可以提高逻辑组织和语言表达能力，还可以培养口译技巧。这种练习方法可以帮助学生快速理解和应用关键词，提高他们在限制条件下进行有效沟通的能力，也就是说，可以帮助学生在口译这种认知任务中进行有效地表达，提升他们的话语构建和口译产出能力。

4.1.2　不流利

提及流利（fluency）的研究，一个重要方面就是考量不流利的一些表现，也就是成功的公共演讲会尽量避免或控制"停顿、重新开始、重复、重新导向"等。高夫曼（Goffman，1981）认为，这些语言上可以发觉的错误是语言产生阶段推理和组织语言的认知努力的外显。成功的公共演讲人如职业演说家、讲师或电台主持人的技巧就是要控制自己的产出，使产出能够掩藏这些努力以及这些努力带来话语上的不流利（disfluency）。最常见的不流利包括迟疑、停顿、嗯啊、纠正、错误开始、重复、插入语、口吃和口误。"停顿"和"嗯啊"分别在技术上被称为"填充停顿"和"无声停顿"："填充停顿"包括错误开始和重复，它们是不流利的重要因素；而无声停顿，并不一定反应迟疑或支吾，有时可用于达成某种修辞效果（Duez，1982）。

无声停顿的情态各不相同，有时可以是换气的空白，特别表现强调或迟疑的有意停顿。迪斯（Deese，1980）认为，有技巧的演讲者可以使自己的迟疑与无声停顿重合，使其出现在话语的自然句法衔接处，也就是说，无声停顿不一定是不流利的一种表现。口语产出比较重要的特点是迟疑，主要分为四种形式：非填充停顿，也就是沉默；填充空白，也就是讲话人毫无意义的填充类表达，比如"嗯、啊、就是、那么、然后"等；重复，也就是讲话人重复同样字词或字词的一部分；错误开始，也就是讲话人突然停下，换了另外一种表达。有研究显示，迟疑现象极大影响听话人对口语话语的理解，尤其是当该语言并非听话人母语的时候。

近年来，研究者们试图创建话语生成的双语模型，早期的模型主要涉及双语话语模式中的具体部分或方面，比如双语词汇的组织或者语码转换现象。关于流利度的测量，研究的突破体现在每分钟内填充停顿的数量。如果该数量比较显著地降低，那就说明流利程度有所提高。这些研究成果支持以下假设：首先，可能对于口译学习者来说，在线话语规划中，比较简单的方式是控制填充停顿，而不是控制无声停顿。也就是说，学习者可以控制发声填充语（fillers）比如"嗯、啊、就是、那么、然后"等，可能对他们来说，将无声停顿缩短或消除反而更加有难度；其次，学习者在线规划的效率看起来提升程度不大，这一点从学习者无声停顿表现未见提升可以看出来。

双语产出中一个经常被忽略的方面是不平衡双语者经常在词汇提取方面存在问题，原因是访问速度较慢，或者因为目标项目从未被习得。德博（De Bot，1992）指出，词汇提取的问题在单语的非失语症患者中比较少见。对于并不能平衡掌握双语的讲者来说，这种问题比较常见。如果激活从概念层蔓延到译员的词汇提取，而并不能激活译语中的任何词元，或仅仅部分激活一个词元，那么译员需要重新产出"前信息内容"，或者采用沟通策略，可能造成二语产出上比较明显的延迟。由此可以得知，译员的不流利是由多种原因造成的，而译员多为不平衡双语者是主要原因之一。金（Jin，2010）的研究指出，不平衡双语者在词汇提取方面可能面临困难，这可能是造成二语产出速度减慢的主要原因。

比较熟知的策略之一是使用通用术语（generic terms），近似表达所需词汇含义的高频词汇（high frequency words），往往所需词汇是译员没有习得的，也可能是"就在嘴边但说不出的"（the tip of tongue phenomenon，TOT）。一定数量和时长的无声停顿是口译流利性的必要组成部分。区别在于，学生译员由于语言或技巧的原因，口译过程中充斥大量不合理的有声停顿，而职业译员能够通过对技巧和策略的娴熟运用，合理地控制不当停顿的产生，并借助标记句法界限的无声停顿来缓解认知负荷（符荣波，2012）。

奥尔特曼（Altman，1994）认为，流利度很大程度上是区分职业译员和受训译员的一个重要方面。语言学习者的一些技巧可以应用到口译教学中，以提升口译产出的流利度，这些技巧包括省略、释义、语义转借、向讲者求助等（Ellis，1994）。这些技巧的熟练应用可以说是流利的重要因素，不论对单语交流来说，还是对口译来说，都是如此。此外，语言外能力（extra-linguistic competences）比如边听边分析的能力、听的过程中以及译语表达过程中使用笔记的能力，与语言技能一样，对译员的流利度起到很重要作用。

从上文中我们可以看出，口译中的不流利主要包括无声停顿和填充停顿，而后者主要表现为"嗯、啊、就是、那么、然后"等填充语、重复、错误开始等现象，是口译训练中需要着重规避的表现。

首先，其实不是每个口译学生都面临这个问题，但确实有些学生这方面的问题较为严重。学生的汉语口语表达习惯会如实反映在外语表达及译语产出中，有时还会随着外语表达及译语产出的难度增加而被无限放大。这就需要学生从平日讲话开始训练自己使用流利的语言，一旦出现多余的填充语，就为自己标记一次错误，一天下来，统计错误数量，假以时日，日常表达不流利的现象定会有所改观。教师可以在课堂上特别关注学生在使用双语表达中的填充语现象，使学生们对此问题提起足够重视，比如，在口译训练初期，甚至整个训练阶段，教师可以根据学生们填充语较多这一习惯的轻重程度，为不同学生设定不同的训练期限以达成最终的目标，也就是将"填充语"控制为"零出现"，可以先将填充停顿过渡到无声停顿，不知下句说什么，那么就停在那里，什么也不说，直至想好要说什么，然后继续。

其次，关于填充语、重复、错误开始等口译中常见的填充停顿，产生的原因比较多样复杂。第一，可能是因为学生在口译中同时进行理解、回忆、组织译语等多任务的处理，其他任务对译语产出的干扰和抑制作用过大，因而学生下意识进行"有声停顿"而不能自控；第二，可能是因为学生的语言运用能力有限，搭配及组句能力较为薄弱，这种情况在使用外语进行译语产出的时候大为常见；第三，学生可能尚未领会"口译即解释"的精髓，而是采用逐词翻译的方式，一旦哪个词想不出对应的译语，就开始使用"嗯啊"或不断地重复前一个词而不能继续；第四，可能是因为学生不能有效区分口译和笔译，试图在口译中每次都产出笔译译文类的译语，以至于不断更改开头的选择，从而造成很多"错误开始"的情况。

口译产出中过分拘泥于源语的字词和句式，比如，源语中的词性和句子数量都要做到一一对应，那么译语产出势必带有浓厚的"翻译腔"，甚至可能会因为译语的可理解度较差而造成听众听不懂译语的情况。在口译训练中，特别是英译中过程中，由于中文是同学们的母语，我们对其驾驭能力稍强，可以理解了源语之后，用自己觉得通顺的汉语产出译语。同样重要的是，不论译语组织是怎样的，一旦产出就不要轻易修正，只要不是出现了错误信息，就一直顺译下去。汉语的小句非常灵活，可以调整源语的词性，打碎源语的句式，完成译语。这样，在降低译语产出负担的同时，还可以保障译语的可理解度（邹德艳，2016）。

实际上，在口译中，不论句子以何种方式开头，都可以继续表达，本句还未包含的信息可以在下句中进行补充，没有必要尝试若干种句子开头的方式，导致原地恋战、踟蹰不前。译语中包含过多重复或重新开始，筛选信息以理解信息的任务就留给了听众，极大增加听众的听解负担，降低译语的可理解度。一旦句子出口，就应该尽量完成整句，而遗漏的信息可以在下句中补充。这样可以避免给听众增加听解负担，提高译语的可理解度，使译语更加"听众友好型"。

4.2　话语整合

　　人类的语言虽然千差万别，但只是表层结构不同。在深层结构层面上，各种语言之间是相似的。在口译听解过程中，译员需要把握好信息的推导，需要知道具体字词句只是用来服务信息传达的，在口译听解的有限时间内，对信息进行有效梳理整合，并根据口译现场需要进行合理产出，这是译员必备的能力。信息缩减练习可以训练学生提炼主要信息的能力，提升口译信息处理的灵活度，进而有效提升其整体口译水平。学生可以尝试计时缩减练习，这个练习由教师准备母语或外语语段，首先计算匀速阅读这些语段所需时间，在这个时间的基础上，对用时进行缩减，缩减程度由学生程度和源语难度来定，比如在正常阅读时间的三分之二时间之内，要求学生在有准备或无准备的情况下，对该语段进行缩减，可以依次尝试同语或译语。这个练习训练学生边产出边辨识冗余信息、留取主要信息的能力，同时需要保持语言产出的连贯性和流利度。下面我们看一个例子。

Make sure you are always prepared for any kind of extreme weather before it occurs. You can do this by regularly checking the weather forecast. Heat waves can often be predicted days or even weeks in advance. Heat waves are simultaneously seen as fun, an opportunity to be in the sun, and a danger that can cause illness. Make sure you drink plenty of water during this time or you could become dehydrated. If you feel hot, find a shady spot. Also watch out for the signs of heat stroke. A person may first become sluggish and lethargic and then confused or incoherent. If you notice these second symptoms, get the person into the shade immediately and take them to an ambulance. If left untreated, heat stroke can eventually lead to death.

以下是一个精简版本。

We should be prepared for extreme weather like a heatwave, which can usually be predicted in advance. A heatwave can be both fun and dangerous, as it can lead to dehydration, heatstroke or even death. So drink plenty of water, find a shady spot and watch out for the signs of heatstroke.

我们注意到，缩减的版本可能是对源语概念及逻辑上的捋顺和整合，需要更快更有效的信息分级、提炼及重组。在这个过程中，我们可以关注以下几个因素。

重复信息的整合。口译源语转瞬即逝，讲话人为了有效传递信息，往往会对特别需要传达的信息进行多种形式的提及和说明。这里需要注意的是，重复信息有时候并不一定是一模一样的信息，可能是同样信息的不同方式的表达和处理。讲话人的这些尝试无疑有助于译员理解源语信息，译员在口译理解过程中可对重复信息进行整合，关注新信息，并在缩减练习中对重复信息进行重组。下面我们看一个例子。

Interpretations are different people's versions of the past. They can be in history books, be shown in documentaries about the past, or even be fictionalised in novels and films. Different people often interpret the same event or person in history very differently, depending on

<u>what evidence they use and consider important</u>. For example, one historian might call the Black Death a "catastrophe", while another sees it as a "turning point for the power of peasantry".

上段中画线的两个句子意思非常接近，后句是前句的解释性重复。因此，我们可以在缩减练习中将其调整为下面的版本。

Different people may interpret the past differently in history books, documentaries or fictional accounts, using different historical evidence. For example, the Black Death can be seen by some historians as a "catastrophe", while others may view it as a "turning point in the power of the peasantry".

同类信息的整合。同类信息指的是在不增加新信息的情况下，源语中使用的发挥同样作用的信息，比如意思接近的一连串形容词、组成接近的一连串平行结构、说明问题的多种解释方法、说明问题的具体事例等。遇到类似的同类信息，我们就可以对其进行整合。下面我们看一个例子。

Today, we are going to talk about the English language, and it has many words. *The Collins English Dictionary* has around 260,000 words! It is worth noting that many of these words come from other languages. We call them "loanwords" or "borrowings", which are derived from other languages. One example is "coffee", which comes from Arabic. Another example is "pyjamas", which comes from Hindi. We also have "pizza" from Italian, and some sports words like "karate" and "kung fu" are borrowed from Japanese and Chinese respectively.

上段举例部分的形式较为分散，可以通过梳理整合使原文更加简洁易懂。以下是一个精简版本。

English has a lot of words, and *The Collins English Dictionary* includes around 260,000 words. Called "loanwords", many English words are borrowed from other languages. Examples are "coffee" from Arabic, "pyjamas" from Hindi, "pizza" from Italian, "karate" from Japanese, "kung fu" from Chinese and many others.

以下是一个更加简略并突出主干信息的版本。

English has a lot of words and many of them are borrowed from other languages. Examples are "coffee" from Arabic, "pyjamas" from Hindi, "pizza" from Italian, "karate" from Japanese, "kung fu" from Chinese and many others.

逻辑的整合。口译源语往往为未加修饰的口语化内容，讲话人随时都会对话语进行调整，这就需要译员不但要注意分析源语意义，而且要挖掘源语的逻辑线索，这样才能在译语产出中对源语不同级别的信息进行有效传递。下面我们看一个例子。

China and the US should work together to avoid the kind of mistakes the US has made in the past. I will give you an example. In the early 1970s, as the price of oil skyrocketed and the cost of gasoline soared, individuals and governments under President Carter and

President Ford before him tried to impose austerity measures and encourage the development of cars that were more fuel efficient and energy efficient. In the early 1980s, the price of petrol went down. So everybody in America said to themselves, "Oh, we do not have to worry about that anymore and we do not need to have fuel-efficient cars, we can continue to have very inefficient cars." And that was a mistake. It set us back. Now if you compare what our whole country has done to what a single state has done, California has continued to push energy conservation. California tried to promote cars that use more gasoline. And even today, California uses less electricity per capita than the rest of the United States because of efficiency measures. So we made a mistake. People thought, "Oh, we do not have to worry about this anymore." We know we have to care, and we will continue to make our own changes.

请注意画线部分的信息，在整合这些信息的同时，整段话的逻辑可以更加清晰。以下是一个精简版本。

China and the US should work together to avoid the mistakes the US made in the past. Back in the 1970s, as the price of oil skyrocketed, individuals along with the Carter and Ford administrations tried austerity measures such as using energy-efficient cars. In the 1980s, the price of oil fell again. Therefore, people in America mistakenly thought that they did not need to use fuel-efficient cars. But the state of California continued to push for energy savings. And today, California still has a lower per capita consumption of electricity. So we made a mistake and we should continue to make changes.

译员在进行口译时，需要快速准确地理解源语信息，并将其转化为目标语言表达，这就意味着他们需要一边产出，一边辨识冗余信息，并留取主要信息，以及对信息进行逻辑组织，这包括整合重复的信息，合并类似的信息以及将信息有序排列。有效的信息处理能力是实现这一目标的关键。通过信息缩减练习，译员可以提高识别和提取关键信息的能力，同时在产出时保持连贯性和流利度。这种练习有助于提高译员的信息处理效率，使其在有限的时间内更好地完成口译任务。

4.2.1　名物化

莱考夫和约翰逊（Lakoff & Johnson，1980）指出，语言中大约70%的表达源于隐喻概念，隐喻度为零或许只是实验状态下的语言。作为系统功能语法的创始人，韩礼德（Halliday，1994）最早提出语法隐喻的概念。不同于传统词汇层面发生的隐喻化过程，语法隐喻发生在词汇语法层，是从意义出发看语言表达上的变异，具体指的是用某一语法类别或结构去代替另一语法类别或结构，而不是用一个词去代替另一个词。韩礼德将语法隐喻分为概念隐喻和人际隐喻，概念隐喻中的名物化（nominalization）是创造语法隐喻最有力的方式。韩礼德指出，名物化是唯一最有效的创造语法隐喻的方式。当动词和形容词不再充当小句中的过程或修饰语，而是转化成名词来体现参与者或者过程，这便产生了名物化。名物化的过程主要是把表达"过程"的动词或说明某一事物的小句加以"物化"，从而使名词（或词组）兼具动词或形容词的意义和名词的语法功能，词性转换是这种现象得以实现的一种方式。在这一过程中，动作过程的参与者丧失了，部分原有信息也损失了，语义上可能产生歧义或模糊。但是，名物化现象是正式语体的一大特征，因为名物化具有浓缩功能，即一个名物化的语句包含了相当大的信息量，具有高度的"信息密度"（Thompson，2000）。凭借其囊括（encapsulation）和浓缩（condensation）的功能，名物化可以提高话语的词汇密度和信息度，进而提升话语的客观性和叙述的不可协商性。

名物化对小句内部结构、语类和语式、话语的组织等都产生影响，语法结构的改变引起语义的变化。韩礼德（Halliday，2004）指出，名物化的实质就是"同样的所指，不同的能指"。从本质上看，"所指"没有变，"能指"改变了，即用不同的说法说明同样或相似的意义。这对翻译，特别是口译实践，具有重要意义，我们主要探讨如何通过去名物化降低口译中源语的隐喻度，从而在降低译员译语产出难度的同时，增强译语的可理解度。

韩礼德（Halliday，2000）指出，决定话语中语法隐喻程度的一个重要因素就是要看该话语是口语体还是书面体，演说和写作的隐喻模式不同，因为二者使用不同的方式去构建复杂的意义。在口译中，讲者使用书面文稿或者译员使用书面译稿的情况也是有的，其中前者的情况多于后者。但口译中源语和译语更多情况下趋向口语体，译员更多情况下作为现场演说的译语产出者，为听众提供口语体的译文。不论从译员产出译语的角度，还是从听众理解译语的角度，口译中不但不应提倡使用名物化来加大话语的隐喻度，相反，应对名物化程度较高的源语进行去名物化，拆卸（unpack）名物化囊括和浓缩的意义，这个过程实际上是对名词结构进行解构和重构，使其内在的过程性、属性性等语义特征得到清晰的呈现。下文对去名物化在口译中的形式及去名物化对译语的影响进行说明。

名物化可分为词汇名物化和小句名物化。前者指词的转换，把动词或形容词名物化成一个新词，表示一般事件或属性；后者指小句作为一个层级在另一小句中发挥名词作用。以下例句说明如何将源语中的名词（结构）去名物化，口译为动词表示过程、形容词表示属性、介副词表示环境成分和小句表示关系的一致式。

1. 名词变动词（过程）

We are working hard to bring peaceful **resolution** there.（我们努力以

和平的方式**解决**那里的问题。）

We need to prioritize the **development** of renewable energy sources to combat climate change.（我们需要优先**发展**可再生能源来应对气候变化。）

The first thing that is important on the healthcare issue is that there should be **access** for all the affordable and quality healthcare, regardless of their socioeconomic status.（讲到医疗保健问题，很重要的一点就是，所有人都应该能够**获得**经济实惠且高质量的医疗保健，无论他们的社会经济地位如何。）

2. 名词变形容词（属性）

When the students get to know each other, they learn the **universality** of many values.（两国学生更加了解对方，可以了解到许多价值观实际是**共通的**。）

The incident has revealed **inadequacies** in the university's scientific and research capabilities.（这个事件显示，这所大学的科研能力是**不足的**。）

The new policy has resulted in increased **accessibility** for people with disabilities.（新政策已经使得残疾人的生活变得更加**无障碍**。）

3. 名词变介副词（环境成分）

The **cause** of the delivery delay was a strike that happened days ago.（货送晚了，**因为**几天前发生了罢工。）

The **concurrence** of their disappearance is the precondition for a breakthrough.（它们**同时**消失，这是取得突破的前提。）

The **reason** for the failure of the project was due to a combination of factors, including a lack of funding from the government, poor management decisions, and unforeseen technical difficulties.（这个项目失败，**因为**多个因素的综合作用，包括政府资金缺乏、管理决策不当和

无法预见的技术困难等。)

4.名词变小句（关系）

I believe the ship's **arrival** in Shanghai today is a **symbol** of the friendship between our two countries in the past 150 years.（我相信，这艘船今天**到达**上海，**象征**着友谊，这友谊一直存在于我们两国之间达150年。）

Analysis of the questionnaire responses revealed a number of female/male **differences**.（我们**分析**了调查问卷，发现男性和女性调查参与人在诸多方面**表现出不同**。）

The **revolutionizing** of our communication methods can be attributed to the **ongoing development** of technology, which has brought about **significant changes** in the way we interact and exchange information.（我们的交流方式**发生了变革**，这归因于技术**在持续发展**，这已经使我们互动和信息交流的方式**大大改变了**。）

总结来看，去名物化的过程在改变小句内部语义、降低隐喻式高度词汇密度的同时，对话语进行了重构，改变了话语衔接方式、主位结构、信息结构等语法层次。拆卸掉的名物化分解出来的意义必须用小句重新来加以囊括。因此，可以对口译中的源语进行去名物化，降低译语话语词汇密度，同时增加其语法复杂度。下面将从词汇密度和语法复杂度两个方面对口译源语去名物化对译语产生的影响进行说明。

为了体现口译源语和译语在真实口译过程中的词汇密度和语法复杂度两个方面的变化，本研究使用中国大学生英汉汉英口笔译语料库中的口译子语料库（PACCEL-S）（文秋芳，王金铨，2008）。该语料库源自全国英语专业八级英汉互译口语考试录音，经过语音转写而成的口译平行语料。本研究对比分析了该语料库中口译源语及译语的词汇（实词）密度和语法特点，探讨译员在句子层面上对源语名物化的处理策略。译语部分选取了得分较高（LEVEL1）的译文，总字数为18698字。

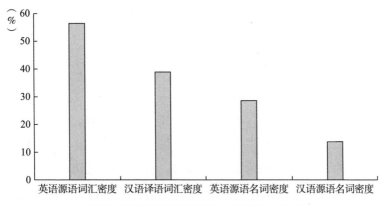

源语与译语的词汇密度和名词密度对比图

　　上图为源语与译语的词汇密度和名词密度对比图，可以看出，译语的词汇密度和名词密度均低于源语。获得较高分数的学生译员在口译中对源语进行了不同程度的去名物化，降低了源语的词汇密度和名物化程度。另外，除了在词汇密度上分析口译中去名物化对译语的影响，我们还可以从语法复杂度的变化上发现去名物化的影响。原因在于，名物化结构可以被看作小句的压缩，使小句能够包容更多的信息。那么，去名物化中被拆卸掉的意义需要用新的小句来囊括，这就增加了译语的语法复杂度。艾金斯（Eggins，1994）提出了量化语法复杂度的方法，即小句与整个句子数量之比。

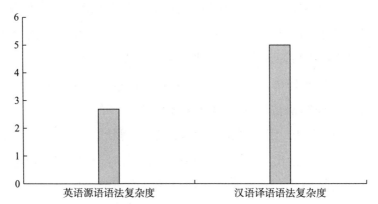

源语与译语的语法复杂度对比图

上图为源语与译语的语法复杂度对比图，可以看出，学生译员的译语语法复杂度比原语高，这说明学生使用了更多小句，以拆卸并包容更多信息。总结来看，口译源语的名物化程度决定译语去名物化的必要程度，去名物化对译语词汇密度和语法复杂度方面的影响是否存在于大多数译语话语转换中，还要看源语的名物化程度。然而，从口译即解释或换种表达的层面看，去名物化为口译提供了多种选择，不同程度的去名物化选择在为译员减轻表达负担的同时，也提升了译语的可理解度。那么，在这个过程中，译员是在自主降低译语产出难度，还是充分考虑听众的接受能力，抑或是两者兼有，这还有待进一步的研究。

首先，在口译译语产出中使用去名物化的策略，可以降低译语产出负担。在学习口译过程中，学生容易进行词对词翻译，主要体现在对源语句子结构和词性亦步亦趋。这就引发一系列问题。由于英汉两种语言结构不同，完全照搬原文结构可能造成译语不知所云，照搬词性对口译学生的词汇量和组句能力是巨大挑战。口译已成为英语本科专业的必修课，而本科学生的英语水平还比较有限，指望学生出口便可产出级阶较高的英语，是不现实的。况且，在口译过程中，译语产出只是一部分任务，学生还要顾及听解、笔记、转换等任务，在口译教学中引导学生熟悉去名物化策略，可以帮助学生在"译得好"之前先达到"张开口"的层级。韩礼德最初是在语言科学中发现了语法隐喻的表达法，对相似意义的多种表达方式产生兴趣并最终提出了语法隐喻的概念。反其道而行之，将隐喻式的表达还原为一致式，为口译译语产出提供了更多解决方案。

其次，在口译译语产出中使用去名物化的策略，可以提升译语可理解度。人们在理解语法隐喻时可能需要付出更多的认知努力去"拆卸"（unpack）语言信息，因而增加了解读难度（胡壮麟，2000）。赵德全和宁志敏（2005）也指出，话语理解难度随着语法隐喻的增多而增大。在口译中进行去名物化，不仅是因为译员译语产出能力的限制，也是基于口语表达的特点。口译表达的信息转瞬即逝，复杂的用词和句式无疑会加重听众的理解负担。口译中的去名物化可以有效降低源语的理解难度，消除隐喻式表达的歧义和含糊，提升译语的可理解度。听众可以付出较小的认知努力而获得更高的理解准确率。如果译语在很大程度上采用一致式表达，那么听众就不需要付出太多努力来"解构"译语，只需要按照小句顺序横向地进行理解。综上所述，口译实践如果亦步亦趋跟从源语的形式，不但增加译员产出译语的难度，同时增加听众理解译语的难度，亦即降低了译语的可理解度。

再次，关注书面语与口语在名物化程度上的差异，可以更加明确笔译与口译"标准译文"不能通用，这对口译教学实践和口译教材编写都具有一定意义。口译类教材的编写一直以来都面临口语化不足的问题。刘和平（2008）指出，现有口译教材的口语特点不突出，书面材料远远多于口语材料。编选口译教材的第一要点就是"真材实景，耳听口说"，"口译教材文字化本身已经为教学效果蒙上了一层阴影，因为这些教材同笔译课教材除选材有所不同外，别无特点"（刘和平，2001）。我们通过英语专业八级口译平行语料库的研究，也发现考试所提供的参考译文与学生真实译文之间在词汇密度、名词密度和语法复杂度上都有所差异。

从数据可以明显看出，与参考译文相比，真实口译译语的词汇密度和名词密度都更低，而语法复杂度却明显更高。这一点还反映在真实译语的平均字数多于参考译文的字数上。这充分说明，在编写口译教材的过程中，除了应该注重选择真实口译材料之外，所提供的参考答案也需接近真实口译产出的特点。由此，我们可以得出结论，在口译中对源语进行去名物化这一策略的使用对口译教学设计、教学评估和口译教材的编写都具有一定的意义（邹德艳，2016）。

总结来看，口语信息转瞬即逝，为了帮助交际顺利有效地进行，人们在口语表达中往往遵循一定的原则。何高大（1997）总结口语用词原则为，"能用人们熟悉的词，就不用牵强的词；能用单个的词，就不用多个的词；能用表示具体概念的词，就不用抽象概念的词；能用短语、简单词，就不用长词、大词"。如果口译译语产出应当遵循以上口语用词原则，那么口译译语产出在语法上也应该遵循去隐喻化或去名物化的原则。

当然，作为一种口译策略，去名物化并不是绝对的，更不是口译的终极目标。首先，名物化表达在语义上可能是模糊的，讲者可能故意使用模糊式表达，也可能是无意中使用，如果是前者的情况，则去名物化可能丧失源语的特殊修辞效果或意图。其次，口译中的去名物化策略并不完全适合对译语精确度要求较高的口译类型，如政治外交口译等。再次，去名物化或一致式表达在降低译语词汇密度的同时增加其语法复杂性，句式相对零散冗长，使得译员可能需要更多时间去翻译同样的信息，并不有利于增强译语的简洁性和省时性。

4.2.2　核心句

句子中的大部分成分是额外信息，最主要的信息都可以通过 SVO，也就是主谓宾的形式得以传达。如果不能听辨出句子的主谓宾，那么句子的其余部分也是没有意义的。有经验的交替传译译员都会指出，交替传译就是在所有信息中辨认出中心信息的过程（Gillies，2009）。《实战交替传译（英汉互译）》（林超伦，2012）提出每三个字记一笔，也是提倡记忆主要信息的意思。

核心句翻译策略旨在分析复杂句的深层结构，找到最深层简单句的施动者及受动者，以分析出每个核心句之间的逻辑关系，并对核心句加以转换、重构和检验，完成翻译。通过采用核心句翻译策略，可以减少口译实践过程中由于复杂句而产生的对原文的误解，使译文更加准确、流畅。核心句翻译策略由美国著名语言学家、翻译家奈达（Nida）提出。译文应达到与原文"最切近的自然对等"（Nida，2001）。为使译文减少模糊、更加清晰，翻译中源语向目的语的转换，是在深层结构层面上进行的，译者必须通过逆向转换法（back-transformation）分析出源语表层结构背后的深层结构，再将源语的深层结构转换成目的语的深层结构，最后重组为符合目的语语法规则和表达习惯的表层结构。

核心句译法首先需要进行核心句分析，即将复杂句分解为只包含单个主谓框架（一个谓语动词）的多个语义相对完整的句子——核心句，分析各个核心句间的语义逻辑关系。然后，按照译语表达习惯，用合适的排列方式对各个核心句进行重构。转换生成语法理论认为，虽然人类语言表层结构千差万别，但在深层结构层面上，各种语言是相似的。语言与语言之间在深层结构层面的相似性，构成了翻译的基础。翻译是一个从源语表层结构到源语深层结构，再经过译语深层结构到译语表层结构的过程。简单来说，核心句译法实际上是将复杂信息简单化，再通过适当衔接加以调整，体现了释意理论"脱离源语语言外壳"的理念，着眼于语义内核的传达。

奈达在转换生成语法理论的基础上，提出了由源语结构转换成译语结构的核心句理论（Nida，1982）。表层结构更为复杂多变，而不同语言在核心结构上有更多的相似之处；翻译时可通过核心句层面的转换作为过渡，译出令人满意的译文。译者不应受源语表层结构的影响，应该避免直接进行句子表层结构的转换。

奈达将翻译活动分成四个阶段，即分析、转换、重组和检验。他认为，源语向译语的转换过程是在语言的深层结构进行的，译者首先通过分析源语的表层结构，得出其深层结构，然后将其转换为译语的深层结构，最后按照目的语的行文规则和表达习惯进行译语表层结构的重组。为此，奈达建议翻译时遵循以下 5 个步骤：1）分析词类；2）将源语中隐含的词显化出来以组成核心句；3）列出核心句；4）厘清核心句之间的关系；5）重组核心句，并向目的语表层转换。

核心句（kernel）就是奈达用于指代源语的深层结构，是"用于建构复杂表层结构的基本句式"。基于词的语义范畴，即事物范畴（O，object）、事件范畴（E，event）、抽象范畴（A，abstract）和关系范畴

（R，relation），奈达将英语句法的深层结构分为 7 个核心句（曹秀萍，2012）。

（1）John ran（quickly）.（任何表示人或物体的名词都可以充当主语。）

（2）John hit Bill.（任何施事都可以对受事施加行为。）

（3）John gave Bill a ball.（任何施事都可以实施"给"的动作。）

（4）John is in the house.（画线部分可以替换为任何其他介词短语。）

（5）John is sick.（画线部分可以替换为描述主语特征的任何形容词。）

（6）John is a boy.（主语是画线部分所指概念中的一员。）

（7）John is my father.（主语与画线部分所指相同，反之亦然。）

陈小全（2008）指出，就句法结构而言，汉语采用简单句依次展开的竹竿句式，但句子之间的关系却多种多样；而英语像一棵多枝共干的大树，往往先确定主句，在主句的基础上搭建其他成分。李长栓（2004）认为，核心句分析的关键是通过逻辑关系、百科知识或常识找到各个动作的逻辑主语。翻译时，按照逻辑关系，对原文进行重组。通过核心句分析可以摆脱原文句法对译文的影响。核心句分析的实质是找到"谁做了什么"。

对于复杂句中出现的系列核心句，应先找到复杂句中最基本的词汇，辨别其性质是动作的施动者，还是受动者，并对它们之间的关系加以说明。核心句翻译策略为翻译实践和翻译研究提供了新的模式，促进了翻译的具体化，对于结构复杂的英语长句汉译具有较好的理论指导意义。在英语长句汉译过程中，先找出源语句子的核心句，并转换成目的语的核心句，得出理想的译文。进行核心句分析时，我们通常需要先找到"动作"。在英语中，动作可能由一个动词表示，也可能由名词化动词（nominalization）表示。找到动作后，再根据逻辑关系、百科知识或常识，找到这个动作的发出者（李长栓，2004）。请看下面的例子。

例 1：The absence of long-term environmental data impeded our assessment of climate change effects on biodiversity in tropical rainforests.

核心句：

① Long-term environmental data is absent.

② We could not assess something.

③ Climate change affects biodiversity.

④ Some rainforests are tropical.

译文：由于缺乏长期环境数据，我们无法评估气候变化对热带雨林生物多样性的影响。

例2：I was inspired by those who came, like Dr. Rajan, who helped start the School Health Programme, and produced the original version of the Child's Health Booklet, which we still use today.

核心句：

① I was inspired by those who came, like Dr. Rajan. (Those who came, like Dr. Rajan, inspired me.)

② Those who came, like Dr. Rajan, helped start the School Health Programme.

③ Those who came, like Dr. Rajan, produced the original version of the Child's Health Booklet.

④ We still use the original version of the Child's Health Booklet today.

译文：来到这里的人们，比如拉詹博士，激励了我。他们帮助启动了《学校健康计划》，制作了第一版的《儿童健康手册》，我们至今仍在使用这个版本。

例3：Although there is evidence that the new treatment may be effective in relieving symptoms, given that the evidence is still inconclusive and long-term side effects have not been thoroughly studied, we cannot recommend the treatment for widespread use at this time.

核心句：

① There is evidence that the new treatment may be effective.

② The evidence is still inconclusive.

③ Long-term side effects have not been thoroughly studied.

④ We cannot recommend the treatment for widespread use now.

译文：有证据表明这种新疗法可能有效缓解症状，但鉴于证据仍不充分，且尚未充分研究长期副作用，我们目前不能推荐广泛使用这种疗法。

例 4：The discovery of penicillin, which revolutionized modern medicine and saved countless lives, was a turning point in the history of medicine and public health.

核心句：

① Penicillin was discovered.

② Penicillin changed modern medicine completely.

③ Penicillin saved many lives.

④ The discovery of penicillin was a turning point in history.

译文：青霉素的发现革新了现代医学，拯救了无数生命，成为医学史和公共卫生史的一个转折点。

例 5：In spite of the more and more economic and technical achievements and progress we have made, we can't afford to be optimistic, faced with the fact that ecological loss is unprecedented, which is demonstrated by the increasingly severe desertification, shrinking resources of fresh water, unbearable scales of air pollution, acid rain, and chemical residues in food, etc.

核心句：

① We have made more and more economic and technical achievements and progress.

② (But), we can't afford to be optimistic.

③ (Because), we face unprecedented ecological loss.

④ (We face) increasingly severe desertification.

⑤ (We face) shrinking resources of fresh water.

⑥ (We face) unbearable scales of air pollution，acid rain and chemical residues in food.

顺译译文：我们在经济和技术上取得了越来越多的成就和进步，但是我们依然不能乐观，因为我们面临前所未有的生态损失：土地沙漠化越来越严重；淡水资源越来越匮乏；空气污染、酸雨、食物中的农药残留越来越让人无法忍受。

调整译文：尽管我们在经济和技术上取得了越来越多的成就和进步，然而我们的生态所遭受的破坏却是前所未有的。诸如土地沙漠化程度越来越严重，淡水资源越来越匮乏，空气污染、酸雨和食物中农药残留已经让我们无法再忍受，所有这一切都不容我们有半点乐观。

综上所述，口译教学中应该加强学生提取句子主干的意识和能力，通过大量练习提升这种转换的自动化程度，使学生在有转换意识的前提下，随时进行核心句分析及重组。核心句是句子中最关键、最核心的部分，包含着最重要的信息和观点。理解和掌握核心句对于口译的准确性至关重要，提取句子主干的意识和能力是口译者必备的基本技能之一。此外，掌握核心句还可以提高口译的流利度。当译员能够迅速准确地提取句子主干并进行重组时，他们可以更快地组织语言，使口译更加流畅。这样，译员能够更好地跟上演讲者的思路，并及时传达信息，保持口译的连贯性和流畅度。加强学生提取句子主干的意识和能力对于口译教学至关重要。它不仅可以提高口译的准确性，还可以增加口译的流利度，使学生能够更好地理解和传达核心句的含义，从而提升口译的质量和效果。

4.3　口译脱壳

"脱离源语语言外壳"是巴黎释意理论学派的核心理论。根据该理论，口译过程中，在话语理解和译语再表达之间，"意义"会"脱离"语言的具体表达形式而独立存在。我们都知道，口头陈述转瞬即逝。我们可以记住听到的整体内容，却几乎忘记了陈述所用的词语。事实上，讲话使用的有声符号逐渐消失，而听者（译员）保持着非语言形式的记忆，即处于意识状态的思想或提到的事实。译员之所以能够记住意义的各种细微差别，并自如完整地将其用其他语言表达出来，是因为启用了一项基本能力，即在词语消失时记住并理解了内容。译员摆脱了原来的语言形式，翻译的是篇章，而不仅仅是语言（邹德艳、张宏宇，2015）。

"脱离源语语言外壳"现象牵扯到了从源语信息储存到译语表达过渡的某种中间状态，是译员译语表达的基础之一。译员在口译工作时，特别是在对源语进行加工的过程中，会使用语言以外的其他诸多载体，这就完完全全脱离了"语言"这一思维的工具。口译中的"脱离源语外壳"现象其实是译员在双语转换之前对源语所代表的信息进行某种"还原"的过程。它在巴黎释意理论中已经构成了口译的一个主要程序。"脱离源语语言外壳"现象在口译过程中十分常见，并且十分自然。"脱离源语语言外壳"的主张对于口译实践及口译教学的贡献在于：首先，该主张为不可译现象提供了适用的方案；其次，该主张推翻了"口译就是语言代码转换"的看法，有助于去除译语产出中的"翻译腔"；最后，该主张有效区分了教学口译与口译教学，教学口译强化语言技能，口译教学注重口译技能。该主张推动了口译的职业化和专业化发展，是把基础理论研究的成果用于指导口译教学实践的典范。

口译表达阶段是展示理解阶段记忆成果的过程，需要译员在表达的同时进行回忆，并尽量使两者互不干扰。为实现这一目标，理解阶段的信息分析必须更加有效，因为经过有效分析的信息结构可以更加持久，即使在受到"说"的认知抑制时，仍能发挥应有的作用。换言之，理解阶段的信息分析需要在持久力和抗干扰力方面达到一定水平，足以支撑一段时间内的口译任务。只有在当下任务完成后，这段信息记忆的作用才算真正发挥完毕。

　　口译的记忆与表达是相辅相成的。记忆越有效，越可以辅助表达，而表达中的诸多不流利现象也可能是记忆不够有效的结果和表现，当然这其中也不能排除个人表达本身存在的各种不流利现象和习惯。反过来看，口译中的表达极大程度影响记忆的回溯。这是因为，相比正常人，译员往往并不具备超凡的记忆容量，在记忆容量有限的情况下，更多的资源被用于组织译语，或对译语作出过多考虑、修改、再修改，这势必影响记忆的回溯，更不用说这样的译语同时还会大大增加听众的理解负担。因此，不论是在口译训练的复述阶段，还是在口译训练的译语产出阶段，我们都需要强调并训练学生的"说话的能力"。

4.3.1　演讲训练

　　美国著名人际关系学大师卡耐基曾经说过，演讲是人人都有的一种潜在能力。口译中的公共演讲与一般情况下的公共演讲既有相同点，也有区别。二者都需经过语言产出的各个阶段，但是，前者不需要自主构思，只需重述源语的内容。这里需要注意的是，同样的意思，可以有多种表达方法。虽然这些表达方法在措辞和结构上会有差异，但在口译中，过分关注这种差异势必影响产出。在口译中，最好的译语不是笔译情况下左思右想、查原引证的结果，而是在口译需要产出的当下，能够想到并成功组织出来的结构和用词，只要不是出现重大错误，最快想到并产出的译语就是最好的。上文提到，不需译者自主构思看似是口译的优势，但是，我们反过来看，正因为有了源语这个框架作为参照点，如果处理不好，这个框架就可能成为表达的桎梏。

　　公共演讲能力一直以来都被认定为会议口译能力的标志，同时也是一项标准，可以用来评价译员的产出（Gile，1995）。对于译员和会议参与者的调查证明了流利度也是非常重要的标准，可以衡量口译的质量（Bühler，1986；Kurz，1993）。奥尔特曼（Altman，1994）曾指出，流利度是口译中的唯一因素，可以清楚区分职业译员与非职业译员的不同。

然而，以往的研究并没有详细描述流利的演讲应该如何定义，以及这种技能应该如何发展并最终习得。比如，塞莱斯科维奇和勒代雷（Seleskovitch & Lederer，1989）只是指出了演说能力以及控制"声音效果"（effects de voix）的重要性。她们还认为，口译学员对于流利的认识应当得到加强，但是口译教师面临教学的时间压力，很多情况下做不到这一点。因此，需要设立专门的公共演讲课程（Weber，1989）。我们可以看出，不论公共演讲训练是否真的能够在每个口译训练项目中得以实施，不论其可行性如何，有一点毋庸置疑，那就是，公共演讲技能对于口译来说至关重要，是译员应该随着其他口译技能一起推进和精练的技能。此外，有研究者针对表演训练对于口译表现的提升效果做了实证研究，经由 7 周职业演员的戏剧技巧训练，邀请外部评审评估，实验班在口译产出的自信度、流利度和问题应对效果等方面都有较好的表现（Cho & Roger，2010）。

总的来说，目前口译教学中关于如何将演讲技巧训练与口译课程设置相结合的描述仍然比较匮乏，对于口译流利度的培养和评估方面的知识也十分欠缺。尽管缺少这方面的具体标准和规范，但在口译教学中训练学生的表达能力非常重要，这有助于提高其译语输出质量，应该贯穿于整个口译训练过程。教师可以在课堂上巧妙设计一些环节，引导学生多说话，为口译输出做好充分准备。同时，教师还应向学生强调，在表达训练中要注意利用停顿来避免口误，反复练习，直到能够在没有口误的情况下，在规定时间内完成训练任务。相关的教学活动包括：即兴演讲、有主题的即兴演讲、有提示的即兴演讲、单词表自由演讲、无声电影配音等极大调动学生自主产出能力的活动；还包括词汇变化练习、句法变化练习等方式，这要求学生用不一样的词汇或句法成分完成句子，可以有效提升学生的语言灵活性。我们接下来主要介绍主题演讲、幻灯片演示文稿（PPT）重组、计时缩减三种练习方式。

主题演讲

在口译训练中提高学生"说话的能力"至关重要。口译产出与自然话语的差异主要在于，前者的话语生成都要基于口译中的输入信息。但是，同样的输入信息经过不同译员的转换，会产生不同的译语效果。这就意味着，输入信息经由译员进行转变，这个过程中结合了译员的个人理解能力、世界知识、长时记忆、表达能力等多方面因素，成为译员的意念。因此，口译中译语的产出虽然基于源语，但势必借由译员的个人认知能力才能得以具化。口译中的话语产出能力是个人能力，是成为译员的必备素质。因此，我们要在口译训练中加大对于口译学习者的话语产出能力的训练。

口译的源语通常是主题演讲，因此，在口译训练中针对主题演讲进行思考和练习，就会让我们对口译中需要翻译的内容有更多的了解，知道讲话人如何组织演讲，为什么会那样组织演讲，演讲主要想要表达的信息和意图是什么，等等。为了提高口译的准确性和流畅度，译员可以通过练习提取主题演讲中的关键词句和梗概来加强对演讲内容的理解。这些关键词句和梗概可以作为"原材料"，帮助译员更好地组织语言，准确地传达演讲者想要表达的信息和意图。此外，针对主题演讲进行思考和练习还可以帮助译员更好地掌握演讲的结构和组织方式。译员可以通过分析演讲者的用词、语调、语速等因素来了解演讲者的表达方式和风格，从而更好地传达演讲者的思想和观点。

我们来看一个例子，以下段落已经给出了主题和开头部分，但是主要内容并未展开，只提供了小标题，需要根据小标题展开篇章。在产出的同时，还可以邀请同学进行翻译。

Please reorganize the following notes, if necessary, in a logical order and expand the notes into sentences, to make your own speech. You may ask your partner to comment on your performance or interpret your speech into Chinese.

Many of us don't know the best ways to look after our eyes. Could you share your ideas on this?

Eye care organizations and health professionals are joining together to promote the importance of eye health and the need for regular sight tests for all. Sight is the sense people fear losing the most. Fight for sight. Here are top tips for healthy eyes:

1. Have regular check-ups
2. Wear protective glasses
3. Limit the use of digital devices
4. Take care of your contact lenses

To what extent has information technology reduced social inequality? Give reasons for your answer and include any relevant examples from your own knowledge or experience.

People who live in highly developed countries often take access to information technology for granted. They find it hard to imagine a world in which this technology does not bring greater prosperity. However, as the IT revolution moves forward in some parts of the world, in other parts of the world the poor are falling further and further behind. Indeed, there are many barriers to wider IT access and its potential benefits.

1. In some countries, fewer than 50% population able to read
2. Use of blocking software and firewalls common
3. Electricity supply irregular
4. Government censorship or Internet widespread
5. Even where IT access available, governments fearful of well-informed public
6. Broadband access only in major cities
7. Illiteracy a major obstacle
8. Basic infrastructure inadequate
9. Women and poor especially likely to be illiterate

我们知道，言语是思想的外在表现形式，好的演讲往往具备明确的思想和鲜明的主题。因此，把握演讲的主题和中心思想，找出各个部分意义的发展脉络，在此基础上记忆讲稿内容就容易多了。比如，大多数演讲通常遵循提出问题、分析问题和解决问题这三个主要环节。从这个意义上说，把握文章的章法结构，可以有效帮助记忆，也就可以进一步辅助译员高质量完成口译。请看下面的例子。

Many species of plants and animals have come and gone throughout the history of the Earth. From this perspective, extinction can be seen as part of a natural process. Some people have argued that we should not, therefore, make efforts to preserve the natural habitats of endangered plants and animals. To what extent do you agree with this?

（我们应当在合理范围内保护濒临灭绝的物种及其自然栖息地吗？）

回应 1:

If you look at it that way, it's true that humans and animals have conflicting interests. People have always exploited animals for food and clothing, and farmers have brought bigger and bigger areas of land under cultivation. But should we keep on doing this? In regions of the world where the population is growing, and there aren't enough resources, the conflict between humans and animals is really bad. If you go to Africa, for example, you can see large nature reserves alongside really poor human settlements. I love the idea of elephants and lions living in the wild. But often it's the poor farmer living nearby who's got to pay the cost in terms of land and lost earnings.

（人与动物利益冲突，保护野生动物的成本由贫困农民承担。）

回应 2:

Looked at from a broad historical perspective, it is true that humans and animals have conflicting interests. People have always exploited animals for food and clothing, whilst farmers have brought ever-increasing areas of land under cultivation. Whether this process should continue is a question that requires careful consideration. In regions of the world where the population is growing, and resources are scarce, the conflict between humans and animals is particularly problematic. This can be seen in parts of Africa, for example, where large nature reserves sit alongside very poor human settlements. People living thousands of miles away may value the idea of elephants and lions living in the wild. However, often it is the poor farmer living nearby who must pay the cost in terms of land and lost earnings.

（人与动物利益冲突，是由于竞争的需求和利益，在平衡动物权利与不断增长的人口需求之间寻求平衡。）

这篇演讲探讨了"我们应当在合理范围内保护濒临灭绝的物种及其自然栖息地吗?"这个问题。文章分为三个部分，首先介绍了地球历史上许多植物和动物的出现和消失，认为灭绝是自然过程的一部分。接着引出一些人认为我们不应该保护濒危植物和动物的自然栖息地的观点。最后提出问题，询问听众对这个观点的看法。回应1认为人与动物利益冲突，保护野生动物的成本由贫困农民承担。回应2也认为人类和动物之间存在利益冲突，是由于竞争的需求和利益，需要在平衡动物权利与不断增长的人口需求之间寻求平衡。

通过这个例子，我们可以更好地了解，不同的表层语言可以构建类似的话语结构，而后者是口译听解中最需要把握的因素。针对某类主题的演讲内容，先进行主题相关文本的输入之后，要求学生针对某个主题自行设计内容，进行即兴演讲。这些主题可以包括：欢迎宴会、感谢致辞、介绍性主题、劝说类主题等。带有主题的即兴演讲还可以由其他同学进行复述、交替传译甚至同声传译。学生自我组篇能力的发展可以提升至其理解讲话人话语的能力。这样的练习还可以针对口译源语进行更深程度的信息处理。超前的逻辑推导会随着言语链的发布和接收得到印证，并为随后信息分析提供可靠的语境和认知环境基础（刘和平，2001）。

幻灯片演示文稿（PPT）重组

幻灯片演示文稿作为一种演示文稿图形程序，具有文稿和音视频的演示功能，可增强演讲的视听效果，已经成为公共演讲的重要组成部分。幻灯片演示文稿演讲在现代社会交流、求职、商务场景下得到广泛应用，是现代人进行有效交流必备的知识与技能。司徒罗斌和杜蕴德（Setton & Dawrant，2016）提到，除了亚洲区域，世界范围内开始更多地使用同声传译，使用幻灯片演示文稿的口译任务比例也大幅增加。随着技术的发展，特别是全球疫情之后，远距离口译已成为常态，以幻灯片演示文稿为主要载体和形式的多模态信息成为远距离口译的主要内容。

远程口译（remote interpreting）通过信息和通信技术在与讲话者和听众不同的地点进行口译，只将讲话者的声音（音频远程口译），或讲话者的声音和图像（视频远程口译）提供给译员。同声传译模式译出与接收源语（听）和产生目的语（说）同时进行的口译。远程视频口译通过信息和通信技术，从不同的地点进行口译，发言者的声音和图像被传输给译员。它的主要特点是译员不直接面对讲话者和听众，视觉输入（演讲者、听众的观点和听众可获得的视觉材料）通过一或多块屏幕显示给译员。成立于1953年的国际会议口译员协会（International Association of Conference Interpreters，AIIC）是唯一的全球会议口译员协会，一直在推动行业的高标准质量和道德规范，并代表其从业者的利益。AIIC规定，由于译员分布在远离会议室的不同地点，其需要通过屏幕或视频监视器获得视觉输入。屏幕（最好是LED显示屏）应足够大，以便译员更清楚地阅读显示文本或看到图像。

如果在会前能拿到幻灯片演示文稿的材料，这可以辅助译前的准备工作；会议过程中，译员也可以通过观看幻灯片演示文稿上的文字和图表，确认讲者的讲话内容。这些无疑都可以减轻译员的记忆负担，有利于译语的产出。但是，大多数情况下，幻灯片演示文稿只是讲话人的演讲纲要，更多的时候讲话人会即兴添加幻灯片演示文稿上没有的扩展内容。此外，幻灯片演示文稿在展现讲话提纲和主旨的同时，还可能链接图片、动画、视听材料等辅助观众理解演讲。这样多模态信息的展现方式可以辅助译员理解讲话人的主旨，但实际上它是一把双刃剑，如果处理不好，则可能提升口译的难度，因为它在口译多任务认知活动上增添了新的任务，使其信息输入模式复杂多样，增加了译员的理解负担。这个时候，译员的精力要多分配出来给幻灯片演示文稿，对其精力分配能力是极大的挑战。研究发现，源语文本的同时输入会显著提升译员的整体口译表现，但学生译员会出现过度关注源语文本信息的情况，这使得他们忽略讲者信息这一输入渠道，过度追求字的准确翻译，耗费过多认知精力，受到源语语言干扰较大（杨姗姗，2023）。而职业译员比学生译员在原文听辨和译文产出之间的协调时间更短，速度更快，反映出译员的口译经验越丰富，其理解原文、转换语义和产出译文的速度越快。也反映出职业译员并没有因为视觉信息的冗余而降低理解和产出的协调速度（苏雯超，2023）。总的来看，在幻灯片演示文稿演讲的中译过程中，译员需要注意以下几点。

第一，口译需要翻译的是讲话人的话语，在讲话人边展示幻灯片演示文稿边演讲的过程中，译员在利用幻灯片演示文稿及其辅助材料理解话语的同时，一定要专注讲话人的话语，不能受到幻灯片演示文稿的影响而分心，导致误听或漏听讲话人的源语。第二，讲话人可能事先将幻灯片演示文稿的材料提供给译员，而后在会议现场又对幻灯片演示文稿进行了修改甚至替换。译员不能受到之前提供的幻灯片演示文稿的影响，会议开始之后不能再翻看之前的幻灯片演示文稿或材料，而要以讲话人现场所使用的幻灯片演示文稿材料为主，更重要的是要以讲话人现场所说的话语为主，以完成口译任务。第三，幻灯片演示文稿演讲的理解很大程度上需要参考幻灯片演示文稿的内容，因此在交替传译中，译员应尽量在演讲者翻到下一页幻灯片演示文稿之前，完成当前幻灯片演示文稿内容的翻译。如果讲话人在一个幻灯片演示文稿页面上的讲话时间过长，可能会涉及多页幻灯片演示文稿的内容，此时译员可以与演讲者沟通，并解释自己需要尽量完成当前幻灯片演示文稿页面内容翻译的原因。

Supermarkets

- **Supermarkets do a few things to make consumers spend more money.**

- **They put freshly baked goods such as bread, as they smell lovely, near the entrance to make us feel hungry, and hungry shoppers spend more.**

- **They also rearrange things and put them in different places this makes us spend more time in the store and that means spending more money.**

主题演讲幻灯片图例

例 1: Supermarkets do a few things to make consumers spend more money. They put freshly baked goods such as bread, as they smell lovely, near the entrance to make us feel hungry, and hungry shoppers spend more. They also rearrange things and put them in different places; this makes us spend more time in the store and that means spending more money. They put sweets and chocolate near the checkout, so it is easy to add bars of chocolate to our basket or trolley while we are waiting in the queue. And they put the most expensive items on the middle shelves where you are more likely to see them. Loyalty cards have their advantages, without a doubt. But deep down the store is probably benefiting more than the loyalty card holder. But who can resist a discount or money off? So, while a loyalty card will give you money off the main reason a supermarket wants you to use it is so they can track your spending habits and learn more about what you buy and when. And be careful of special offers, for example, three for the price of two, buy one get one free. People often buy more than they need and throw away half of it. So, every part of the supermarket from entrance to checkout counter is designed to make you spend more money and buy more things than you need. There's a reason your mother told you to make a grocery list and stick to it.

实际上，幻灯片演示文稿内容与讲话内容不对应，是译员在口译过程中面临的较大问题。对幻灯片演示文稿内容不予理会，显然是不必要和不明智的，但过度依赖幻灯片演示文稿内容会影响听解，更何况幻灯片演示文稿内容与实际讲话内容有差别是常态，且两者的不匹配的情况千差万别。就这个例子来说，讲话内容可能总结出来的要点就可以包括多个版本。

• Supermarkets strategically place tempting items near the entrance to stimulate hunger and increase spending.

• Loyalty cards offer benefits to consumers, but supermarkets also benefit by tracking consumer spending habits.

• Creating a shopping list helps control spending and avoid impulsive purchases.

• Supermarkets place tempting items near the entrance to stimulate hunger and increase spending.

• Special offers can lead to unnecessary purchases and potential waste, so creating a shopping list helps control spending.

• Loyalty cards offer benefits to consumers, but supermarkets also benefit by tracking consumer spending habits.

• Supermarkets employ strategies to increase consumer spending.

• Placing tempting items near the entrance to stimulate hunger.

• Rearrange products to prolong shopping time and encourage more purchases.

• Placing sweets and chocolates near the checkout for impulse buying.

• Highlighting extensive items on middle shelves for better visibility.

• Loyalty cards benefit both consumers and supermarkets.

• Special offers can lead to unnecessary purchases and waste.

• Creating a shopping list helps control spending.

在幻灯片演示文稿口译过程中，译员付出更大的认知努力以解决视听信息的不一致，但同时也能灵活识别有助于听觉加工的视觉信息，解决多模态信息之间的冲突和不一致往往需要增加认知控制（Chmiel，2020；苏雯超，2021）。所以，为确保较好的幻灯片演示文稿口译效果，

译员需要专注于讲话人的话语，并确保准确地传达讲话人的意思和信息。这需要对讲话人的语言、表达方式、语调等进行细致的观察和理解，以便更好地传达他们的意思。同时，译员也应该注意口译的流畅性和连贯性，以便让听众更好地理解讲话内容。在这个例子中，幻灯片演示文稿的内容以文字为主，因此还可以对译员理解源语起到一定的提升和佐证的作用。我们看下一个例子，幻灯片演示文稿内容仅有图片，几乎没有或者缺少文字内容。

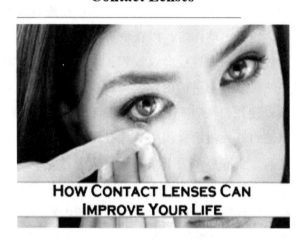

Contact Lenses

主题演讲幻灯片图例

例 2：Take care of your contact lenses. Nowadays, people wear contact lenses to improve poor vision, or to improve the quality of vision for those who wear high power glasses. Some people wear contact lenses that can enhance or change the eye color, known as cosmetic contact lenses. If you wear contact lenses, make sure you look after them properly. Thoroughly wash and dry your hands before inserting or removing your contact lenses. Your lenses and their case should only be cleaned with the lens solution recommended by your optometrist. Serious sight threatening infections can occur with contact lens wear, and one should be aware of these. The important point to note with any contact lenses is not to share the lenses with friends as this can increase the risk of infections in the eye. Always follow the instructions given to you by your optometrist or the lens manufacturer. This way, you should be able to be comfortable with lens wear with good vision.

当幻灯片演示文稿内容仅包含图片而缺少文字内容时，译员需要针对这种情况进行调整，以下是一些可能的方法：仔细观察图片内容，包括图像中的人物、场景、动作等，以获取更多关于讲话内容的线索；结合幻灯片演示文稿所属的主题或会议议程，以及其他演讲者的发言，来推测图片所代表的意思和与讲话内容的关联；如果图片无法完全传达讲话内容，译员可以使用口头补充语言来解释或补充图片所缺少的信息；如果译员事先知道幻灯片演示文稿中只含有图片而没有文字内容，可以提前与讲话人沟通，获取更多关于图片所代表意思的信息，以便更好地进行口译。

实际上，在幻灯片演示文稿内容与实际讲话内容的匹配度方面，以上两种情况只涉及了两个较为简单的情况：第一种是两者的匹配度较高，第二种是两者的匹配度较低。而更多情况是处于中间段的各种模态信息的不同组合和变体，也就是说，译员需要同时处理讲话人的讲话和幻灯片演示文稿上的文字、图像、表格等视觉信息，以及讲话人的手势等非语言信息。我们来看一个例子。

例 3 的幻灯片演示文稿主要描述的是页岩油气和常规油气提取的区别以及它们的特点，与其匹配的话语也大概会围绕这样的内容进行，但具体的展开方式可能有所差别，下面列出来两个可能的版本，大家感受一下，幻灯片演示文稿内容与实际讲话内容的匹配方式，是如何既殊途同归又有所差异的。

Shale gas is natural gas!

Land surface

Overburden

Trap

Reservoir

Seal

Source rock

Basement

Shale oil and gas are exactly the same product as oil and natural gas from conventional extraction.

The difference is the source: conventional exploits reservoir, shale exploits source rock

Conventional hydrocarbons are found in reservoirs:
1.Coarse grains
2.High permeability
3.Limiited extension(at most as largo as Greater London)

Hydrocarbons migrate from source rock and are sometimes trapped in a reservoir

Shale is found in the source rock:
1.Very fine grains
2.Very low permeability
3.Very large extension(it could be as large as half of France)

主题演讲幻灯片图例

例 3 版本 1：Let's look at this slide. Shale gas is a type of natural gas that is found trapped within shale formations. It is considered an unconventional natural gas because it is extracted from source rock rather than from traditional reservoirs. Shale oil and gas are extracted from the source rock, whereas conventional oil and gas are found in reservoirs. Shale has very fine grains, low permeability, and a large extension, while conventional hydrocarbons have coarse grains, high permeability, and limited extension. Hydrocarbons migrate from the source rock and can be trapped in a reservoir. Here are three questions you might be asking: What is the difference between shale oil/gas and conventional oil/gas extraction? What are the characteristics of shale and conventional hydrocarbons in terms of grain size, permeability, and extension? How do hydrocarbons migrate and get trapped in a reservoir? I'm going to answer these questions one by one.

例 3 版本 2：Let's look at this slide. Shale gas is a type of natural gas that is found trapped within shale formations. It is considered an unconventional natural gas because it is extracted from source rock rather than from traditional reservoirs. Shale oil and gas extraction differs from conventional oil and gas extraction. Shale oil and gas are extracted from source rock, while conventional oil and gas are found in reservoirs. Shale has very fine grains, low permeability, and a large extension, whereas conventional hydrocarbons have coarse grains, high permeability, and limited extension. Hydrocarbons migrate from the source rock and can be trapped in a reservoir. Shale oil and gas extraction often involves hydraulic fracturing, or fracking, which opens more natural gas for production but adds costs to the extraction process. On the other hand, conventional oil and gas extraction typically relies on natural pressure within the reservoir to bring hydrocarbons to the surface. In summary, the key differences between shale oil and gas and conventional oil and gas lie in their extraction methods, the characteristics of the rocks they are found in, and the migration and trapping of hydrocarbons.

这里的核心问题是探究译员如何整合多模态信息，以更好理解和传达源语内容。研究者通过操纵听觉信息和视觉信息的一致性来研究这个问题，换句话说，他们研究译员如何同时处理多个感官通道的信息，并将它们整合成一个连贯的意义表示，以便进行准确的翻译。在有稿同声传译中，多模态信息整合过程中的一个重要组件，当遇到视听信息不一致时，往往会加强认知控制，以解决视听信息之间的冲突。此外，优秀的译员能够判断哪些视觉信息有助于视听信息的整合，并更多地关注可以促进口译加工的视觉信息，例如与听觉信息在语义上一致的图片（Chmiel，2020；苏雯超，2021）。

在口译训练中，可以采用幻灯片演示文稿重组练习。通过依次展现一场演讲的多张幻灯片演示文稿，要求学生根据幻灯片演示文稿内容自行产出、添加并丰富讲话内容。将自行产出的内容与实际会议发言对比，学生会发现，只要对主题理解正确，辅以相关知识和从容表达，即便具体表述有差异，但不影响幻灯片演示文稿主旨的传达。这种练习可以提升学生的语言灵活性、即兴演讲能力、主题敏感度和辨识能力。译员必须提高自身的公共演讲水平，才能更好地理解讲话人的话语组织方式和思路脉络，从而在口译中更快跟上讲话人的思路，完成口译任务。通过幻灯片演示文稿重组练习，学生可以模拟真实的口译场景，锻炼快速理解、归纳和表达的综合能力，为未来的口译工作做好准备。

计时缩减

计时缩减练习是由教师准备母语或外语语段，计算匀速阅读这些语段所需的时间，再在这个时间的基础上对用时进行缩减，缩减程度由学生学习水平和难度要求来定，比如在正常阅读时间三分之二的时间内，要求学生在有准备或无准备的情况下，对该语段进行缩减，同语或译语可以依次尝试。这个练习训练学生边产出译语边辨识冗余信息、留取主要信息的能力，同时需要保持语言产出的连贯性和流利度（Andres & Behr，2015）。下面我们看一个例子。

We know that the United States, like South Africa, had to overcome centuries of racial subjugation. Sacrifices were needed here too - the sacrifice of countless people, known and unknown, to see the dawn of a new day.

以下是一个精简版本。

We know that both our countries had to overcome racial subjugation. Many have made sacrifices to bring about this change.

再来看另外一个例子。

And because he was not only a leader of a movement but also a skilled politician, the constitution for South Africa that emerged was worthy of this multiracial democracy. It was in keeping with his vision of laws that protected the rights of minorities as well as those of the majority and the precious freedoms of every South African.

以下是一个精简版本。

Due to his skills as a political leader, he was able to negotiate a constitution which protects the rights of every South African.

此外，同一篇源语可以进行不同程度的缩减，随着要求的不断变化，引领学生积极思考，勇敢尝试，增强学生理解能力及产出的灵活度。我们来看一个逐级缩减的例子。以下例子将逐级对源语进行 1/2 和 1/4 的缩减产出，直至最后，只用一句话总结源语。

	Brain Food
Source Language	Three recent scientific studies suggest that your mother was right when she advised you to eat fish if you want to become smart. All the studies suggest that cognitive performance is improved by eating omega-3 fatty acids, which are found in fish. The smallest study looked at 404 Dutch people aged between 50 and 70 over a three-year period. It found that people with higher levels of omega-3 fatty acids tended to experience significantly slower cognitive decline. Norwegian scientists studied more than 2,000 older people and came to a similar conclusion: they found that those who ate more than 10 grammes of fish per day performed better on cognitive tests than those who ate less than 10 grammes of fish per day. Those who ate more fish did even better. The best test results were achieved by those who ate about 75 grammes of fish per day. The largest study looked at more than 2,400 people in New Zealand. It found a convincing link between omega-3 fatty acids and mental health that was less consistent, but the results were still consistent with those of the other two studies. These studies show that there may well be a link between the consumption of omega-3 fatty acids in fish and brain function. However, more clinical trials are needed to determine with certainty whether eating fish reduces the incidence of age-related cognitive decline. (230 words)

1/2 of the SL	**Brain Food** Three recent scientific studies suggest that your mother was right when she advised you to eat fish if you want to become smart. All the studies suggest that cognitive performance is improved by eating omega-3 fatty acids, which are found in fish. The smallest study looked at 404 Dutch people aged between 50 and 70 over a three-year period. It found that people with higher levels of omega-3 fatty acids tended to experience significantly slower cognitive decline. Norwegian scientists studied more than 2,000 older people and came to a similar conclusion. They found that those who ate more than 10 grammes of fish per day performed better on cognitive tests than those who ate less than 10 grammes of fish per day. (122 words)
1/4 of the SL	**Brain Food** Three recent scientific studies suggest that your mother was right when she advised you to eat fish if you want to become smart. All the studies suggest that cognitive performance is improved by eating omega-3 fatty acids, which are found in fish. The smallest study looked at 404 Dutch people aged between 50 and 70 over three years. (58 words)
Bullets	**Brain Food** • All the studies suggest that cognitive performance is improved by eating omega-3 fatty acids, which are found in fish. • The largest study looked at more than 2,400 people in New Zealand. • These studies show that there may well be a link between the consumption of omega-3 fatty acids in fish and brain function. • However, more clinical trials are needed to determine with certainty whether eating fish reduces the incidence of age-related cognitive decline.
Bullets	**Brain Food** • Studies show that there may well be a link between the consumption of omega-3 fatty acids in fish and brain function. • However, more clinical trials are needed to determine with certainty whether eating fish reduces the incidence of age-related cognitive decline.
One Sentence Summary	**Brain Food** Eating fish improves cognitive performance, but more research is needed to determine if it reduces age-related cognitive decline. (18 words)

这样逐级缩减练习口译产出，可以提高学生信息筛选和处理的能力，并增强学生的语言表达能力。随着信息量的减少，学生需要用更简练的语言表达主要的意义，锻炼语言表达能力。同时还可以训练学生在有限时间内做出快速决策。不同程度的缩减要求，需要学生不断调整策略，提高处理信息的灵活性。同样重要的是，练习从较为简单的开始，逐渐增加难度，这可以帮助学生积累成功经验，增强信心。我们再来看一个逐级缩减的例子。

Source Language	**The Biggest Challenge that Humans Face Today** The topic is the biggest challenge that humans face today. I have decided to talk about food and water, so here we go. According to the United Nations, by 2030, there will be 8.5 billion people on earth, by 2050 there will be 9.7 billion and by 2100 there will be more than 11 billion people on our planet. They said that in seven years India will have a higher population than China. The average person can live 15 days without food and three days without water. So if we look at the current consumption, the problems of developing countries and the growing birth rate, we will face a big problem. So what are the problems we face and what are the possible solutions to them? What does the future of the human race really look like? Today I will talk to you about food and water. I will talk about the main problems we face, their causes and consequences, and of course some solutions. First of all, there is enough food on our planet, but all the food is in the wrong place. The food is not evenly or fairly or equally distributed. This becomes clear when we look at the top 10 countries that consume the most food in the world. I'll start with the first country. Not surprisingly, it is the United States of America, closely followed by Austria, Greece, Belgium, Luxembourg, Italy, Malta, Portugal, France and Israel. It is quite shocking that two rather small nations like Malta and Israel are in the top ten. But what about the countries that eat the least food in the world? These include the Democratic Republic of Congo, Eritrea, Burundi and Haiti. It is quite disturbing that the countries that eat the least are the countries with the lowest incomes, those that have to spend an average of 50 percent of their income on food. The top ten countries only spend between 5 and 20 percent of their income on food. This is a complete imbalance that will only get worse as the population grows and food prices rise. But what about food waste? Well, about one-third of the world's food is wasted every year. Every year, consumers in rich countries waste almost as much food 222 million tonnes as the food produced in sub-Saharan Africa 230 million tonnes.

Source Language	In the United States, exactly 30 percent of food is thrown away each year, and half of the water used to produce the food is wasted. But what happens to the food? Well, it usually ends up in landfills, where a large amount of methane is produced, and the environment is heavily polluted. But why is food wasted in the first place? Well, it's because of the sell-by-dates, expiration-dates, and best-before-dates, which are often not very accurate. The supermarkets do not want to be sued if someone gets sick, and people do not use common sense to decide whether they should eat something or not. So they just throw it in the rubbish. But consumers are not the only ones to blame. Supermarkets also dispose of the food themselves. But the worst thing is that, in the UK, one-third of the crops is not even harvested. (536 words)
1/2 of the SL	**The Biggest Challenge that Humans Face Today** The greatest challenge facing humanity today is food and water. According to the United Nations, by 2030 there will be 8.5 billion people on earth, by 2050 there will be 9.7 billion, and by 2100 there will be more than 11 billion. The average person can live 15 days without food and three days without water. So if we look at the current consumption, the problems of developing countries and the growing birth rate, we are facing a big problem. The top 10 countries that consume the most food are the United States of America, Austria, Greece, Belgium, Luxembourg, Italy, Malta, Portugal, France and Israel. Two small nations, Malta and Israel, are also in the top ten. // The countries that eat the least food include the Democratic Republic of Congo, Eritrea, Burundi and Haiti. This is because the lowest-income countries spend on average 50% of their income on food, while the ten highest-income countries spend only between 5% and 20%. Furthermore, one third of the world's food is wasted each year, with consumers in rich countries wasting as much as food produced in sub-Saharan Africa. Why is food wasted in the first place? It's because of inaccurate sell-by, expiry and best-before dates. It's not only consumers who are to blame, supermarkets also dispose of the food themselves. (217 words)
1/4 of the SL	**The Biggest Challenge that Humans Face Today** The United Nations estimates that in 2030 there will be 8.5 billion people on earth, in 2050 there will be 9.7 billion and in 2100 there will be 11 billion. The 10 countries with the highest food consumption are the United States, Austria, Greece, Belgium, Luxembourg, Italy, Malta, Portugal, France and Israel. The countries that consume the least food are the Democratic Republic of Congo, Eritrea, Burundi and Haiti. Every year, one third of global food waste is caused by inaccurate use-by, expiry and best-before dates. Consumers are not the only ones to blame, as supermarkets dispose of the food themselves. (101 words)

Bullets	**The Biggest Challenge that Humans Face Today** • By 2030, humanity will face a major population growth challenge of 8.5 billion people. • There is enough food on Earth, but it is not evenly distributed. • The countries that eat the least are the countries with the lowest incomes, and this imbalance will only get worse. • Consumers and supermarkets are both responsible for food waste caused by inaccurate shelf life.
Bullets	**The Biggest Challenge that Humans Face Today** • There is enough food on Earth, but it is not evenly distributed. • The countries that eat the least are the countries with the lowest incomes, and this imbalance will only get worse.
One Sentence Summary	**The Biggest Challenge that Humans Face Today** The world has enough food, but it is not evenly distributed, with the lowest income countries eating the least, and the imbalance is widening. (24 words)

　　需要注意的是，逐级缩减的练习本身也需要循序渐进，可以选择不同长度和难度的源语，以适合学习者的需求和其训练的目标要求。每一级缩减的信息量应适当减少，不能跳跃太大，否则会影响学习者的跟踪和理解。

　　综上所述，口译中的公共演讲训练需要引导学生在特定约束条件下进行有效表达。这些约束条件可能包括语言方向、主题、语速、时长、关键词等。通过在这些条件下的练习，学生可以提高语言表达的灵活性、准确性和适应性，从而更好地应对口译任务中的各种挑战。此外，口译中的演讲与一般公共演讲相似的地方往往在于，场景中少不了观众的参与。口译中的公共演讲训练应该给予学生更多"站在前台"的表现机会，"逼迫"学生适应在观众面前"自如表现"的口译需要。经过了这种模式的训练之后，学生们面对观众时的紧张感会减少，也会更加渴望面对观众，从而将其紧张情绪对语言水平发挥的负面影响降到最低。这样，学生能够更快适应真实口译的需要，更快成为口译职业所需要的适用人才。

4.3.2 复述训练

复述就是用言语重复识记内容，复述需要对话语的信息理解和逻辑把握有较高要求，可以检验我们是否理解所听内容，是否能够将各信息点有逻辑地联结起来。复述可以锻炼我们的记忆力，还可以锻炼我们的逻辑分析能力和有序表达能力。在日常生活中，我们常常需要将他人的话转述给第三者听，或将刚刚听到的故事讲给他人。这时，我们首先要保证听懂别人的话或是理解故事内容，才能在脑中形成有逻辑的记忆，然后复述出来（柴明颎，2014）。

在复述中，区分主要信息和次要信息非常重要。主要信息是话语中最能体现讲者意图的信息，是讲者最希望传达给听众的信息，也是我们进行复述时必须把握的信息。将这些信息串起来就是话语的大意，即是话语的骨架，加上补充信息将最终形成一个完整的话语。此外，复述还应把握的基本原则就是，不能曲解或改变原文的观点及主要事实。在口译教学中，复述是最为常见和实用的练习方法之一，因为复述可以考查学生是否真正理解了源语，更重要的是，复述在理解源语的同时记忆并回溯源语，正是对口译真实模式极大程度的模拟。从复述练习的语言组合来看，一般认为母语到母语难度最小，之后是外语到外语，再是外语到母语，最后是母语到外语，其中后两者进入了译述的阶段，也就是翻译阶段了。

此外，针对复述应该把握的原则，口译教学界也有诸多建议，对源语主要信息的把握和复述语言的连贯性基本上是主要关注的两点，也有一些学者对复述过程总结了具体的评估标准，比如鲁索和萨尔瓦多（Russo & Salvador，2004）在口译评估中，主要关注同义词的使用和连贯性的维持，以确保复述训练能够真正提高学生的思维灵活性和表达能力。通过评估学生在复述过程中是否恰当地运用同义词，以及是否能够保持表达的连贯性，教师可以判断学生的语言组织和表达能力是否得到提升。这种评估方式有助于学生在口译实践中更加灵活、准确地传递信息，同时也能提高其语言表达的流畅度和连贯性。根据鲁索（Russo，2014）的最新研究，复述过程中"寻找同义词"的能力与学生的学习成绩和完成学业所用时间相关。复述需要把握源语的主要观点和概念，并尽量采用灵活的方式将其重组。这样的理念需要通过由浅入深的练习来逐步渗透。首先从句子层面入手，让学生理解基本方法；其次进入话语练习。

在句子层面上，我们至少可以通过以下三种方式来对源语进行重组，也就是复述，这三种方式是：改变词性、改变句子结构、将长句打散为若干小句。下面我们看几个例子。

1. 改变词性。

源语：**He learns things very slowly.**

复述：He is a slow learner.

源语：**Tourism earns a lot of foreign exchange for Spain.**

复述：Tourism is a big foreign exchange earner for Spain.

源语：**The reason for the delay in delivery was a strike that happened days ago.**

复述：The delivery was delayed because of the strike that took place days ago.

源语：**An analysis of the responses to the questionnaire revealed a number of differences between women and men.**

复述：They analysed the questionnaire responses and found that female and male subjects differed in several ways.

源语：I believe that the arrival of the ship in Shanghai today is a symbol of the friendship between our two countries over the past 150 years.

复述：The ship's arrival in Shanghai today is symbolic of the friendship between our two countries over the past 150 years.

2. 改变句子结构。

源语：The centre and its website are available to anyone in the country who is interested in researching demographic data.

复述：Anyone in the country who wants to research demographic data can visit the centre and its website.

源语：He did not go to sleep until his mother came back.

复述 1：He did not fall asleep until his mother came back.

复述 2：After his mother came back, he went to sleep.

源语：Only by eliminating corruption and bureaucracy can we build a clean, small and efficient government.

复述 1：We must eliminate corruption and bureaucracy before we can build a clean, small and efficient government.

复述 2：We must eliminate corruption and bureaucracy before we can build a clean, small and efficient government.

源语：The book he wrote 20 years ago has always been his drive and pride.

复述 1：The book he wrote 20 years ago has always inspired him and made him proud.

复述 2：He wrote a book 20 years ago. This book has always been his pride and adornment.

复述 3：He wrote a book 20 years ago. He was always proud of that book.

源语：**The boom in the aviation industry that started about 30 years ago led to a corresponding boom in the hotel industry.**

复述：The boom in the aviation industry began about 30 years ago. This boom led to a similar boom in hotel construction.

3. 将长句打散为若干小句（综合以上两种方法）。

源语：**With all its weaknesses, this historic measure or something similar would greatly improve health security in the US.**

复述：This historic measure has its weaknesses, but measures like this would greatly improve health security in the US.

源语：**Advertising includes any activity in which visual or verbal messages are conveyed to the public to inform and induce them to purchase goods or services（with the aim of）.**

复述：Advertising includes those activities by which visual or oral messages are conveyed to the public with the aim of informing and persuading them to purchase goods or services.

源语：**As New Zealand's most populous city, Auckland is both a reflection of New Zealand and a showcase to the wider world, with its diversity of industries, manufacturing, services, finance, entertainment and education, as well as its diverse ethnic background.**

复述：Auckland is New Zealand's most populous city. Its diverse economy includes manufacturing, services, finance, entertainment, and education. It is also a city with a variety of ethnic backgrounds. Its industrial diversity and ethnic diversity make the city a mirror of New Zealand and a window on the wider world.

源语：Learners assessed as dyslexic can be supported either one-to-one or sometimes in small groups which are facilitated by a specialist support tutor, who will provide handouts on different coloured paper or present information more visually.

复述：Dyslexic learners can get one-to-one or small-group support. They will be helped by a specialist tutor. And the handouts provided by the tutor will be in different colors, in order to make the information more visible.

源语：Although fossil fuels such as oil, gas, coal and peat are used by power stations to generate electricity and fuel our cars, and are essential to modern lifestyles, their use comes at the expense of the environment, as damage is caused at every step of extracting and processing these fuels.

复述：Fossil fuels such as oil, gas, coal and peat are used by power plants to generate electricity and fuel our cars. In this sense, fossil fuels are very important for us to maintain our modern lifestyle. But in this way, we are damaging the environment. The reason is that damage is caused at every stage of the use of these fuels, from extraction to processing.

在学生经过一定句子层面的复述练习，对复述要旨有了更清晰的认识后，可以进一步发挥其在复述中的灵活性。这时，学生可以仅根据关键词构建源语信息框架。一旦确定了信息结构，如何用语言外壳进行表达就成为体现译员说话能力的关键环节。诺兰（Nolan，2008）通过举例说明，同一段源语可以采用多种表达方法和组织方式，而在效果上不会有巨大差异。换言之，在同一种语言中，语言外壳也有多种可接受的模式和选择。这意味着译员可以根据自身的语言风格和偏好，灵活选择恰当的表达方式，只要准确传达了源语的信息内容即可。

源语的信息框架	译语的产出可能包括
Government's plan for education: Train teachers Build schools Provide scholarships Help rural families Publish textbooks Improve television programs	My government's plans for education include training more teachers, building more schools, providing more scholarships, helping families in rural areas where there are no schools, publishing affordable textbooks and improving educational television programmes.
	To improve education, my government will train more teachers, build more schools, provide more scholarships, help families in rural areas without schools, publish affordable textbooks and improve educational television programmes.
	Train more teachers, build more schools, provide more scholarships, help families in rural areas without schools, publish affordable textbooks and improve educational television: These are some of the measures my government is taking to achieve its education goals.

在多种语言外壳中进行选择，有诸多原则和因素如场合、语速等需要考虑。比如，较为正式的场合倾向于选择语域较高的组合，比如名词性结构；又比如，同声传译尤其需要考虑源语速度，产出结构和用词需尽量简洁，以便跟上源语速度。但不论交替传译还是同声传译，译员并没有太多时间考虑语言外壳的选择，即便在交替传译记笔记阶段，可能更多需要关注信息结构中的主要信息。因此，在一般场合，口译产出的语言外壳的选择标准似乎很简单，那就是"开口如何便如何"。一旦开口的结构确定下来，就要保持结构平衡和语言准确，继续下去。因为不论使用哪套语言外壳，在信息结构的构建方面，也就是意义表达方面并无差异。

这一点在口译训练初级阶段尤为重要，学员总是试图找到"最好"或者"更好"的表达法，反复自我否定，更换已经出口且并没有错误的结构和词汇。须知与笔译不同，口译中最好的选择就是第一选择，一旦出口，除非是纠正错误，不然，任何第二选择，不但不能提升口译效果，反而会大大降低流利度，降低听众对译语的理解度和对译员的信任度。这里的指导思想在于，教师不应该把具体的句词或话语看成独立的教学材料，为了翻译好某个单独的句词或话语而翻译，翻译不出"范文"式的语言就是失败或错误。须知学生不会翻译的句词或话语是永远客观存在的，那么是不是只有学会了翻译所有的句词，学生才能够开始"职业口译"呢？显然，这有悖于口译原则。波赫哈克（Pöchhacker，2004）指出，interpreter 源于拉丁词 interpres，意思是人们解释意思（explaining the meaning）。"解释"这个词道出了口译的真谛。教师评价学生口译的效果，应该看学生是否能够在有限时间内自然、清晰、有逻辑地传达源语的意思。据此，在口译教学中，教师应该教会学生把握口译的"灵活度"，着重口译的整体效果，避免学生产生只顾"字典意义"而不顾语境意义的"死译"现象（邹德艳，2011a）。

首先，在口译训练的初级阶段，教师应该强调单语或双语复述的重要性，在学生能够较为全面、流畅地进行复述的基础上，再转向"传译"。这种训练方式教会学生"脱离源语语言外壳"，将源语的意义附加上译语语言外壳，并按照目的语言可接受的方式重组源语意义。口译实践和研究人员总结出来的一些具体口译技巧如断句、转换、重复、增补、省略、反说、归纳等等，都证明了释意派理论中心思想"脱离源语语言外壳"的有效性。换言之，只要把握住了"脱离源语语言外壳"这个中心思想，译员会在口译中自觉使用断句、转换、重复、增补、省略、反说、归纳等技巧。

其次，要真正提高学生口译的"灵活度"，教师需要帮助学生树立这样的认识，即口译中的"解决方案"绝不仅仅只有一个，更没有所谓"范文"的终极目标。刘和平（2001）引用塞莱斯科维奇（Seleskovtich）的观点指出，语言教学是教言语，翻译教学旨在使学生明白大多数与原文一致的对等词义不是固定的。在这种认识指导下，尤其因为口译具有很强的"即时性",那么口译学生就需要在有限时间内大胆使用能够想到的最便利的词语完成口译,以传达源语的意义。译语与源语之间在内涵或外延上的不契合是口译中难以避免的,译员可以通过解释传达文化之间的差异来弥补这种不契合,或者在任务完成之后思考更加契合的表达,以提高自身的双语转换能力。在口译教学实践中,学生出现卡壳的情形,有的是因为自己当时大脑一片空白,任何一个可以表达某意思的词都想不出来;有的是因为虽然可以想到一个词,却总觉得应该有更好的,进而左挑右选。以上两种情况都造成卡壳,影响口译的流利度和可理解度,破坏学生学习口译的积极性(邹德艳,2011a)。

综上所述,单个句子或段落的口译是口译教学中必不可少的一部分,但教师不应该仅仅关注学生是否能够使用最恰当的"笔译范文"似的语言,而应该更多鼓励学生采用灵活的方式表达源语的意思,应该高屋建瓴地教学生如何应对不同语言结构或篇章组织的转换。口译学生需要掌握口译中通用的一般技能,只有这样,他们才有可能通过译前准备来应对不同主题的口译任务。将这样的理念应用于口译中的复述练习,可以更好地结合记忆回溯和语言组织。这样的练习可以有效夯实口译多种技巧的综合运用,最终提升口译效果。在这个过程中,译语应该做到比源语更加简洁精练,从而突出对意义的把握和传达。请看下面的例子。

Sleep researchers have found that traditional remedies for insomnia, such as counting sheep, are ineffective. Instead, they have found that imagining a pleasant scene is likely to put you to sleep quickly. The research team divided 50 people who suffered from insomnia into three groups. One group imagined watching a waterfall, while another group tried counting sheep. A third group was given no special instructions on how to fall asleep. It turned out that the group that thought of a waterfall fell asleep 20 minutes faster. Mechanical tasks like counting sheep are apparently too boring to make people sleepy. There are many practical applications for insomnia research. It is estimated that about one in ten people suffers from severe insomnia.

口译学习者产出的复述版本可能如下。

Results from sleep researchers suggest that established remedies for insomnia, such as counting sheep, do not work, although imagining an attractive view can significantly promote sleep. The researchers divided 50 insomniacs into three groups. The first thought of falling water, the second tried counting sheep. A third group was not specifically instructed. The results show that the group that thought of waterfalls fell asleep faster. It seems that repetitive situations are not effective because they are too boring. The study is of great use because it is believed that 10% of the population suffers from sleep problems.

　　用多种方式表达同一意思，这在笔译中是较少采用的。笔译往往要求译者通过多方比照和鉴别，找到一种最为恰当的表达。但是，这种"精雕细琢"在口译中是与其即时加工的工作性质相冲突的。在口译训练中尤其要避免学习者养成字对字、句对句的口译习惯。口译实践的首要目的和原则是促成交际双方的交流与沟通，这就要求译员要在短时间内完成源语核心信息的有效传递。"逐字对译"或"逐句对译"并非口译实践的常态，"信息对等"和"功能等效"才是评价口译质量的首选因素（刘和平，2002）。

　　林超伦（2012）提到，多人听同一段话，之后凭记忆把原话写出，结果就是没有一个人的版本是完全一样的，与原文一模一样也是不可能的。原因在于：首先，环境和讲者的干扰可能导致无法每个人都清楚听到每个字；其次，听话是逐字逐句听的，但回忆并不是逐字逐句进行的，回忆不遵循听话的顺序，先说的字后回忆或者后说的字先回忆都是常见现象；最后，不同人对同样的话会有不同的理解，这也会导致回忆的不同。

不论从实践还是从理论层面，我们都可以知道，对源语的回忆和重建从来都是以主旨为主，字面的语言外壳是根据产出需要变换的，这种需要有来自语言组织上的，有来自文化层面上的，也有来自现场特殊情况限制的。为此，在口译训练中，针对同样的概念，我们要引导学生进行资源扩展及储备。如果储备较多，瞬时可用的资源就比较多，从中选择一个就显得绰绰有余；反之，如果储备较少，就容易出现张口结舌、捉襟见肘的情况。这样的储备训练可以从字词开始，进而扩展到句子甚至篇章，针对句子或篇章进行同义语主旨反复，也就是复述。下面，我们分别从字词、句子、篇章三个层面进行举例说明。

教师可以通过同义词搜集练习来帮助学生进行词汇上的联想和积累，在句子层面上，也可以鼓励学生将同样的源语用不同目的语句型表达出来。有了更多选择之后，学生不至于面临"无米之炊"的窘境。比如，汉语"建立"就有很多英语译法：create，construct，establish，build，set up，work up，frame，found，等等。学生译员首先要做到的是能够使用其中任意一个译法来完成口译。在这个阶段之后，才需要考虑分辨各个表达法之间的细小差别，进而有能力选择更加契合的一个。这样练习的好处是可以培养学生在口译中的灵活应变能力，同时可以帮助学生判断不同译语之间的优劣，从而提升自己的口译能力（邹德艳，2011a）。

针对词汇储备的练习，仅提供同义词是不够的。更好的方式是：在给出同义词的基础上，提供句子让学生使用这些词汇，或给出部分完整的句子，只留关键词让学生填空。这样不仅能帮助学生理解和掌握词语用法，还可以训练他们在实际语境中运用词汇的能力，对提高学生的语言运用能力很有帮助。

例如，"感到兴奋、热情、激励或印象深刻"的英译可以使用 inspire，attract，interest，motivate，excite，intrigue，enthuse，dazzle，fire someone with enthusiasm，capture someone's interest/imagination/attention 等表达，利用这些表达完成句子，可以让学生感受同义表达的不同形式如何灵活使用，完成句意。

1. Her story **captured** the interest of the world's media.

2. We must **motivate** students to take charge of their own learning.

3. We were hoping to **interest** the buyer in our new line of merchandise.

4. The film has so far **excited** little interest outside the art-house cinemas.

5. Tourists are **attracted** by its endless sandy beaches and perfect weather.

6. We use interactive displays to inspire children to read and write for **pleasure**.

7. Her resignation will do little to **inspire** confidence in a company that is already struggling.

8. I am **glad** I am not a freshman now, because I do not think I would have ever wanted to give up the dorm experience.

9. We could not be **happier** to help the company develop the tools that brands and publishers need to move the podcast industry forward.

10. Exploring new destinations and immersing myself in different cultures always brings me a sense of **thrill and excitement**.

例如，"目的、目标"的英译可以使用 so as to，in order to，with the object of，to achieve（goals），for the purpose of，with the aim of 等表达，利用这些表达完成句子，可以让学生感受，同义表达的不同形式可以灵活使用，完成句意。

1. They **aim at** quality rather than quantity.

2. After you reach your **goal**, you can get a generous reward.

3. Our ultimate **objective** is the removal of all nuclear weapons.

4. Three complementary **objectives** towards attaining this **goal** have been established.

5. This indicates that intent is a calculated, **purposeful** act aimed at injuring or harming another.

6. The ultimate **goal/aim/purpose** of an enterprise participating in an exhibition is to market its products in the area.

7. Most countries had erected barriers to trade of agricultural products **so as to** (**in order to/ to**) protect either their farmers or their consumers.

8. Advertising includes those activities by which visual or oral messages are delivered to the public, **the aim of which is to** inform them and influence them to buy merchandise or services.

9. Some developing countries have taken measure to compel multinationals to enter in partnership with local investors. **The purpose** is to gain firm control over some of their important industries and products, as these industries and products are strategically significant (for the host countries) .

10. The company implemented a comprehensive training program **with the intention** of improving employee productivity and performance.

综上所述，我们可以看出，对词汇的灵活使用往往也连带着句式的变化，而句式的变化也对词和词组的使用形式提出不同的要求，二者紧密联系，不可分割。在句子层面，教师可以针对同一源语句子，采用不同的句子成分开头，"强迫"学生按照所给开头继续句子，完成源语的主要意思的表达。经过这样的训练，学生将逐渐意识到，同一种意思的表达可以借由不同的表达方式来完成，流利的、重复和修改较少的产出才是口译中需要的表达，于是逐渐减少不必要的自我修订。请看下面的例子。

源语	皮尤研究中心进行的一项调查研究显示，超过一半的美国人从社交媒体平台获取新闻，这比从报纸和电视频道等传统媒体获取新闻的美国人的比例更高。
笔译	**A survey study** conducted by the Pew Research Center shows that more than half of Americans get their news from social media platforms, which is a higher percentage of Americans who get their news from traditional media such as newspapers and TV channels.
同声传译	**The Pew Research Center** conducted a survey study showing that more than half of Americans get their news from social media platforms, newspapers and TV channels, these traditional media, have a lower percentage of American viewers.
交替传译 1	**Acccording to** the Pew Research Center, more than half of Americans get their news from social media platforms, a higher percentage of Americans who get their news from traditional media such as newspapers and TV channels.
交替传译 2	**More than half** of Americans get their news from social media platforms, more than those who get news from newspapers, TV channels, and other traditional media. This is the research result of the Pew Research Center.

以上表格列出了针对同一源语句子的多种不同译文版本，让我们一起感受笔译与口译之间细微却关键的差异。表格中的同声传译版本并非唯一，但一般来讲，同声传译，尤其在无稿情况下，译员需把握顺译原则，尽量"顺句驱动"，先听到的先译，后出现的内容顺句加入，信息加工顺序需要遵循的原则是"first come, first served"。

相比同声传译来说，交替传译的优势是时间充裕，组织译语以句子甚至话语为单位，也就是说，字词甚至句子都可根据需要调整顺序。但这往往造成口译初学者的一种错误认识，那就是交替传译译员"可以"也"一定"要将译语组织到"最好"。他们试图开始时使用一个句式，又换一个句式，半个句子还都没有译出来，已经换掉多个主语了。事实上，为了纠正或杜绝这种"踟蹰不前""原地踏步"的错误做法，我们可以采用关键词产出训练法，目的就是训练学生一旦张口用哪个词，就怎么都可以顺着这个词把所有意思译出。也就是说，同一句源语可以有多种译语，适当练习，可以让学生逐步知晓并接受这种状态。我们再看下面的例子：

源语	美国消费者研究机构 Attest 日前发布了《美国媒体消费报告》。该报告指出，美国人媒体消费方式发生了结构性变化，社交媒体收割了 93% 的美国用户，美国传统媒体作为用户获取新闻首选渠道的地位，正在被社交媒体所颠覆。
笔译	Attest, a US consumer research firm, recently released its "US Media Consumption Report". The report points out that there has been a structural change in the way Americans consume media, with social media harvesting 93% of US users, and the status of traditional US media as the preferred channel for users to get news is being displaced by social media.
同声传译	**US consumer research firm** *Attest*, recently released "US Media Consumption Report", saying that Americans' media consumption has undergone structural changes. Social media has harvested 93% of US users. Traditional US media is losing its users and is being displaced by social media.
交替传译 1	**"US Media Consumption Report"** was recently released by *Attest*, a US consumer research firm. It says that Americans' media consumption has undergone structural changes. Social media has harvested 93% of US users. US Traditional media is losing its users and being displaced by social media.
交替传译 2	Attest is a US consumer research firm, and it recently released its "US Media Consumption Report". It says that Americans' media consumption is going through structural changes. Social media has harvested 93% of US users, and traditional media is losing its users and being displaced by social media.

这句话虽然短小，但囊括了多层逻辑关系。消费者研究机构 Attest 日前发布了《美国媒体消费报告》。该报告指出，美国人的媒体消费方式发生了结构性变化，传统媒体正在被社交媒体所颠覆。

笔译译文用一句话囊括所有句法关系，地道明晰，水平高的译员也可能在口译状态下产出这样的译语。但是，在口译训练中，学生语言水平不能一下子提高到这种程度，过分要求学生字对字、句对句，就会造成他们的译语破碎不堪，流利度下降。参考表格中的交替传译译语，可以鼓励学生采用不同方式开始句子，随后用断句的方式完成全部译语。

　　此节我们从演讲训练和复述训练两个方面探讨了口译脱壳。口译中词汇和句法使用需要更加灵活，这样才可以在需要的时候马上加以使用。但这不意味着口译中的词汇和句式越丰富越好，越花哨越好。相反，所选的词汇和句式应以简洁达意为主，难词、偏词和过于复杂的句式并不建议选用，因为这会加大译语的理解难度。口译研究也表明，相对于新手译员来说，有经验的职业译员可以产出更高质量的译语。但是，职业译员的译语在词汇多样性上低于新手译员（Timarová et al., 2014）。也就是说，可能正是因为职业译员可以大量并有效使用常用词汇，才可以空出更多认知资源，参与源语理解和译语产出，进而保障译语质量。

4.4　口译分脑

　　译员听到源语信息，必须同时进行解码分析以形成短时记忆，并快速转换代码表达给听众。如果我们把人脑看作信息处理通道，它的容量有限，不能同时处理过多任务。精力分配合理，便能较好完成任务；反之，分配不合理，译语就要受到影响。实际上，口译的最大难点就是多任务性，也就是通称的分脑。多任务处理最初是用来指计算机同时运行两个或多个程序的能力。比如，计算机可以同时下载文件和浏览网页。同样地，计算机使用者也可以进行多任务处理，比如，我们可以同时在一个窗口查询信息而在另外一个窗口与网友聊天。现实生活中，我们经常可以自如地进行多任务处理，比如：一边打电话，一边记下信息；一边看报纸，一边吃早餐；一边听音乐，一边工作；一边做饭，一边与家人聊天。

　　以上提及的多任务处理一般属于两种情况，一种情况是我们可以在两个或多个任务中自由快速地转换；另外一种情况是多种任务中的一种或几种几乎不需要太多的注意力，已经具备高度的自动化。口译是多任务处理的典型认知活动，难点就是需要成功克服对源语信息的预测、理解、记忆、转换和目的语的计划、组织、表达、监听、修正，同步说出目的语等多重任务间的交织、重叠和干扰给大脑造成的注意力分配困难，使听说并行不悖。在训练中要使受训者能够在多种任务之间自由、快速地转换，或者通过训练使其中某些任务的处理达到自动化的程度，进而可以有效将注意力分配给更加复杂的任务，进而保障并提升口译质量。

多任务处理训练也称分脑训练，目的是让学生了解多任务处理的运作特点，感受多任务处理的紧迫，自我调节多任务处理过程中有效分配工作记忆的能力。本节提供一些提升多任务处理能力的训练方法。首先，选择逻辑较清晰的篇章，按照自然段正常顺序交替进行听、读，并感受听、读任务频繁交替，检验自己是否可以不受干扰依然能够把握文章的主旨。其次，同时听、读一篇文章，感受听与读之间的平行进行，体验这个过程是否比单独听或读该篇文章更难，难在哪里，自己是否可以应对。此外，还可以准备两段长度相近、内容不相关的文字，在听其中一段文字的同时，阅读另外一段文字，听、读两个任务同时进行，同时结束。结束后，分别尝试复述两段的内容。可以进行小组练习，复述所读与所听的要点，然后互相做出评判。在以上训练中，任务语言的选择可以从全部汉语过渡到全部英语或两语夹杂。这样，同样的训练方式也会展现出由易到难的变化。在复述任务中，从用源语复述到用译语复述同样展现出由易到难的变化。

4.4.1　影子跟读

影子跟读练习又叫源语或单语复述练习，就是用同种语言几乎同步地跟读发言人的讲话或事先录制好的新闻录音、会议资料等。该训练的目的是培养译员的注意力分配和听说同步的技能。有关影子跟读练习的文献表明，影子跟读练习与听力理解和注意力集中有关。影子跟读类似鹦鹉学舌，跟读者紧接讲话者后面，保持几个词、半句话，甚至一句话的距离，尝试边听边重复听到的内容。但是，影子跟读又不能完全是鹦鹉学舌，跟读者要保证在跟读的同时能够听懂源语发言，且要发音清晰，音量适中，语句完整连贯。切忌机械地模仿发音，要做到耳朵听源语，嘴巴说同种语言复述，脑子想语言内容（邹德艳、刘芷岑，2020）。

源语跟读

影子跟读练习的第一阶段一般只要求紧跟源语发言，用同样的语言复述出发言内容。练习初期可以与源语的间隔时间较短，在熟练掌握要领之后尝试将时间间隔延长。

Bangladesh has achieved an economic **miracle** in the last 20 years. Just a few **decades ago**, it was one of the **poorest** countries in the world, ravaged by famine and floods. **Now** it is one of the **middle-income** countries. It is **now** the second largest clothing exporter in the world. **Textile factories** employ millions of **young women**, giving them economic power, encouraging **rural families** to invest in education and triggering a demographic dividend.

在跟读此段落时，要把握句子中的关键词和段落的主要结构。首先，关键词通常是表达句子核心意思的词语，跟读时应该着重强调它们，以确保目标语言表达的准确性和流畅性。例如，在上述例子中，"Bangladesh" "economic miracle" "poorest countries" "middle-income countries" 等都是关键词，需要在跟读时加以注意。其次，句子结构也是理解和跟读源语的关键。在跟读时，应该注意源语句子的主谓宾结构、从句和修饰语等语法成分，以确保目标语言表达的准确性和连贯性。例如，在上述例子中，"Just a few decades ago, it was one of the poorest countries in the world, ravaged by famine and floods. Now it is one of the middle-income countries. It is now the second largest clothing exporter in the world." 这三句话是并列句，需要在跟读时注意其结构，以确保目标语言表达的连贯性。

源语概述

源语概述练习是影子跟读练习的延续。用源语跟读完一段讲话内容后，停下来凭记忆力对跟读内容用同种语言概述，归纳讲话内容的核心思想。

China has dramatically expanded its universities. Some in China may be concerned that not all university graduates find jobs immediately. I suspect that this is not a problem of oversupply of graduates, but the need for a more efficient labour market for talented people. It also suggests that young people are willing to move to less urban areas for their first job after university. Besides, the competition for the best jobs in big cities keeps us all on our toes, does not it? China cannot have too many talented people.

此段落可作如下概括。

China has expanded its universities and some fear that the graduates will not find jobs. I do not think China has too many graduates or talented people. Rather, the country needs a more efficient labour market. And there are not enough young people willing to work in rural areas, while competition in the cities remains fierce.

在源语概述练习中，需要通过对源语内容的理解和记忆，用同种语言对其进行概括和归纳。为了准确地概括源语内容，需要注意以下几点：首先，要抓住源语内容的核心思想。在跟读时，应该着重关注源语中表达的关键信息和主要观点，以便在概述时能够准确地表达出来。例如，在上述例子中，核心思想是中国需要一个更高效的劳动力市场，而不是过多的毕业生或人才。其次，要注意源语内容的逻辑结构。在跟读时，应该注意源语中句子之间的关系和逻辑连接词，以便在概述时能够准确地表达出来。例如，在上述例子中，"China has expanded its university"和"some fear that the graduates will not find jobs"是因果关系，"there are not enough young people willing to work in rural areas"是一个结果，"competition in the cities remains fierce"是一个对比。最后，在概述时，应该用简洁明了的语言表达出源语内容的主要观点和核心思想。为了使概述更加清晰易懂，可以使用简单的句子和常用词汇，避免使用过于复杂或专业化的术语。同时，也要注意语言的流畅性和连贯性，以便让听众更容易理解和接受概述内容。

上文我们说过，影子跟读类似鹦鹉学舌，但又不能完全是鹦鹉学舌，需要保证在跟读的同时能够听懂源语发言的意思。实际上，在正常跟读的基础上刻意安排一些无关的练习，能够培养我们合理分配注意力的能力。比如，我们可以针对具体语段，在用源语跟读的同时完成注意力干扰练习。具体要求为，同学们从 1 开始顺写，或从 999 开始逆写。或从 10 开始每 10 个数字跳写，或者写下有意义的句子。跟读结束后，可以通过多种方式检验跟读的效果。比如，将跟读的产出内容录音，或由同伴听取跟读的产出，检查跟读话语的流畅性和可理解度。或者，检查跟读过程中数字记录等无关练习的结果是否正确，还可以在影子跟读之后，复述或概括听到的讲话内容。接下来，我们看一个例子。

可以请同伴阅读段落，我们边听边练习影子跟读，然后根据自己对文章的理解和记忆，填写表格。也可以在我们跟读的同时，让同伴边听边填写表格，检验我们跟读任务的完成情况，检验跟读产出的清晰度和可理解度。

Hi, I am April, and I am a university lecturer. I chose this profession because I wanted to do something meaningful. When I started my career years ago, I enjoyed it: preparing and giving lectures, discussing with students about their presentations and projects. But the workload overwhelmed me. I knew, of course, that the work could be difficult at times, but it was stimulating and challenging, in a word, difficult, but in an enjoyable way.

Hi, my name is Buster, and I am a software engineer. Lately I have been feeling overwhelmed by work and the pressure is increasing. I feel like work is too competitive. I know that a lifestyle that is less stressful is hard to have. So, I need to be able to deal with the stress and strain of my job. I do not want to be so stressed that I have a nervous breakdown due to overwork. Nowadays burnout is an increasingly common problem among colleagues in my profession.

Hi, I am Carroll, and I am a freelance designer, a freelancer. That means I work for myself and am self-employed. To use the official term, I am a sole trader. Deciding what you want to do for a living is the most important professional decision you can make, the second is deciding how you want to do it. Becoming a freelancer is a serious life decision that should not be taken lightly. I have made my living exclusively as a freelancer for the past few years and plan to continue doing so for years to come. This by no means makes me a guru in this field, but it does mean that I have experienced many of the joys and disasters that come with it.

Hi, my name is David and I volunteer for charities, also called non-profit organisations. Organisations of this type are also known as charities and make up the voluntary sector, which relies heavily on volunteers. They are usually run by paid professionals and pursue social goals such as helping the sick or the poor or promoting artistic activities. They do a lot of fundraising to get people to give money to the organisation in the form of donations. Non-profit organisations are not to be confused with loss-making businesses. Employees in the non-profit sector earn five to ten percent less than in the private sector. Research shows that volunteers help people the most, so I am proud of my job.

Name of the Person	His/Her Profession	Words Used to Describe His/Her Profession (As Many Words as You Can)
April	university lecturer	rewarding; stretched; difficult; stimulating; challenging; enjoyable
Buster	software engineer	overwhelmed; pressure; competitive; stressful; overwork; nervous breakdown; burnout
Carroll	freelance designer	self-employed; sole trader; vocational decision; guru; joys and disasters
David	volunteer	non-profit organization; not-for-profit organization; charities; voluntary sector; professionals; fund-raising; donations; loss-making companies; private sector

　　综上所述，影子跟读是多任务处理的典型训练，占用较多认知资源，甚至会出现"跟不上"和"跟丢了"的任务超负荷状态。这种情况下，对源语主要内容进行记忆和回溯的任务要求难度更大，因人而异，也因任务内容而异。记忆很少或者完全不记得跟读了什么内容是非常常见的，这也是跟读练习中难度较高的阶段。可以先采用源语概述练习，然后采用译语概述练习。练习时不必过度强调句子结构和具体内容，而要尽量用简练的译语传达源语中心思想和主要信息点。这样的练习如果可以循

序渐进，逐渐加大难度，则有助于学习者尽量接近并感受口译中多任务同时进行的状态，为口译的精进学习打下良好的基础。

4.4.2 限时视译

视译的产出形式是口语，似乎意味着已经对其产出速度或时限有所要求，但实际上视译的定义中，较少明确提及视译的速度或时限。视译的同时，播放原文的声音，是同声传译中常见的有稿同传；如果不同时播放原文的声音，视译任务是否要在限定时间内完成，是没有严格规定的。莫泽－默瑟（Moser-Mercer，1995）的研究发现，不限时的视译实践中，老手可以同时处理多任务，新手一般在阅读完后再翻译。这造成两者在视译速度上差异较大，前者每分钟 115 词，后者每分钟 60 词。赫米尔和利耶夫斯卡（Chmiel & Lijewska，2019）也发现，职业译员的视译用时比学生译员少。安杰莱利（Angelelli，1999）指出，视译译语听起来应该如同译员在使用译语朗读文本，译语产出应尽量流利，避免迟疑和停顿。司徒罗斌和杜蕴德（Setten & Dawrant，2016）认为，既然视译产出的是口语，那么听众理应对流利度有所期待，视译产出应是清晰、易懂、自然的，并对视译给出了相对具体的要求：从 C 语或 B 语译入到 A 语，产出用时不应超过阅读原文用时；从 A 语译入到 B 语，产出用时不应超过阅读原文用时的 20%。

视译定义中，自然语速产出似乎是视译的时限，但这一标准不够确切。我们可以将上文提到的视阅口译和视听口译看作视译时限的两端，一端是无时限视译，一端是可以叠加到有稿同传多个认知任务中的有时限视译。总结来看，我们可以这样定义限时视译：不同于自定步速视译（Self-Contained，Self-Paced ST），限时视译（Time-Limited，Time-Constrained ST）是通过外部条件控制视译原文输入速度，从而引导译员在一定时限内产出译语的视译方式（Zou & Chen，2023）。探讨视译时限的意义不仅在于明确其连续统的两端，还在于我们也可以对中间区间的时限予以更多关注，将限时要求结合进视译训练中，以凸显限时条件下视译的认知过程及其技能组成，进而更好发挥视译衔接笔译和口译的中介作用。

吉尔（Gile，1995/2009）的认知负荷模型（Effort Model）：同声传译＝听力理解（Listening）＋记忆（Memory）＋产出（Production）＋协调（Coordination）；视译＝阅读理解（Reading）＋记忆（Memory）＋产出（Production）＋协调（Coordination）；视译与同声传译只在信息输入模式上有所差异，但因读和听都是各自过程的首要部分，其余部分都因之发生并因之变化，所以两者的认知过程虽类似但不同。视译的视觉输入可回访，似乎比同声传译的听觉输入更简单，但实际上视觉输入长时存在也是一种干扰，且阅读的视觉干扰使译员更多关注词义，"得义忘言"更困难。视译对口译初学者更困难，因为他们还未掌握与语言形式拉开距离，并保持语言形式脱离外壳之后的心理表征（Gile，2020）。

口译过程中，如果译员不能有效将有限的认知资源分配在源语听辨、译语表达及工作记忆之间；或由于口译任务本身难度过高而导致认知资源短缺，就会出现认知负荷失衡。认知负荷应用于翻译认知研究，可识别翻译过程的重要特征；可揭示注意、意识、问题解决、自动化和专长等因素之间的复杂关系（Munoz Martin，2012）。关注视译的时限及其带来的认知负荷变化，可凸显视译的多任务性，细化视译认知研究。在限时翻译活动如同声传译、交替传译、视译、视听翻译中，完成任务、避免宕机不仅是一种"自我保护"，更是"生存选择"。那么，限时视译中，译员是如何在认知负荷内完成多个共时任务的呢？

输入输出时差在同声传译中体现为"听说时差"（EVS，Ear-Voice Span），指的是译员听到源语，到产出译语之间的时间差；在视译中体现为"视说时差"（EVS，Eye-Voice Span），指的是译员看到原文，到产出译语之间的时间差。研究表明，同声传译的听说时差基本处于0.5至11秒之间，平均在2至4秒之间（Barik，1973）；视译中的"视说时差"也可以参照这样一个跨度，具体研究显示，视译中的这个数值是8秒

（Chmiel & Lijewska，2022）。虽然在视译中"超前阅读"是常态，但总是要先看明白才可以开口翻译，也就是说，视译过程中眼睛看到并加工的信息的位置往往超前于口头产出的信息，但因为视译中文本不会像语音一样消失不见，视译回视的存在使得视译的"视说时差"变得更为复杂。司徒罗斌和杜蕴德（Setten & Dawrant，2016）发现，视译中增加阅读量可保障译语质量，但更多信息摄入会占用时间和精力。因此，为确保"视说时差"保持在可控范围，视译译员需在摄入一定量信息之后就完成片段的翻译，避免认知超负荷。

部分研究者（丹尼尔·吉尔、雷炳浩，2021）认为，视译的困难在于原文信息的保持使得译员一直受到干扰。实际上，这只是问题的一个方面。人类语言不可或缺的部分是从口语和书面语中提取语义的能力，语义表征不受感觉模态的影响（Binder et al. 2009；Price 2012）。对视译来说，一方面，与同声传译中的源语转瞬即逝不同，视译中的文本信息一直存在，在工作记忆广度和认知负荷总量允许的情况下，可多次访问，有助于理解原文，且输入输出时差可以更加灵活；另一方面，兰伯格-费尔伯和施奈德（Lamberger-Felber & Schneider，2008）发现，视译和同声传译中，视觉和听觉输入对译语产出的干扰程度和频率，并非取决于具体的翻译方式，而更多取决于译员个人的表现差异。也就是说，译员个人的能力和状态，对翻译过程中视听输入对产出的影响程度起着更关键的作用，而不是翻译方式本身的差异。

视译与其他限时翻译活动一样，是多任务同时进行的认知过程，对学生译员的源语理解、翻译思维、拆分重组、顺译使用及译语表达等均有积极影响（刘进，2011；邓玮，2017）；帮助学生译员感受并适应"脱离源语语言外壳"的过程。宋（Song，2010）指出，视译与同声传译的技能迁移，如不能顺利进行，主要原因是视译不限时的话，其静态特征与同声传译在线动态信息加工模式不能更好契合。可以看出，作为一种限时翻译活动，视译的时限发挥重要作用，可凸显视译促进译员高效分析原文、脱离原文结构、形成译文策略的作用。限时视译需在时间限制下协调完成原文阅读、短时记忆、译语产出，而所有任务都要竞争有限的认知资源，因而要确保任务叠加不超出可用的加工容量。以下从快速阅读、工作记忆、译语产出三个方面说明限时视译的技能组成及训练方法。

　　限时视译需要较高的阅读理解能力。快速阅读的研究表明，阅读效率需要在阅读速度和准确性之间要进行权衡。那么，对限时视译来说特别重要的阅读效率体现在哪些方面呢？高效阅读者可注视到对信息建构贡献更大的实词，在注视词上所用时间更少，眼跳距离更大，很少回看。低效阅读者注视的不见得是实词，注视词所用时间更多，眼跳距离较小，经常回看。所以，注视词是否为建构信息更有效的实词，注视词用时多还是少，眼跳距离大还是小，回看多还是少等，都是决定阅读效率的重要因素。这一点对视译来说非常重要，成为高效阅读者，才能做好视译。下图是阅读时眼动的典型模式，包括注视和扫视，眼睛在静止文本上移动时从来都不是平稳的（Shah，2018）。

眼动仪下的阅读过程

　　那么如何在限时视译训练中提升快速阅读能力？卡利纳（Kalina，2000）、山德雷利和霍金斯（Sandrelli & Hawkins，2006）认为，在视译中，控制时间的重要性突出了快速阅读和理解的关键作用。与同声传译相比，视译要求译员在有限时间内快速阅读、理解源语信息，并迅速转换为目标语输出。因此，培养译员的快速阅读能力和瞬时理解能力，对提高视译质量至关重要。卡蒙等（Cammoun et al.，2009）建议在文本准备过程中，特别关注主要观点、复杂句法、习语表达等元素；特别是在准备时间有限的情况下，优先采用以下技巧：在关键元素周围使用画圈、高亮、下划线以辅助理解；快速浏览文本以把握主要观点，例如正面与负面、支持与批评等；查看开头和结尾段落。宋（Song，2010）通过使用定时幻灯片演示文稿，帮助学生掌握口译尤其是与同声传译相关的技能和策略。司徒罗斌和杜蕴德（Setten & Dawrant，2016）建议将原文语义单元进行标记，避免学生紧贴原文表面结构，帮助学生根据语义和结构提示生成译语；或者将文本分成信息块，依次呈现，可按照训练需求调整呈现速度，训练学生断句，让学生感受信息有限而又不得不在冒险和谨慎中权衡，完成口译任务。

此外，快速阅读不仅是语言学习的方法和路径，更是人类快速摄入信息的需要和趋势。个人通信设备的普及使信息的获取无处不在，我们可支配的信息处理时间不能够满足我们需要获取的信息量，于是快速阅读成为刚需。可以帮我们实现快速阅读的方法包括移动窗口、时报广场、高亮显示、一行一行呈现、句子呈现和快速序列视觉呈现（Rapid Serial Visual Presentation，RSVP）等。RSVP首次被吉尔伯特（Gilbert，1959）应用于阅读研究，之后被福斯特（Forster，1970）用于研究书面语言的理解和处理。RSVP是一次显示一个或多个词语，按顺序呈现，避免眼睛平移和回视，最小化阅读时的眼动，促使阅读者快速阅读。这些方法可在限时视译训练中加以借鉴。

限时视译需要更高效的工作记忆能力。如何在限时视译训练中提升工作记忆能力？心理学研究发现，通过训练中央执行系统的抑制、转换、刷新功能，可提高个体的工作记忆能力（周仁来、赵鑫，2010；赵鑫、周仁来，2011）。工作记忆与口译的结合研究也发现，译员比一般双语者展现出认知转换上的优势（赵宏明、董燕萍，2021）；工作记忆中央执行系统的抑制功能与口译经历长短有关，抑制功能越好，输入输出时差越短，口译准确率有上升趋势（Timarová et al.，2014；邹德艳，2017；Chmiel，2021）。传统口译训练方法如跟读、跟读并复述、多任务跟读、听读同步等分脑练习都可提升译员的多任务处理能力。可借鉴的工作记忆训练方法包括视觉空间工作记忆任务、数字广度任务、词语广度任务、选择反应时等工作记忆训练任务、复述等策略训练任务、n-back 任务等（王勤勤，2013）。此外，使用专业工作记忆训练软件如认知训练程序（Lumosity）或个性化训练程序（CogniFit），连续训练 4~5 周，工作记忆水平可得提高（刘春雷、周仁来，2012）。在限时视译训练中应用工作记忆训练方法，借鉴跨学科成果，可丰富翻译训练方法的科学性及可持续性。

　　限时视译需要更高效的译语产出能力。视译译员可控制感知信息的节奏，但只有在阅读的同时进行译语产出，才能保障流利度。研究表明，有经验的视译译员更关注整体意思，使用自上而下策略（top-down strategy）；新手更关注具体字词，特别是造成困难的词，使用自下而上策略（bottom-up strategy）（Davis & Bistodeau 1993；Liu et al.，2004）。王斌华（2012）研究发现，有经验的译员善于以已知推断未知，且在未知信息属于冗余或可忽略情况时会选择跳过未知信息，但新手往往把注意力放在未知信息上，并因此"卡壳"。时间限制下，译员只能更关注主要信息和信息结构，在保持一定预测成功率的同时，较高质量完成顺译。视译中原文存在，更难以脱离源语语言外壳；所以，译员表现出来的"脱壳"速度和能力，是口译刻意训练才能达成的效果。

　　那么，如何在限时视译训练中提升译语产出能力？提升译语表达能力的方法往往基于提升双语表达能力的一般方法，如通过平行文本输入练习及翻译练习来补充相关认知知识；通过单词表自由演讲、关键词输出、填空输出、压缩输出等练习进行主题框架下的灵活产出。但在限时视译中，指导原则是克服原文文本的过度影响，尽量在一定速度下顺译。此外，主要概念的快速转换和句法差异的灵活处理，分别如同砖头和水泥，如有机融合，可更快更好建构译语。其中，砖头不仅包括负载专题和世界知识的术语，还包括常用词汇：可通过"快速连续视觉呈现"或"滚屏呈现"的方式，针对术语进行双语转换准确度和速度的训练，提升术语"基线"转换效率；水泥指的是句法灵活处理，承认并充分利用语言可塑性，抑制语言干扰，更加线性产出，保持产出地道的同时尽可能接近原文语序。法尔博（Falbo，1995）建议使用"伪视译"（Pseudo ST）的方法，即便原文和译文之间存在直接对应，也要求学生将原文的句法和词汇进行刻意转换，以训练学生灵活产出；司徒罗斌和杜蕴德（Setten & Dawrant，2016）也指出，句法灵活处理可更好应对口译中的时间限制，保障译语流利度。

　　总结来看，提高限时视译能力可以从以下几个方面着手。首先，提高快速阅读能力。可以通过文本标记、快速浏览、关注开头结尾等技巧快速抓住文本主旨；也可以借鉴快速阅读软件的设计，进行更有效的训练。其次，提高工作记忆能力。可以通过工作记忆相关的心理学训练任务，以及传统的口译训练方法，来增强工作记忆容量，还可以利用认知训练软件进行系统训练。最后，提高译语产出能力。可以注意运用自上而下的处理策略，关注主要信息，跳过冗余信息；重点加强关键概念的快速转换和句法的灵活处理，还可以通过快速呈现关键词、进行伪视译等训练来达到训练目的。

后　记

国际会议口译员协会（AIIC）在其工作任务的"培训和专业发展"部分指出：不论对于学生、专业译员，还是对于翻译教师来说，适当的培训能够对其工作表现、专业能力和职业满意度产生积极影响。培训至少包括三类：对希望成为译员的学生进行初步培训；为希望磨炼技能或获得竞争优势的译员提供持续的专业发展；为希望将技能传授给下一代译员的翻译教师提供培训。

翻译教育教学是我们培养高层次翻译人才、助力翻译人才队伍可持续发展的重要议题。口译话语与普通话语既有相似之处，又有独特性。本书认为，在口译教学中，应该重视对口译话语的分析和重构，并将其贯穿于整个口译训练过程。也就是说，口译话语分析应当贯穿口译训练的全过程，而不应仅限于某个特定环节。通过对口译话语的深入分析和重建训练，可以帮助学习者更好地掌握口译的实践技能。本书从话语的形式和话语的理解入手，从话语难度、信息权重、信息结构、信息推进的角度探讨口译中的话语分析，从话语生成、话语整合、口译脱壳、口译分脑的角度探讨口译中的话语重构，将可操作的话语分析和重构方法整合在一起，为口译的技能习得提供理论支撑和教学建议。在阅读本书后，我们与读者共同思考并探讨两个问题，以厘清我们的出发点和目的地。

口译还需要学习吗？随着人工智能的发展，语音识别、机器翻译、强化学习等复杂的学习任务都可以由机器完成，效果可以匹敌乃至超过人类表现，于是，"外语无用论""翻译无用论"甚嚣尘上，以色列学者赫拉里在《未来简史——从智人到智神》里甚至提出了人类将逐步成为"无用阶层"。在机器面前，人类只能缴械投降、步步后退、苟延残喘吗？从实质上看，"无用论"把人和人工智能当作并行的主体，即把作为生产工具的人工智能主体化了，因此导致生产力发展的双目的性，既为了人，也为了机器，从而导致逻辑的根本错误（杨青峰，2020）。此外，"无用论"只关注了结果，忽略了过程；完成翻译任务、达成结果绝不是翻译的全部，翻译是人类消除误解和偏见、增进理解与互信的桥梁，更是人类本身通过语言学习、语言转换，来贯通古今、交流中外、开阔视野、精进思考的过程。人类的智力劳动始终是人工智能存在的逻辑前提，这就告诉我们，在人机互动的过程中，在人机共治的时代中，我们有所为，亦有所不为；面对机器大潮的汹涌来袭，需保持最大程度的"淡定"。

口译应该怎么学呢？进入新时代，翻译实践方式及学习模式都发生了翻天覆地的变化。"人工智能语言服务"丰富并扩展了翻译活动的内涵和外延，语言服务行业迎来跨越式发展。海量移动学习资源支撑下的泛在学习对传统教学的路径方法和师生角色发起挑战，这都要求我们对学习本身进行思考。对学习过程及结果的考量从传统的学习评价（assessment of learning）逐渐转变到了以评促学（assessment for learning）、以评为学（assessment as learning）。口译学习过程需要学习评价，需要以评促学，更需要以评为学，也就是"学评融合"——学生通过自我评估、自我监控、自我调节来逐步缩小学习差距并明确更高的学习目标，促进其主动发展，更好地培养其核心素养。所以，本书从口译过程的多个维度对口译进行探讨，对口译教师及口译学习者都有帮助，通过"知己知彼"的反思来扩展口译思维的深度和广度，帮助不同级别口译学习者对学习过程和目标达成进行思考，发展学习者的元认知能力和达成学习标准的意识，达成泛在学习环境中的学习效果。

本书的教学设计和建议不仅适合口译教师将其应用于教学实践，还可供口译学习者作为参考，自行提升口译话语分析及重构能力。同时，我们要知道，口译不是教会的，而是练成的。练习是成为译员最重要的方法，如今泛在学习的资源条件下，我们可以随时随地练脑、练口。除此之外，要有意识地在一周之内与同学一起多练习几次，因为积极练习是我们将口译技巧内化并熟练运用的唯一方法。

笔者的另一本拙作《口译的记忆训练——理论与实践》于 2016 年出版，市场反响较好，在 2017 年进行了第二次印刷，2021 年获得了辽宁省哲学社会科学奖·成果奖二等奖。回头看那本书，疏漏颇多，实与读者厚爱不相匹配。另外，如今距 2016 年已过去 7 年，行业发展及翻译实践日新月异，笔者自身对专业的认识也有所增进。因此，有了再写一本书的想法，也就有了本书的出现。笔者水平有限，书中错误或不妥之处在所难免，希望读者多多批评指正，希望与口译研究者、教学人员和自学人员共同探讨，共同进步。

2023 年秋 于大连旅顺

参考文献

一 中文著作和中文译著

鲍刚:《口译理论概论》,旅游教育出版社,1998。

曹雪虹、张宗橙编著《信息论与编码(第2版)》,清华大学出版社,2009。

柴明颎主编《英语口译——公共演讲与复述》,上海交通大学出版社,2014。

〔英〕东尼·博赞:《博赞记忆术》,陆时文译,化学工业出版社,2014。

〔英〕东尼·博赞:《思维导图——大脑使用说明书》,张鼎昆,徐克茹译,外语教学与研究出版社,2005。

桂诗春:《心理语言学》,上海教育出版社,1998。

桂诗春:《新编心理语言学》,上海外语教育出版社,2005。

〔美〕哈里·洛拉尼:《哈佛记忆课》,陈嘉宁译,北京联合出版公司,2014。

何高大主编《实用英汉汉英口译技巧》,中南工业大学出版社,1997。

胡壮麟、朱永生、张德禄、李战子:《系统功能语言学概论》,北京大学出版社,2005。

胡壮麟、朱永生、张德禄:《系统功能语法概论》,湖南教育出版社,1989。

黄国文:《话语分析的理论与实践——广告话语研究》,上海外语教育出版社,2004。

李长栓:《非文学翻译理论与实践》,中国对外翻译出版公司,2004。

林超伦主编《实战交替传译(英汉互译)》,中国出版集团公司,2012。

刘和平:《口译技巧——思维科学与口译推理教学法》,中国对外翻译出版公司,2001。

屈承熹、潘文国:《汉语话语语法》,北京语言大学出版社,2006。

万宏瑜:《视阅口译的认知研究》,中国海洋大学出版社,2017。

文秋芳、王金铨:《中国大学生英汉汉英口笔译语料库》,外语教学与研究出版社,2008。

席晓青:《话语分析:思维、策略与实践》,厦门大学出版社,2011。

徐赳赳:《现代汉语篇章语言学》,商务印书馆,2010。

杨承淑:《口译教学研究:理论与实践》,中国对外翻译出版公司,2005。

张德禄、苗兴伟、李学宁:《功能语言学与外语教学》,人民教育出版社,2005。

张今、张克定:《英汉语信息结构对比研究》,河南大学出版社,1998。

邹德艳:《交替传译工作记忆能力的差异研究》,中央编译出版社,2017。

邹德艳:《口译的记忆训练——理论与实践》,中央编译出版社,2016。

邹德艳主编《听辨与译述》,北京师范大学出版社,2020。

二 中文论文

蔡曙山:《论语言在人类认知中的地位和作用》,《北京大学学报(哲学社会科学版)》2020年第1期。

蔡曙山:《认知科学研究与相关学科的发展》,《江西社会科学》2007年第4期。

曹思琪、汤晨晨、武海燕、刘勋:《价值计算决定何时与如何努力》,《心理科学进展》2022年第4期。

曹秀萍:《认知语法视角下的"功能对等"翻译观——从奈达的7个核心句谈起》,《湖北文理学院学报》2012年第9期。

曾守锤、李其维：《模糊痕迹理论：对经典认知发展理论的挑战》，《心理科学》2004 年第 2 期。

陈明瑶：《论语篇连贯与话语标记语的汉译》，《上海翻译》2005 年第 4 期。

陈小全：《汉英翻译中的句法结构转换》，《中国翻译》2008 年第 5 期。

丹尼尔·吉尔、雷炳浩：《认知负荷模型在口译教学中的建构》，《翻译界》2021 年第 1 期。

邓玮：《国内视译研究 30 年（1987—2016）回顾与反思——基于中国知网（CNKI）的文献计量分析》，《外国语文》2017 年第 5 期。

董燕萍、王斌华：《口译过程的两阶段解读——以一般语言理解和产出为参照》，《中国翻译》2013 年第 1 期。

符荣波：《英汉双向交替传译中译语停顿的对比研究》，《外语教学与研究》2012 年第 3 期。

高莹、樊宇、王亚非：《口语非流利性现象与内在的语言发展之间的相关研究》，《外语与外语教学》2014 年第 4 期。

胡壮麟：《评语法隐喻的韩礼德模式》，《外语教学与研究》2000 年第 2 期。

胡壮麟：《语篇分析在教学中的应用》，《外语教学》2001 年第 1 期。

鞠玉梅：《信息结构研究中的已知信息》，《天津外国语学院学报》2003 年第 5 期。

李美霞：《论话语类型分析和小句关系分析的互补性》，《外语教学》2001 年第 4 期。

刘春雷、周仁来：《工作记忆训练对认知功能和大脑神经系统的影响》，《心理科学进展》2012 年第 7 期。

刘和平、鲍刚：《技能化口译教学法原则——兼论高校口译教学的问题》，《中国翻译》1994 年第 6 期。

刘和平、雷中华：《对口译职业化＋专业化趋势的思考：挑战与对策》，《中国翻译》2017 年第 4 期。

刘和平：《对口译教学统一纲要的理论思考》，《中国翻译》2002 年第 3 期。

刘进：《以视译促交传——一项基于实证的相关性研究报告》，《中国翻译》
　　2011年第3期。

刘文翠、崔桂华：《主述位结构与信息结构的比较研究》，《东北师大学报
　　（哲学社会科学版）》2005年第6期。

庞继贤、叶宁：《西方语类理论比较分析》，《浙江大学学报（人文社会科
　　学版）》2011年第2期。

苏雯超：《带稿同传认知加工过程中的眼动研究》，《中国外语》2023年第
　　3期。

苏雯超：《同声传译视觉信息加工中的眼动研究》，《中国科技翻译》2021
　　年第2期。

王斌华：《从口译能力到译员能力：专业口译教学理念的拓展》，《外语与
　　外语教学》2012年第6期。

王洪林：《全球化时代跨学科与跨界翻译研究——苏珊·巴斯奈特〈翻译〉
　　介评》，《东方翻译》2019年第4期。

王穗苹：《当前篇章阅读研究的争论与分歧》，《心理科学》2001年第3期。

王军：《错拼词及其基于能指所指关系的解读理据》，《外语教学》2014年
　　第4期。

王勤勤：《工作记忆训练对流体智力的影响研究评述》，《心理技术与应用》
　　2013年第4期。

伍铁平：《语言的模糊性和词源学》，《外语教学》1986年第1期。

肖福寿：《口语和笔语语域特征与二语写作质量和年级之间的关系研究》，
　　《中国外语》2013年第6期。

徐光国、张庆林：《习得性勤奋的实验研究和理论假设》，《心理科学》
　　1996年第3期。

徐然：《"专注听力"——口译听力培训方法之我见》，《中国翻译》2010
　　年第3期。

杨青峰：《对人工智能"无用阶层论"的辨析——基于马克思主义哲学视

角》,《新视野》2020 年第 5 期。

杨姗姗:《源语文本输入下数字同传表现研究——来自新手译员的证据》,
《外语与翻译》2023 年第 3 期。

易伟、梅舒婷、郑亚:《努力:成本还是奖赏?》,《心理科学进展》2019
年第 8 期。

赵德全、宁志敏:《解读报刊英语中的语法隐喻》,《国外外语教学》2005
年第 1 期。

赵宏明、董燕萍:《口译员的认知转换优势》,《心理科学进展》2021 年第
4 期。

赵鑫、周仁来:《工作记忆中央执行系统不同子功能评估方法》,《中国临
床心理学杂志》2011 年第 6 期。

钟丽佳、盛群力:《如何调控认知负荷"最优化":发展综合认知努力——
访谈国际著名认知科学家弗莱德·帕斯》,《现代远程教育研究》
2017 年第 4 期。

周仁来、赵鑫:《无所不能的"小矮人"到成长中的"巨人"——工作记
忆中央执行系统研究评述》,《西北师大学报》(社会科学版)2010
年第 5 期。

邹德艳、刘芷岑:《跨界融合视角下的口笔译再思考》,《外文研究》2020
年第 4 期。

邹德艳、张宏宇:《模糊痕迹理论观照下的释意》,《外文研究》2015 年第
2 期。

邹德艳:《口译教学与教学口译》,《长春理工大学学报》2011 年第 5 期。

邹德艳:《语言输出自动化与口译》,《鸡西大学学报》2011 年第 5 期。

三 英文著作

Andres, Dörte, and Martina Behr. 2015. *To Know How to Suggest: Approaches
to Teaching Conference Interpreting*. Frank & Timme Verlag für

Wissenschaftliche Literatur.

Baddeley, Alan D. 1986. *Working Memory*. Oxford University Press.

Baddeley, Alan D. 1990. *Human Memory: Theory and Practice*. Allyn & Bacon.

Baker, Mona. 1992. *In Other Words*. Routledge.

Bassnet, Susan. 2014. *Translation*, Routledge.

Bell, Roger T. 2005. *Translation and Translating: Theory and Practice*. Foreign Language Teaching and Research Press.

Biber, Douglas. 2012. *Variation Across Speech and Writing*. Cambridge University Press.

Carroll, David W. 1999. *Psychology of Language*. Cole Publishing Company.

Cruse, Alan. 2002. *Meaning in Language: An Introduction to Semantics and Pragmatics*. Oxford University Press.

Eggins, Suzanne. 1994. *An Introduction to Systemic Functional Linguistics*. Printer Publishers.

Gigerenzer, Gerd, Peter M. Todd, and the ABC Group. 1999. *Simple Heuristics that Make us Smart*. Oxford University Press.

Gile, Daniel. 1995/2009. *Basic Concepts and Models for Interpreter and Translator Training*. John Benjamins Publishing Company.

Gillies, Andrew. 2009. *Note-Taking for Consecutive Interpreting: A Short Course*. Shanghai Foreign Language Education Press.

Goffman, Erving. 1981. *Forms of Talk*. University of Pennsylvania Press.

Gutt, Ernst-August. 1991/2000. *Translation and Relevance: Cognition and Context*. Saint Jerome Press.

Halliday, Michael A.K. 1967. *Intonation and Grammar in British English*. Mouton.

Halliday, Michael A.K. 1985. *Spoken and Written English*. Deakin University.

Halliday, Michael A.K. 1994. *An Introduction to Functional Grammar*. Edward Arnold.

Halliday, Michael A.K. 2000. *Introduction to Functional Grammar*. Foreign Language Teaching and Research Press.

Halliday, Michael A.K., and Ruqaiya Hasan. 1976. *Cohesion in English*. Longman.

Hatch, Evelyn M. 1983. *Psycholinguistics: A Second Language Perspective*. Newbury House.

Jones, Roderick. 2008. *Conference Interpreting Explained*. Shanghai Foreign Language Education Press.

Kade, Otto. 1968. *Zufall und Gesetzmäßigkeit in der Übersetzung [Chance and Regularity in Translation]*. Enzyklopadie.

Kahneman, Daniel. 1973. *Effort and Attention*. Prentice-Hall.

Krashen, Stephen D. 1985. *The Input Hypothesis: Issues and Implications*. Longman.

Labov, William. 1972. *Language in the Inner City*. University of Pennsylvania Press.

Lakoff, George, and Mark Johnson. 1980. *Metaphors We Live By*. The University of Chicago Press.

Levelt, Willem J.M. 1989. *Speaking: From Intention to Articulation*. The MIT Press.

Martinet, Andre. 1960. *Elements of General Linguistics*. Faber and Faber.

McCarthy, Michael, and Ronald Carter. 1994. *Language as Discourse*. Longman.

McCarthy, Michael. 2001. *Discourse Analysis for Language Teachers*. CUP.

Miller, George A., Eugene Galanter, and Karl H. Pribram. 1960. *Plans and the Structure of Behavior*. Holt, Rinehart and Winston.

Munday, Jeremy. 2001/2008. *Introducing Translation Studies: Theories and Applications*. Routledge.

Nida, Eugene A., and Charles R. Taber. 1982. *The Theory and Practice of*

Translation. E. J. Brill.

Nolan, James. 2008. *Interpretation: Techniques and Exercise.* Shanghai Foreign Language Education Press.

Pöchhacker, Franz. 2004. *Introducing Interpreting Studies.* Routledge.

Reza, Fazlollah. 2012. *An Introduction to Information Theory.* Dover Publication.

Seleskovitch, Danica, and Marianne Lederer. 1989. *Pedagogie Raisonnée de L'interpretation [Reasoned Pedagogy of Interpretation].* Luxembourg Didier Erudition.

Setton, Robin, and Andrew Dawrant. 2016. *Conference Interpreting: A Complete Course.* John Benjamins.

Setton, Robin. 1999. *Simultaneous Interpretation: A Cognitive-Pragmatic Analysis.* John Benjamins.

Solso, Robert L. 1998. *Cognitive Psychology (5th ed.).* Allyn & Bacon.

Sperber, Dan, and Deirdre Wilson. 1986. *Relevance: Communication and Cognition.* Blackwell.

Thompson, Geoff. 2000. *Introducing Functional Grammar.* Foreign Language Teaching and Research Press.

Wanat, Stanley F. 1971. *Linguistic Structure and Visual Attention in Reading.* International Reading Association.

Weber, Wilhelm K. 1984. *Training Translators and Conference Interpreters.* Harcourt.

Zipf, George K. 1949. *Human Behavior and the Principle of Least Effort.* Addison-Wesley.

四 英文论文

Agrifoglio, Marjorie. 2004. "Sight Translation and Interpreting: A Comparative Analysis of Constraints and Failures." *Interpreting* 6(1)

Altman, Janet. 1994. "Error Analysis in the Teaching of Simultaneous Interpretation: A Pilot Study." In *Bridging the Gap-Empirical Research in Simultaneous Interpretation*, edited by Lambert, Sylvie, and Moser-Mercer, Barbara. Philadelphia-Amsterdam: John Benjamins.

Angelelli, Claudia V. 1999. "The Role of Reading in Sight Translation." *The ATA Chronicl* 28(5).

Ariel, Robert, and Alan D. Castel. 2014. "Eyes Wide Open: Enhanced Pupil Dilation When Selectively Studying Important Information." *Experimental Brain Research* 232(1).

Atkinson, Richard C., and Richard Shiffrin. 1968. "Human Memory: A Proposed System and Its Control Processes." *The Psychology of Learning and Motivation*, Vol. 2.

Ayasse, Nicolai D., Alana J. Hodson and Arthur Wingfield. 2021. "The Principle of Least Effort and Comprehension of Spoken Sentences by Younger and Older Adults." *Frontiers in Psychology*, Vol.12.

Baddeley, Alan D., and Graham J. Hitch. 1974. "Working Memory." In *The Psychology of Learning and Motivation*, edited by Bower, Gordon H. Academic Press.

Barik, Henri C. 1973. "Simultaneous Interpretation: Temporal and Quantitative Data." *Language and Speech* 16(3).

Barton, David, Mary Hamilton, and Roz Ivanić. 2008. "Introduction." In *Situated Literacies: Reading and Writing in Context*, edited by Barton, David, Hamilton, Mary, and Ivanić, Roz. Routledge.

Binder, Jeffrey R., Rutvik H. Desai, William W. Graves, and Lisa L. Conant. 2009. "Where Is the Semantic System? A Critical Review and Meta-Analysis of 120 Functional Neuroimaging Studies." *Cereb Cortex* 19(12).

Blaise, Max, Tamara Marksteiner, Ann Krispenz, and Ale Bertrams. 2021.

"Measuring Motivation for Cognitive Effort as State." *Frontiers in Psychology* Vol. 12.

Brainerd, Charles J., and Valerie F. Reyna. 1990. "Gist is the Grist: Fuzzy-Trace Theory and the New Intuitionism." *Developmental Review* 10(1).

Brehm, Jack W., and Elizabeth A. Self. 1989. "The Intensity of Motivation." *Annual Review of Psychology* Vol. 40.

Bühler, Hildegund. 1986. "Linguistic (Semantic) and Extra-Linguistic (Pragmatic) Criteria for the Evaluation of Conference Interpretation and Interpreters." *Multilingua* 5(4).

Cacioppo, John T., and Richard E. Petty. 1982. "The Need for Cognition." *Journal of Personality and Social Psychology* 42(1).

Cacioppo, John T., Richard E. Petty, Jeffrey A. Feinstein and W. Blair G. Jarvis. 1996. "Dispositional Differences in Cognitive Motivation: The Life and Times of Individuals Varying in Need for Cognition." *Psychological Bulletin* 119(2).

Camitta, Miriam. 1993. "Vernacular Writing: Varieties of Literacy Among Philadelphia High School Students." In *Cross-cultural Approaches to Literacy*, edited by Street, Brain V. Cambridge University Press.

Campbell, Stuart. 1999. "A Cognitive Approach to Source Text Difficulty in Translation." *Target* 11(1).

Carruthers, Peter, and David M. Williams. 2022. "Model-Free Metacognition." *Cognition*, 225(9).

Case, Donald O. 2005. "Principle of Least Effort." In *Theories of Information Behavior*, edited by Fisher, Karen E., Erdelez, Sanda, and McKechnie, Lynne. Information Today.

Chang, Anna C.S., and Sonia Millett. 2015. "Improving Reading Rates and Comprehension Through Audio-Assisted Extensive Reading for Beginner

Learners." *System* 52(5).

Chaudron, Craig, and Jack C. Richards. 1986. "The Effect of Discourse Markers on the Comprehension of Lectures." *Applied Linguistics* 7(2).

Chmiel, Agnieszka, and Agnieszka Lijewska. 2019. "Syntactic Processing in Sight Translation by Professional and Trainee Interpreters: Professionals are More Time-Efficient While Trainees View the Source Text Less." *Target* 31(3).

Chmiel, Agnieszka, and Agnieszka Lijewska. 2022. "Reading Patterns, Reformulation and Eye-Voice Span (IVS) in Sight Translation." *Translation and Interpreting Studies*. Web: 11 October 2022.

Chmiel, Agnieszka, Przemyslaw Janikowski, and Agnieszka Lijewska. 2020. "Multimodal Processing in Simultaneous Interpreting with Text: Interpreters Focus More on the Visual than the Auditory Modality." *Target* 32(1).

Chmiel, Agnieszka. 2021. "Effects of Simultaneous Interpreting Experience and Training on Anticipation, as Measured by Word-Translation Latencies." *Interpreting* 23(1).

Cho, Jinhyun, and Peter Roger. 2010. "Improving Interpreting Performance Through Theatrical Training." *The Interpreter and Translator Trainer (ITT)* 4(2).

Clay, George, Christopher Mlynski, Franziska M. Korb, Thomas Goschke, and Veronika Job. 2022. "Rewarding Cognitive Effort Increases the Intrinsic Value of Mental Labor." *PNAS Proceedings of the National Academy of Sciences of the United States of America* 119(5).

Cohen, Arthur R., Ezra Stotland, and Donald M. Wolfe. 1955. "An Experimental Investigation of Need for Cognition." *Journal of Abnormal Psychology* 51(2).

Cowan, Nelson. 2001. "The Magical Number 4 in Short-Term Memory: A Reconsideration of Mental Storage Capacity." *Behavioral and Brain*

Sciences 24(1).

Cronin, Michael. 2002. "The Empire Talks Back: Orality, Heteronomy, and the Cultural Turn in Interpretation Studies." In *Translation and Power*, edited by Tymoczko, Maria, and Gentzler, Edwin. University of Massachusetts Press.

Dam, Helle V. 2001. "On the Option Between Form-based and Meaning-based Interpreting: The Effect of Source Text Difficulty on Lexical Target Text Form in Simultaneous Interpreting." *The Interpreters' Newsletter* Vol.11.

Davis, James N., and Linda Bistodeau. 1993. "How do L1 and L2 Reading Differ? Evidence from Think Aloud Protocols." *The Modern Language Journal* 77(4).

Davison, Alice, and Georgia M. Green. 1988. "Introduction." In *Linguistic Complexity and Text Comprehension: Readability Issues Reconsidered*, edited by Davison, Alice, and Green, Georgia M. Erlbaum.

De Bot, Kees. 1992. "A Bilingual Production Model: Levelt's 'Speaking' Model Adapted." *Applied Linguistics* 13(1).

De Morree, Helma M., and Samuele M. Marcora. 2010. "The Face of Effort: Frowning Muscle Activity Reflects Effort During a Physical Task." *Biological Psychology* 85(3).

Deese, James. 1980. "Pauses, Prosody, and the Demands of Production in Language." In *Temporal Variables in Speech*, edited by Dechert, Hans W., and Raupach, Manfred. Mouton.

Dragsted, Barbara, and Inge Gorm Hansen. 2009. "Exploring Translation and Interpreting Hybrids: The Case of Sight Translation." *Meta* 54(3).

Duez, Danielle. 1982. "Silent and Non-silent Pauses in Three Speech Styles." *Language and Speech* 25(1).

Eisenberger, Robert. 1992. "Learned Industriousness." *Psychological Review* 99(2).

Ellis, Rod. 1994. "A Theory of Instructed Second Language Acquisition." In *Implicit and Explicit Learning of Languages*, edited by Ellis, Nick. Academic Press.

Estes, W.K. 1980. "Is Human Memory Obsolete?" *American Scientist* 68(1).

Fabbro, Franco, and Laura Gran. 1997. "Neurolinguistic Aspects of Simultaneous Interpretation." In *Conference Interpreting: Current Trends in Research*, edited by Gambier, Yves, Gile, Daniel, and Taylor, Christopher. John Benjamins.

Falbo, Caterina. 1995. "Interprétationconsécutive et exercicespréparatoires [Consecutive Interpretation and Preparatory Exercises]." *The Interpreters' Newsletter* (6).

Felberg, Tatjana R., and Anne Birgitta Nilsen. 2017. "Exploring Semiotic Resources in Sight Translation." *The Journal of Specialised Translation* Vol. 28.

Ferreira, Fernanda, and Nikole D. Patson. 2007. "The 'Good-Enough' Approach to Language Comprehension." *Language and Linguistics Compass* 1(1-2).

Ferreira, Fernanda, Karl G.D. Bailey and Vittoria Ferraro. 2002. "Good-Enough Representations in Language Comprehension." *Current Directions in Psychological Science* 11(1).

Flesch, Rudolf. 1948. "A New Readability Yardstick." *Journal of Applied Psychology* 32(3).

Flowerdew, John, and Steve Tauroza. 1995. "The Effect of Discourse Markers on Second Language Lecture Comprehension." *Studies in Second Language Acquisition* 17(4).

Forster, Kenneth I. 1970. "Visual Perception of Rapidly Presented Word Sequences of Varying Complexity." *Attention, Perception & Psychophysics* 8(4).

Fraser, Janet. 2004. "Translation Research and Interpreting Research: Pure, Applied, Action or Pedagogic?" In *Translation Research and Interpreting Research: Traditions, Gaps and Synergies*, edited by Schäffner, Christina. Multilingual Matters.

Gado, Sabrina, Katharina Lingelbach, Maria Wirzberger and Mathias Vukelić. 2023. "Decoding Mental Effort in a Quasi-Realistic Scenario: A Feasibility Study on Multimodal Data Fusion and Classification." *Sensors* 23(14).

Gerver, David. 1969. "The Effects of Source Language Presentation Rates on the Performance of Simultaneous Conference Interpreting." In *Proceedings of the Second Louisville Conference on Rate and/or Frequency-controlled Speech*, edited by Emerson, Foulke. Center for Rate-controlled Recordings, University of Louisville.

Gilbert, Luther C. 1959. "Speed of Processing Visual Stimuli and Its Relation to Reading." *Journal of Educational Psychology*, 55(1).

Gile, Daniel. 1990. "Scientific Research vs. Personal Theories in the Investigation of Interpretation." In *Aspects of Applied and Experimental Research on Conference Interpretation*, edited by Gran, Laura, and Taylor, Christopher. Campanotto Editore.

Gile, Daniel. 1991. "Methodological Aspects of Interpretation (and Translation) Research", *Target* 3(2).

Gile, Daniel. 2004. "Translation Research Versus Interpreting Research: Kinship, Differences, and Prospects of Partnership." In *Translation Research and Interpreting Research: Traditions, Gaps and Synergies*, edited by Schäffner, Christina. Multilingual Matters.

Gobet, Fernand, and Gary Clarkson. 2004. "Chunks in Expert Memory: Evidence for the Magical Number Four...or is it Two?" *Memory* 12(6).

González, Marta Abuín. 2012. "The Language of Consecutive Interpreters' Notes:

Differences Across Levels of Expertise." *Interpreting* 14(1).

Goodman, Kenneth S. 1967. "Reading: A Psycholinguistic Guessing Game." *Journal of the Reading Specialist* 6(4).

Gorszczyńska, Paula. 2010. "The Potential of Sight Translation to Optimize Written Translation: The Example of the English-Polish Language Pair." In *Translation Effects: Selected Papers of the CETRA Research Seminar in Translation Studies 2009*, edited by Azadibougar, Omid.

Halliday, Michael A.K. 2004. "Things and Relations: Regrammatizing Experience as Technical Knowledge." In *The Language of Science, Volume 5 in the Collected Works of M.A.K. Halliday*, edited by Webster, Jonathan J. Continuum.

Inzlicht, Michael, Amitai Shenhav and Christopher Y. Olivola. 2018. "The Effort Paradox: Effort is both Costly and Valued." *Trends in Cognitive Sciences* 22(4).

Jensen, Kristian Tangsgaard Hvelplund. 2011. "Distribution of Attention Between Source Text and Target Text During Translation." In *Cognitive Exploration of Translation*, edited by O'Brien, Sharon. Continuum.

Kalina, Sylvia. 2000. "Interpreting Competences as a Basis and a Goal for Teaching." *The Interpreters' Newsletter*. Vol.1.

Kintsch, Walter, and Janice Keenan. 1973. "Reading Rate and Retention as a Function of the Number of Propositions in the Base Structure of Sentences." *Cognitive Psychology* 5(3).

Kintsch, Walter, and James R. Miller. 1984. "Readability: A View from Cognitive Psychology." In *Understanding Reading Comprehension: Cognition, Language, and the Structure of Prose*, edited by Flood, James. International Reading Association.

Kintsch, Walter, and Teun A. van Dijk. 1978. "Toward a Model of Text

Comprehension and Production." *Psychological Review* (85).

Kintsch, Walter, Ely Kozminsky, William J. Streby, Gail Mckoon and Janice M. Keenan. 1975. "Comprehension and Recall of Text as a Function of Content Variable." *Journal of Verbal Learning and Verbal Behavior* 14(2).

Kirchhoff, Hella. 1976. "Das Simultandolmetschen: Interdependenz der Variablenim Dolmetschprozess, Dolmetschmodelle und Dolmetschstrategien [Simultaneous Interpreting: Interdependence of Variables in the Interpreting Process, Interpreting Models and Interpreting Strategies]." In *Theorie und Praxis des Ubersetzens und Dolmetschen [Theory and Practice of Translation and Interpreting]*, edited by Drescher, Horst W., and Scheffzek, Sigrid. Peter Lang.

Korpal, Paweł, and Katarzyna Stachowiak-Szymczak. 2020. "Combined Problem Triggers in Simultaneous Interpreting: Exploring the Effect of Delivery Rate on Processing and Rendering Numbers." *Perspectives Studies in Translatology* 28(1).

Kurzban, Robert, Angela Duckworth, Joseph W. Kable and Justus Myers. 2013. "An Opportunity Cost Model of Subjective Effort and Task Performance." *Behavioral and Brain Sciences* 36(6).

Lamberger-Felber, Heike, and Julia Schneider. 2008. "Linguistic Interference in Simultaneous Interpreting with Text: A Case Study." In *Efforts and Models in Interpreting and Translation Research: A Tribute to Daniel Gile*, edited by Hansen, Gyde, Chesterman, Andrew, and Gerzymisch-Arbogast, Heidrun. John Benjamins.

Lee, Jieun. 2012. "What Skills do Student Interpreters Need to Learn in Sight Translation Training?" *Meta* 57(3).

Levý, Jiři. 1967. "Translation as a Decision Process." In *To Honor Roman Jakobson: Essays on the Occasion of his 70. Birthday (Vol.2), Volume 32 in the Series Janua Linguarum. Series Maior*, edited by Schooneveld, C.H. van. De Gruyter Mouton.

Li, Xiangdong. 2014. "Sight Translation as a Topic in Interpreting Research: Progress, Problems, and Prospects." *Across Languages and Cultures* 15(1).

Liu, Minhua, and Yu-Hsien Chiu. 2009. "Assessing Source Material Difficulty for Consecutive Interpreting: Quantifiable Measure and Holistic Judgment." *Interpreting* 11(2).

Liu, Minhua, Diane L. Shallert, and Patrick J. Carroll. 2004. "Working Memory and Expertise in Simultaneous Interpreting." *Interpreting* 6(1).

Macizo, Pedro, and M. Teresa Bajo. 2006. "Reading for Repetition and Reading for Translation: Do They Involve the Same Processes?" *Cognition* 99(1).

Mankauskienė, Dalia. 2016. "Problem Trigger Classification and Its Applications for Empirical Research." *Procedia-Social and Behavioral Sciences* Vol. 231.

Mikkelson, Holly. 1994. "Text Analysis Exercises for Sight Translation." In *Vistas: Proceedings of the 31st Annual Conference of ATA*, edited by Krawutschke, Peter W. Learned Information.

Miller, George A. 1956. "The Magical Number Seven, Plus or Minus Two: Some Limits on Our Capacity for Processing Information." *The Psychological Review* 63(2).

Moser-Mercer, Barbara. 1995. "Sight Translation and Human Information Processing." In *Basic Issues in Translation Studies: Proceedings of the 5th International Conference-Kent Forum on Translation Studies*, edited by Neubert, Albrecht, Shreve, Gregory M., and Gommlich, Klaus. Kent State University Press.

Muñoz Martín, Ricardo. 2012. "Just a Matter of Scope: Mental Load in Translation Process Research." *Translation Spaces* 1(1).

Musslick, Sebastian, and Jonathan D. Cohen. 2021. "Rationalizing Constraints on the Capacity for Cognitive Control." *Trends in Cognitive Science* 25(9).

Musslick, Sebastian, Biswadip Dey, Kayhan Ozcimder, Md. Mostofa Ali Patwary, Theodore L. Willke and Jonathan D. Cohen. 2016. "Parallel Processing Capability Versus Efficiency of Representation in Neural Networks." *Network* 8(7).

Ochs, Elinor. 1979. "Planned and Unplanned Discourse." In *Syntax and Semantics, Vol. 12. Discourse and Syntax*, edited by Givon, Talmy. Academic Press.

Pickering, Martin J., and Victor S. Ferreira. 2008. "Structural Priming: A Critical Review." *Psychological Bulletin* 134(3).

Price, Cathy J. 2012. "A Review and Synthesis of the First 20 Years of PET and fMRI Studies of Heard Speech, Spoken Language and Reading." *Neuroimage* 62(2).

Rayner, Keith, Timothy J. Slattery, Denis Drieghe, and Simon P. Liversedge. 2011. "Eye Movements and Word Skipping During Reading: Effects of Word Length and Predictability." *Journal of Experimental Psychology: Human Perception and Performance* 37(2).

Reyna, Valerie F., and Charles J. Brainerd. 1990. "Fuzzy Processing in Transitivity Development." *Annals of Operations Research* 23(1).

Richter, Michael, Guido H.E. Gendolla and Rex A. Wright. 2016. "Three Decades of Research on Motivational Intensity Theory." In *Advances in Motivation Science*, edited by Elliot, Rex A. Elsevier Inc..

Rubin, Donald L. 2012. "Listenability as a Tool for Advancing Health Literacy." *Journal of Health Communication* 17(3).

Russo, Mariachiara, and Pippa Salvador. 2004. "Aptitude to Interpreting: Preliminary Results of a Testing Methodology Based on Paraphrase." *Meta* 49(2).

Russo, Mariachiara. 2014. "Testing Aptitude for Interpreting: The Predictive Value of Oral Paraphrasing, with Synonyms and Coherence as Assessment Parameters." *Interpreting* 16(1).

Sabandal, John Martin, Jacob A. Berry and Ronald L. Davis. 2021. "Dopamine-Based Mechanism for Transient Forgetting." *Nature* 591(7850).

Schäffner, Christina. 2004. "Introduction." In *Translation Research and Interpreting Research: Traditions, Gaps and Synergies*, edited by Schäffner, Christina. Multilingual Matters.

Setton, Robin, and Manuela Motta. 2007. "Syntacrobatics: Quality and Reformulation in Simultaneous-With-Text." *Interpreting* 9(2).

Simon, Herbert A. 1956. "Rational Choice and the Structure of the Environment." *Psychological Review* 63(2).

Song, Zhongwei. 2010. "Skill Transfer from Sight Translation to Simultaneous Interpreting: A Case Study of an Effective Teaching Technique." *International Journal of Interpreter Education* 2(1).

Swain, Merrill. 1985. "Communication Competence: Some Roles of Comprehensible Input and Comprehensible Output in Its Development." In *Input in Second Language Acquisition*, edited by Gass, Susan M., and Madden, Carolyn G. Heinle & Heinle.

Székely, Marcell, and John Michael. 2020. "The Sense of Effort: A Cost-Benefit Theory of the Phenomenology of Mental Effort." *Review of Philosophy and Psychology* 12(4).

Tannen, Deborah. 1982. "The Oral/Literate Continuum of Discourse." In *Spoken and Written Language: Exploring Orality and Literacy*, edited by Tannen, Deborah. Ablex Publishing Co.

Tannen, Deborah. 1985. "Relative Focus and Involvement in Oral and Written Discourse." In *Literacy, Language and Learning: The Nature and*

Consequences of Reading and Writing, edited by Olson, David R., Torrance, Nancy, and Hildyard, Angela. Cambridge University Press.

Timarová, Šárka, Ivana Čeňková, Reine Meylaerts, Erik Hertog, Arnaud Szmalec, and Wouter Duyck. 2014. "Simultaneous Interpreting and Working Memory Executive Control." *Interpreting* 16(2).

Treadway, Michael T., Joshua W. Buckholtz, Ashley N. Schwartzman, Warren E. Lambert and David H. Zald. 2009. "Worth the "EFFfRT"? The Effort Expenditure for Rewards Task as an Objective Measure of Motivation and Anhedonia." *PLoS One* 4(8).

Tversky, Amos, and Daniel Kahneman. 1981. "The Framing of Decisions and the Psychology of Choice." *Science* 211(4481).

Tyler, Sherman W., Paula T. Hertel, Marvin C. McCallum and Henry C. Ellis. 1979. "Cognitive Effort and Memory." *Journal of Experimental Psychology: Human Learning and Memory* 5(6).

Ure, Jean. 1971. "Lexical Density and Register Differentiation." In *Applications of Linguistics: Selected Papers of the Second International Congress of Applied Linguistics*, edited by Ernest, George, and Trim, John Leslie Melville. Cambridge University Press.

Wang, Lei, Jiehui Zheng and Liang Meng. 2017. "Effort Provides Its Own Reward: Endeavors Reinforce Subjective Expectation and Evaluation of Task Performance." *Experimental Brain Research* 235(4).

Weber, Withelm K. 1989. "Improved Ways of Teaching Consecutive Interpretation." In *The Theoretical and Practical Aspects of Teaching Conference Interpretation*, edited by Gran, Laura, and Dodds, John. Campanotto Editore.

Westbrook, Andrew, and Todd S. Braver. 2015. "Cognitive Effort: A Neuroeconomic Approach." *Cognitive, Affective, & Behavioral*

Neuroscience 15(2).

Westbrook, Andrew, Daria Kester, and Todd S. Braver. 2013. "What is the Subjective Cost of Cognitive Effort? Load, Trait, and Aging Effects Revealed by Economic Preference." *PloS One* 8(7).

Wurm, Svenja. 2014. "Deconstructing Translation and Interpreting Prototypes: A Case of Written-to-Signed-Language Translation." *Translation Studies* 7(3).

Zadeh, Lotfi A. 1965. "Fuzzy Sets." *Information and Control* 8(3).

Zou, Deyan, and Jing Chen. 2023. "Cognitive Process and Skill Training of Time-Limited Sight Translation." *Theory and Practice in Language Studies* 13(9).

Zou, Deyan, and Jiadong Zhang. 2023. "Measuring the 'Invisible': Clarifying the Concept of Cognitive Effort in Translation and Interpreting Processes." *Current Trends in Translation Teaching and Learning E* 10.

Zou, Deyan, and Jiahao Guo. 2024. "Parallel Translation Process in Consecutive Interpreting: Differences Between Beginning and Advanced Interpreting Students." *Acta Psychologica* 248.

五　网络、会议及其他资料

Cammoun-Claveria, Rawdha, Catherine Davies, Konstantin Ivanov, and Boris Naimushin. 2009. *Simultaneous Interpretation with Text: Is the Text 'Friend' or 'Foe'? Laying Foundations for a Teaching Module.* Master of Advanced Studies in Interpreter Training Seminar Paper. University of Geneva.

Gile, Daniel. 2021. "Cognitive Load and Effort in Translation and Interpreting: Methodological Issues." Lecture at CRITT@kent Translation Colloquium.

"International Association of Oil and Gas Producers," IOGP, https://www.iogp.org/.

Jin, Ya-shyuan. 2010. *Is Working Memory Working in Consecutive Interpreting?* Doctoral dissertation, University of Edinburgh.

Rawlinson, Graham E. 1976. *The Significance of Letter Position in Word Recognition*, Doctoral dissertation, University of Nottingham.

"Redundancy (Linguistics)." Wikipedia, http://en.wikipedia.org/wiki/Redundancy_(linguistics).

Sandrelli, Annalisa, and Jim Hawkins. 2006. *From Black Box to the Virtual Interpreting Environment (VIE): Another Step in the Development of Computer Assisted Interpreter Training*, The Future of Conference Interpreting: Training, Technology and Research, conference held in University of Westminster.

Shah, Bhavin. "Visual Tracking: The Hidden Cause of Poor Reading Skills." Central Vision Opticians, https://www.centralvisionopticians.co.uk/visual-tracking/.

Speechpool, http://www.speechpool.net/en/.

刘和平:《口译培训的定位与专业建设》,《进入 21 世纪的高质量口译——第六届全国口译大会暨国际研讨会论文集》,外语教学与研究出版社,2008。

孙海琴:《源语专业信息密度对同声传译"脱离源语语言外壳"程度的影响——一项基于口译释意理论的实证研究》,博士学位论文,上海外国语大学,2012。

图书在版编目（CIP）数据

　口译中的话语：分析与重构 / 邹德艳著 . -- 北京：
社会科学文献出版社，2024.8（2025.9 重印）. -- ISBN 978-7-5228
-3954-7

　Ⅰ . H315.9

　中国国家版本馆 CIP 数据核字第 2024EJ5952 号

口译中的话语
——分析与重构

著　　　者 / 邹德艳

出　版　人 / 冀祥德
组稿编辑 / 高明秀
责任编辑 / 宋　祺
责任印制 / 岳　阳

出　　　版 / 社会科学文献出版社 · 区域国别学分社（010）59367078
　　　　　　地址：北京市北三环中路甲29号院华龙大厦　邮编：100029
　　　　　　网址：www. ssap. com. cn
发　　　行 / 社会科学文献出版社（010）59367028
印　　　装 / 唐山玺诚印务有限公司

规　　　格 / 开　本：787mm×1092mm　1/16
　　　　　　印　张：13.75　字　数：191千字
版　　　次 / 2024年8月第1版　2025年9月第2次印刷
书　　　号 / ISBN 978-7-5228-3954-7
定　　　价 / 79.00元

读者服务电话：4008918866

▲ 版权所有 翻印必究